dispatches from
the field

dispatches from the field

neophyte ethnographers in a changing world

Andrew Gardner
David M. Hoffman

WAVELAND

PRESS, INC.

Long Grove, Illinois

For information about this book, contact:
    Waveland Press, Inc.
    4180 IL Route 83, Suite 101
    Long Grove, IL 60047-9580
    (847) 634-0081
    info@waveland.com
    www.waveland.com

10-digit ISBN 1-57766-451-5
13-digit ISBN 978-1-57766-451-2

Printed in the United States of America

8 7 6 5 4 3

Contents

Acknowledgements

This book has been in the making for several years, and over that period of time a wide variety of individuals both inside and outside of academia have been involved in our incremental steps toward publication. While the list of those individuals would be too long to print here, we would like to express our gratitude to Noel Salazar Medina, Tara Hefferan, Aomar Boum, Nina Siulc, and Anna Wex for their key contributions to the idea behind this book. Furthermore, James Clifford found time in his busy schedule to read a subset of the essays included here, and his support buoyed us for the better part of a year. Jennifer Shepherd also provided valuable comments on the penultimate manuscript, while Kristin Giordano, in addition to providing her perspective on the drafts of these chapters, also quickly pulled together the design for the cover of this book.

Both of us used early versions of this manuscript in the courses we taught, and we benefited greatly from our students' perspectives on the successes and failures of draft versions of these essays. Our thanks go out to the students of World Ethnography at the University of Arizona (Summer 2004), of Cultural Anthropology at the University of Puget Sound (Fall 2005), and of Frontiers of Cultural Anthropology at the University of Colorado—Boulder (Spring 2005, Summer 2005).

David Hoffman would like to acknowledge his family, especially Marty and Linda Hoffman and Bennett and Mary Abrams, whose support and pride in his achievements was always inspirational. Finally, David thanks his wife Amy Moe-Hoffman for her tolerance of the many late nights of reading and writing, the many discussions about this volume, her unwavering support, and her faith. Andrew Gardner would particularly like to thank Kristin Giordano, Mary K. Good, and Mara Leichtman for their comments and critiques on various portions of the manuscript.

Fieldwork and Writing *From* the Field

David M. Hoffman and Andrew M. Gardner

In 1914, Bronislaw Malinowski arrived in Australia as part of the Robert Mond Anthropological Expedition to British New Guinea. The expedition fit within the larger research interests of the social sciences at the turn of that century. As the European empires expanded to the corners of the globe, they encountered—and frequently came to dominate—peoples with dramatically different ways of living in the world. Mapping these different cultures and societies was certainly part of the agenda of these social scientists; explaining the nature of the differences encountered was another. In the currents of anthropology in the late nineteenth century, those explanations typically focused on how these various groups of people fit in the larger evolutionary schemes configured by armchair anthropologists who, in the comforts of their libraries and offices, poured over the musings and reports of colonial travelers, missionaries, and the miscellany of Europeans and Anglo-Americans traveling at the fringes of the "civilized" empires.

Perhaps if not for a confluence of historical happenstance, Malinowski might have followed in the footsteps of the anthropologists of the previous generation, and an attenuated visit with the Melanesian peoples north of Australia would have led back to the university in Europe. Malinowski could have hardly guessed that his trip to Australia would coincide with Austro-Hungarian Archduke Ferdinand's assassination on the streets of Sarajevo, the first in a cavalcade of events that precipitated the First World War. Although educated in England, Malinowski was an Austrian citizen and, suddenly, an enemy alien in Australia. Eventually the budding anthropologist negotiated a compromise with Australian authorities: he would wait out the end of the war under a sort of "house arrest" in the colonial backwater of coastal Papua New Guinea or, more specifically, on the Trobriand Islands.

Only a handful of anthropologists prior to Malinowski had spent time among the members of the cultures they wrote and theorized about, and it was this young anthropologist who codified the practice within the discipline. His recommendations—to live amongst the people one wishes to study, to participate in their everyday life, to communicate with them in their native tongue, and to remain isolated from one's own cultural emissaries—became the template for successive generations of anthropologists. Fieldwork became the rite of passage in anthropology, the singular experience that, more than any other, defines membership in the discipline of anthropology. Today, years of graduate-level coursework prepare students for this experience and, perhaps more to the point, for constructing the grant proposals to fund a year or more in the field. Upon acceptance by a granting institution, she or he departs for the field shortly thereafter, often accompanied by grandiose intentions of reshaping the contours of social theory. If all goes well, the student returns to the university in a year or two and then begins the long struggle to corral fieldnotes, interviews, and other ethnographic data into a coherent doctoral dissertation. Only a portion of the students who begin graduate school in anthropology actually make it to the field. Of those who do, some decide not to come home, and only some of those who do return actually complete a doctoral dissertation. An even smaller percentage of those dissertations make their way to the academic presses and, eventually, to the bookshelves of colleagues, students, and the interested public.

The essays in this book are not about the theory and empirical data anthropologists detail in these doctoral dissertations. Rather they are about the *experience*—namely the difficulties—of conducting ethnographic fieldwork. In that sense, they hardly provide anything new, for the anthropological literature is burgeoning with tomes about the difficulties anthropologists encounter in the field. Like most anthropologists preparing for fieldwork, the contributors to this volume consulted many of these texts as we made preparations for our own departures to points far and near. It was through the experience of consulting these other fieldwork volumes that the seed for this volume was planted, and the idea took root once we became immersed in our own fieldwork. In short, the great majority of anthropological essays on the difficulties of fieldwork, we discovered, have a subtle retrospective tone to them: the problems encountered in the field are described, neatly packaged, and then quickly resolved. Lessons are learned, and the anthropologists departing for the field, ideally, emerge from reading these volumes with one or more new tools in their ethnographic toolkit.

Why is this retrospective tone so characteristic of fieldwork writing? Certainly high on the list of explanations would be that the majority of the essays about fieldwork are constructed well after fieldwork is complete—after, for example, the anthropologists have returned from the field, and after they have met the more pressing demand of completing a dissertation, a process that often takes years. Furthermore, although many anthropologists, building upon the reflexive turn in the discipline, seek to include more detail about their own positionality vis-à-vis their subject population in the text of their dissertation, in the final accounting the vein of anthropological writing that explores the emotional and conceptual undercurrents of ethnographic fieldwork is frequently penned well after fieldwork is complete. We suggest that somewhere in the interim—between the actual experience and writing about it—the dilemmas and problems of the field become reduced and simplified into neat packages that can be quickly resolved.

What we had hoped to find prior to our own departure for the field, and what we have tried to produce here, is a set of essays situated squarely within the problems and dilemmas contemporary anthropologists face in the field. Rather than present another compendium of fieldwork recollections, we believe these essays will convey the process of problems in the making, of dilemmas expanding before the eyes of the aspiring anthropologist, as well as the ethnographer's struggle to keep him- or herself together, to stay focused on the problem at hand, and to keep the projects they designed over years moving forward. To capture these fieldwork problems in the making, all the essays collected in this volume were written *in the field*, albeit with minor alterations, editing, and an occasional postscript or epilogue added in the post-fieldwork phase. What the reader won't find in these essays is a checklist of problems accompanied by solutions, for many of the problems and dilemmas described here remain partially or fully unresolved by the conclusion of the essay. Nor will the reader find a single central and connecting thread in most of the essays included here. Instead, the various logistical hurdles, reflexive concerns, theoretical dilemmas, and ethical quandaries bleed in to one another, oftentimes expanding before the anthropologist or building a cumulative momentum.

The scope of the problems described, as well as the immediacy we've sought to capture by constructing these essays in the field are, in our perception, central to the strength of this collection. Similarly, even readers new to the methods of ethnographic research will perceive that among the diverse fieldwork experiences described here, many mistakes have been made. We see these mistakes as endemic to ethnographic fieldwork or, as Clifford Geertz described it so many years ago, to "the strange anthropological laboratory in which none of the parameters can be manipulated" (Geertz 1973: 22). In the dissertations and articles that will hopefully emerge from these fieldwork experiences, these mistakes will probably be, in large part, omitted or skirted. In some, the problems described here may emerge as central to some portion of the dissertation; more than likely they will be subservient to or demonstrative of a larger theoretical agenda. Alternatively, these essays provide a venue for

directly confronting the difficulties—be they logistical, conceptual, or emotional—of conducting ethnographic research.

Like any volume of essays, the value this collection carries is more than the sum of its
individual parts, for like fieldwork collections of the past, in charting a series of individual
dilemmas and hurdles these essays simultaneously map a particular historical moment in
both the discipline of anthropology and in the world. While the essays visit a breadth of topics, in the sections that follow we provide a sketch of some of the threads that connect the
fieldwork experiences of the essay authors, and hence describe the particular historical
moment in which this fieldwork was conducted. In part, these connecting threads address
recent paradigmatic shifts that have reshaped the way anthropologists examine society and
culture. The tectonic shifts in the discipline, however, have coincided with dramatic changes
in the distribution and location of the populations and communities anthropologists study.
The continuities described below chart the intertwined nature of these two processes.

Fieldwork and the Ethnographer's Identity

What came to be called the "the reflexive turn" in anthropology and closely related dis-
ciplines emerged in the 1980s as a critique of the long-standing belief that anthropologists
could function as objective observers of social and cultural worlds. Critics of this objective,
scientific perspective argued that anthropologists were hardly the unbiased observers they
often claimed to be. Rather, they were unique individuals situated in particular ways within
the social worlds they sought to describe, and their specific position shaped their observations and, hence, the data they collected. These are not idle concerns, for the subjectivity of
the anthropologist was magnified through the power of anthropologists to represent these
social and cultural worlds in ethnography. Thus there were two overlapping correctives: one
was concerned with the power to define and describe others, and the other focused on how
what is written is a product of the anthropologist's own context and identity. In this way,
anthropology and anthropologists became much more reflexive, exploring the role their
own class, ethnicity, nationality, gender, and, in a comprehensive sense, their personality
played in shaping the data from which conclusions were drawn. These concerns permeate
the essays collected in this volume and demonstrate that the identity of the anthropologist
plays a crucial role in the acquisition of social data, in the very formulation of a research
question, and in the shape of the social world that is, in the end, investigated.

These issues play a particularly central role in Greg Simon's contribution to this collection. Confronted by the rampant stereotyping of his American identity by the Indonesian
men and women in the city of Bukittinggi, Simon grows increasingly frustrated with his
inability to shake the attributes the Indonesians assign to him and increasingly preoccupied
with the person who, over the course of fieldwork, he has become. Like Graham Jones, who

uses his essay to explore the disjuncture between the person he was at home in New York City and the *fieldself* he assumed amongst the magicians of Paris, Simon begins to see himself and his emotions as central to his ethnographic experience—as a "tool for research." These concerns with the ethnographic encounter and the identity of the anthropologist are, at times, deeply personal; they also connect to global politics and the historic moment in which the fieldwork described in this volume was conducted. Karen Greenough, for example, struggles with her own position of power relative to the nomadic Wodaabe Fulbe of Niger. Andrew Gardner negotiates the difficulties of conducting ethnographic fieldwork in the Persian Gulf as war breaks out in Iraq, much like Caroline Conzelman's subjects assume her complicity in America's "War on Drugs" in highland Bolivia, and again as echoed in David Hoffman's struggle with a rural Mexican community's skepticism of his identity as a neutral emissary of the U.S. and Mexican governments. As Simon suggests in his description of fieldwork in Indonesia, the fact that anthropologists have a long history of essentializing the peoples they study, while undeniable, must not eclipse the fact that anthropologists' subject populations often essentialize the anthropologist. Through this confluence of processes, the anthropologist's *fieldself* reflects not only the tumultuous and localized dilemmas of fieldwork but also the social, political, and economic processes working at a global level—processes that, at a minimum, shape the willingness of subject populations to speak openly and honestly with foreign (and often Western) ethnographers.

Gender also plays an important role in the fieldwork experiences described in this volume. Kristen Drybread, in her intrepid ethnographic fieldwork conducted in a Brazilian juvenile prison, finds herself in a constant battle against the gendered expectations held by prison officials, an experience that points to the fact that ethnographic fieldwork is often conducted under almost constant duress. Kate Goldade's essay directly engages with the ways in which being a mother alters the social terrain of her fieldwork and, simultaneously, raises crucial ethical issues. In addition, Hoffman's essay, while focused on the construction of trust, reveals that a significant portion of this process depended on his willingness and ability to engage in the activities and discourse central to male identity in a small, coastal village, a process with striking echoes in Nathalie Peutz's description of her own experience adapting to the gendered expectations of villagers on the Yemeni island of Soqotra. Each of these authors explores the influence of gender roles upon the way they are perceived in the communities in which they work and, alternatively, how these perceptions influence the way they see the field and their informants.

Religion also plays an important role in some of the contributions. This theme is perhaps most apparent in Gwen Ottinger's exploration of her relationship with an African American church and its members in rural Louisiana. As we follow her own inquiries into the nature of that belief, she suggests that religious communities can be about more than faith.

While anthropology—and many ethnographers—sit firmly within the secular-humanist tradition, Ottinger's piece examines the importance of faith to many of the communities in which anthropologists work, a fact that can structure a variety of dilemmas in the field. In Ottinger's case, her immersion in the spiritual community of New Sarpy, Louisiana, leads her to ponder her long-standing disregard for religion and its potential positive contribution in the contemporary American political arena.

Ultimately, issues of the anthropologist's identity and its intersection with the people and cultures studied indicate the ongoing resonance of the reflexive turn in the discipline of anthropology. In exploring these issues, however, the essays included here frequently pose more questions than answers: How much of your personal identity should be revealed to one's informants? If you are candid about yourself will this be a boon or a bane to your relationships with informants and potential informants? When your subjects say or do things that are deeply offensive to you, do you confront them or remain quiet in order to maintain their continued contribution to your field project? How will your beliefs create bonds or rifts with the intended subjects of your field project? In engaging with these questions many of the authors in this volume are attempting to understand the relationship between their personhood and their fieldwork, while at the same time struggling with the notion of objectivity ingrained into the discipline of anthropology by some of its earliest practitioners in their quest for scientific and systematic knowledge of the world's cultures. While faith in cultural anthropology as a positivist and scientific endeavor has long been questioned, what we witness throughout these essays is the struggle to resolve an observed "reality" with the ways in which fieldwork delineates and solidifies particular aspects of one's own identity in the course of conducting ethnographic research.

Building Rapport and Trust in the Field

From the earliest days of ethnographic fieldwork, descriptions of the many hurdles between arrival in the field and immersion in the culture focused on building rapport and trust with one's informants. As Bronislaw Malinowski, Franz Boas, Margaret Mead, E. E. Evans-Pritchard, and numerous other early ethnographers made clear, it takes more than a keen eye and persistence to gain an understanding of people's behaviors and thoughts: in most fieldwork descriptions, anthropologists build bonds of friendship and trust in the communities in which they work, and the line between informant and friend, historically a blurry one in the discipline, remains so in contemporary anthropology. While much has changed over the last hundred years, the struggle to establish these bonds of trust, as well as the tension between the ethnographic subjects as, alternatively, either informants or friends, represents a particularly strong set of continuities between early ethnographic efforts and the experiences described in this volume. Hence the struggle to build rapport and trust are central elements of many of the author's essays in this volume.

Field methods courses and texts discuss rapport building *ad nauseam*, but rarely do they yield insights into the unpredictability inherent in this process. Clearly, trust and rapport hinge on the subject community's perception of the anthropologist and his or her actions. Several of the essays collected here point to the unexpected and serendipitous events that oftentimes play a significant role in shaping this relationship. David Hoffman and Kristen Drybread discuss the unanticipated events that emerged as key junctures in construction of close relationships with members of the communities in which they worked. Kate Goldade describes the positive impact of her infant daughter on trust building among Nicaraguan transmigrant women in Costa Rica. Graham Jones, like Drybread and Hoffman, reflects on the troubling realization that breaking this trust—whether intentionally or accidentally—represents a difficult and sometimes dangerous juncture in ethnographic fieldwork. While the risks associated with the breakdown of trust range from fear for personal safety to concern over access to particular informants and the integrity of ethnographic project, together these authors offer insight into the fragility and responsibility inherent to bonds anthropologists establish in the field.

What the contributors seek to demonstrate in this volume is the ongoing process by which these relationships are constructed and maintained. What is conveyed here, we think, is not a series of lessons about how this trust and rapport are built and maintained, but instead a portrait of anthropologists struggling with the diverse dilemmas that are part and parcel of this process. Oftentimes, these dilemmas are unique to the particular cultural context described. In another sense, however, the process of building trust and rapport overlap with the individual personality and identity of the anthropologist in the field. The successes and failures described in these essays, many of which were in progress at the time of writing, must be measured against the shifting political tectonics of the contemporary world. Suspicions that the anthropologist is actually an agent of the CIA, FBI, or DEA surface in many of these essays, a fact that clearly shows that as representatives of American academia (as most of the contributors are), we can't easily shake off the ways our identity as "Americans" both facilitates and impedes the trust and rapport that is essential to collaboration with informants.

The Ethnographer as an Emotional Being

If one only reads ethnographies and dissertations that are the end products of ethnographic fieldwork, one could conclude that ethnographers easily set aside their own emotional states in the pursuit of ethnographic data. Even today, the process of constructing a dissertation, journal article, or ethnography from fieldnotes often disguises the true emotional roller coaster that conducting fieldwork can be. In that sense, these essays have provided an opportunity for the authors to explore the tumultuous emotional experience of conducting ethnographic fieldwork and to reflect on how that experience shaped their perception of the communities in which they worked.

Deep and sustained frustration permeates many of the fieldwork experiences described in this volume. For Greg Simon, as discussed above, this frustration stemmed from twin forces of the stereotyping he faced from the urban Indonesian community around him and, at the same time, from his internal struggle over the *fieldself* he had assumed in this context. Eric Haanstad, David Hoffman, Akihiro Ogawa, and Andrew Gardner also explore the intertwined confusion and frustration that is seemingly a hallmark of the first months in the field, while Karen Greenough and Kristin Drybread share a concern for the ways in which this frustration, anger, and disappointment, oftentimes stemming from the behavior of a few individuals, nonetheless holds the potential to reshape relations between the anthropologist and the community in which he or she works. Megan Tracy's essay on her experience with SARS in China candidly engages with the fear that not only gripped her informants but also crept into her own psyche at the beginning of the outbreak. At the same time, the emotional currents experienced in the field are not all negative: Haanstad, like many of the contributors, quite adeptly points to the ways in which the feelings of desperation can so quickly change to elation after an unexpected turn of events in the field.

Frustration and elation are two of the many emotional states described in the essays collected here. The diversity of these emotions suggests, foremost, that anthropological researchers are human, as are the subjects that they are studying. Part of being human is having emotions, and despite attempts at remaining objective, human emotions are at the foundation of the ethnographic experience. In most cases these essays show the emergence of emotion is not necessarily detrimental to gathering ethnographic data. Instead, it is often a route to deeper understanding of the communities and cultures we study, for the emotional conflicts encountered in the field can be enabling as well as disabling. Ultimately, we feel it is important to honestly and openly engage with the fact that emotions do occur in the field, and although it can be fraught with peril, emotion can also shed light on some of the deeper cultural and social rifts that often exist between anthropologists and their informants. In another sense, introspection is often the path toward the deeper understanding of other ways of living.

Activism, Advocacy, and Scientific Objectivity

Another theme that connects the chapters is the urge to "make a difference" in the lives of those in the various fieldsites described in the essays. The thematic consistencies in this volume also include the development of bonds that are deeper than a superficial informant–anthropologist relationship. Clearly this is related to the discussion on emotions in fieldwork outlined above and is in some ways more of an outgrowth of that subject. However, it is important to note that many of the volume's essays in some way address the role that anthropologists ought to play in the lives of the people they study. Thus, these essays discuss how fieldwork establishes ties, which are oftentimes deep and meaningful, with people and communities—ties often driven as much by the urge to empower these communities as by the urge to extract some contribution to the social sciences' understanding of culture and society in the contemporary world.

That said, many of the authors express their interests in "making a difference" for the situations in which they find their informants and in how to maintain this connection after fieldwork is complete. Gwen Ottinger, Karen Greenough, David Hoffman, Andrew Gardner, and especially Akihiro Ogawa express concern over whether they are or aren't facilitating the types of positive change towards equity, fair wages, political expression, peace, or the environmental quality that many of us take for granted in our daily lives. Caroline Conzelman's essay discusses the ways in which she relies on reciprocity, central to Aymara people and their cultivation of coca, to guide her actions in the field. She uses this Aymara practice as a guiding principle in her work as an anthropologist; the extraction of information from informants and friends must be balanced reciprocally in her own efforts to give something back to the community. Conzelman convincingly argues that anthropologists should use their cultural, economic, and social capital in ways that empower the people and communities that are the subjects of our study.

Doing fieldwork can also distance anthropologists from their informants and friends. From Karen Greenough's piece we discover that the anthropologist's agenda of garnering data for scholarly writing can interfere with friendships and engagement in the daily activities of the host community. She aptly portrays the struggle she faced in striking a balance between fieldwork as an academic endeavor and the urge to simply "live life" among the people for whom she cares so deeply. Greenough's struggle and discomfort revolves around the fundamentally extractive and, from some angles, exploitative relationship anthropologists establish with informants. Her desire to give up on recording fieldnotes and abandon methodical data collection arises from her conflicted feelings about how her anthropological fieldwork will, in the final accounting, serve the Wodaabe Fulbe people.

Elly Teman's essay on her relationship with surrogate mothers and expectant parents in Israel highlights an aspect of anthropological fieldwork that is rarely, if ever, engaged with in print: the intense anxiety over departing the field. Many anthropologists discuss the melancholy and culture shock they experience re-entering their native social milieu (typically elite, Western, university settings), but few recognize that part of this anomie is attached to the separation from the people they have come to like and love. Teman's essay discusses the ways in which she struggles with her exit from fieldwork and from the lives of women she has so closely followed for an extended period of time. This dilemma is echoed by Greenough, who describes a deep ambivalence concerning her return to Kentucky, a return that is equally a departure from the friends and family she has come to know and love in Niger.

For Nathalie Peutz, the discipline's urge to make a difference in the lives of the Soqotri islanders is matched by an explicit discourse permeating her field site: "What are you giving to Soqotra?" the islanders ask of researchers. She describes an interesting scenario where her own internal struggle to contribute to the betterment of the small, rural Soqotri village is redoubled by the constant assessment of her contributions by the Soqotrans. Her struggle to negotiate the barometer of the Soqotrans' expectations with her own need to cull meaningful and useful ethnographic data from that experience represents a central tension in her fieldwork experience and similarly marks one aspect of the significant changes that have altered the fieldwork experience over the last century.

For many anthropologists, fieldwork is about more than the extraction of data or expanding our collective knowledge of the human condition.[1] For many anthropologists, immersion in another culture is part and parcel of a desire to empower these communities, to directly engage the vast inequities of global capitalism and to improve the welfare of those who have fared poorly in its calculus. While this approach to anthropological research has a significant legacy in anthropology, these essays collectively demonstrate that meeting these goals remains a difficult venture, one that exposes deep and longstanding fissures in the discipline. As these essays suggest, anthropological versions of activism and advocacy also interweave with the intensely personal nature of ethnographic fieldwork and with the friendships and relationships that anthropologists develop in the communities in which they work.

New Geographies and New Methods

The final recurring theme we identified in these essays involves the changing structure and shifting geographies of the populations that anthropologists study. Many of the earliest anthropologists found—or at least described—populations that were culturally discrete, often rural, and certainly much different than the societies from which the anthropologist came. Many of the authors in this volume reflect on the ways that the globalized world in which we live affects the actual methods of doing fieldwork.

Andrew Gardner's essay on his work in Bahrain engages with the difficult nature of conducting work in transnational contexts. Gardner's essay points out that studying the migration of people to new lands necessitates not only new methods but also requires fieldworkers to make conscious decisions about what is and isn't feasible in the amount of time that typical fieldwork grants fund. Gardner's case illustrates the ways in which studying transnational populations disrupts the standard techniques of anthropology: while anthropologists strive to obtain the *emic*, or insider's perspective, how does one account for the confluence of many—and in this case oppositional—perspectives encountered in pluralistic contexts? Do you learn the language of the migrants, the host culture, or a *lingua franca?* How does one understand the plight of a migrant group without also studying the social and cultural milieu from which they have come? While there are no clear answers to these questions, Gardner's dilemmas provide a glimpse at the difficulties anthropologists face when working in socially and culturally heterogeneous contexts.

Another important aspect of the contemporary ethnographic experience is the use of communication technologies. While Eric Haanstad elicits the "nightmare scenario" of hard drive crashes, David Hoffman and Megan Tracy focus on the ways in which technology is both limiting and liberating. Hoffman discusses how e-mail and communication connections can distract anthropologists from the very context they have come to study. No longer do we work in completely isolated places where all of our attention is focused on what Bronislaw Malinowski called the "impoderabilia of everyday life" (1922: 18). Instead, contemporary ethnographers are expected to keep in contact with home and up to speed with regional and global processes that impact the communities they study. While Hoffman felt that e-mail and global communication was in some ways limiting, Tracy's experience in China demonstrates that the exact same technologies can enable research to continue despite events that threaten her ability to press on. Without communication technology, Tracy would have lacked information about the SARS outbreak and also been unable to conduct any sort of interview. Moreover, as the scenario described by Tracy demonstrates, e-mail and other communication technologies are often integral components of the sociocultural worlds we study.

In fact, the coalescence of this volume depended upon these very technologies. During 2002 and 2003, many of us were in the field conducting the ethnographic fieldwork described here. The Internet provided us with the ability to begin the process of writing, editing, and sharing notes on the individual chapters. Thus, contemporary communication technologies not only enabled us to advance this volume, but they also allowed the contributors to share their field experiences with each other. Ultimately, the process of sharing drafts in the field facilitated the realization of both similarities and differences in our fieldwork experiences, decreasing the isolation and the daunting nature of the often-frightening task of carrying out an ethnographic research project in a cultural domain foreign to the anthropologist.

The effects of communication technology in a globally connected world extend beyond facilitating or disrupting fieldwork. As noted above, and in contrast to anthropology's past, today's informants and collaborators are also able to employ these technologies to inform themselves about the world and global political economy. That said, many of the contributors suggest that how they were received by community members was based on images and stereotypes produced by globalized communication media. In more concrete terms, the contributions from Greg Simon, Andrew Gardner, Carol Conzelman, David Hoffman, Kristen

Drybread, and Eric Haanstad reflect on how they were viewed and the dangers their American identities posed. Our research subjects are no longer disconnected, naïve, tribal groups but instead have a distinct awareness of contemporary global geopolitics.

While the effects of communication technologies aren't a threat to the anthropological endeavor itself, they do reveal the world to be a different place than it was for anthropologists conducting fieldwork prior to the development of the information highway. Many of the subject populations described in this volume's essays are connected to these global circuits of information (and misinformation). Thus, the actions of governments are now more readily exposed and will affect contemporary fieldwork in a more direct way. The bulk of this volume's essays were written in 2002 and 2003, the very historical juncture in which the United States instigated a preemptive war against Iraq and further extended its global war against terrorism. Whether or not the anthropologists in this volume agreed with these violent projects is beside the point: What is salient is that the images produced by these actions dramatically reshaped the social and political context in which much of this fieldwork was conducted, thereby complicating the field situation in a variety of ways.

Conclusion

The themes described above, while overlapping, represent four connecting threads woven through the essays that follow. At the same time, they hardly encapsulate the diversity of problems and issues described by the authors. We hope that the readers of this volume will find their own connecting threads in the various chapters and that the dilemmas, problems, and mistakes described by the volume's contributors will foster discussion concerning the inner mechanics of the process of conducting ethnographic fieldwork.

For many of the anthropologists the process of constructing these essays was both cathartic and worrisome. As a cathartic exercise, the essays provided an opportunity to formally describe the dilemmas that preoccupy us in the course of conducting ethnographic fieldwork, which are oftentimes relegated to personal conversations with colleagues. At the same time, for many of the contributors these essays are worrisome; in frankly charting the mistakes, ethical dilemmas, and the emotional tumultuousness of the fieldwork experience, the authors have laid bare a portion of the fieldwork process that is typically buffed and polished by the time it reaches print. We hope that readers will profit from these essays and understand that the dilemmas and mistakes described here are an integral part of the ethnographic pathway; they are part of the reason that ethnographic research remains such an interesting and unpredictable facet of the social sciences.

Note

[1] Much of the discussion surrounding these topics also questions who, exactly, is empowered and served by that collective knowledge.

References

Geertz, Clifford. 1973. *The Interpretation of Cultures.* New York: Basic Books.

Malinowski, Bronislaw. 1922. *Argonauts of the Western Pacific.* Repr., Prospect Heights, IL: Waveland Press, in 1984.

Swimming Through Fieldwork: Constructing Trust in the Mexican Caribbean

David M. Hoffman
University of Colorado–Boulder

It is eight weeks into my dissertation fieldwork, and I am crossing the crystal blue waters of the Mexican Caribbean towards a fishing camp located within a world biosphere reserve about 40 kilometers offshore from the town I have chosen as my field site. Through a combination of persistence and good fortune I have finally managed to convince a group of fisherman to take me along with them on an extended fishing trip.

This is my first opportunity to engage in participant observation, to see how these men make a living. Aside from basic personal belongings, I bring along my professional agenda of documenting my companions' actions and perceptions regarding the environment and conservation. However, these issues are far from my mind as we cross outside the protection of the offshore barrier reef, where we immediately encounter a souped-up Mexican military gunship setting out on its routine drug interception patrol. Our captain pauses to let them pass, and as soon as they are out of sight we pop open bon voyage beers and a joint is lit. I had expected the beer as a celebration of cutting ties with the land and comforts of home, but I was not expecting the marijuana.

I am not shocked by the presence of marijuana, but at the same time I am suddenly thrust into an awkward anthropological position; what are the limits of participant observation? If I accept their invitation to smoke, what type of reputation will I build in the small town of 350 that I am living in? Surely my actions will become part of the town *chisme* (rumor) upon the return of my companions. If I decline, I may be perceived by my companions as a wimp, a teetotaler, or uninterested in truly participating in the lifestyle of these fishermen. Worse yet, refusal to participate could endanger my ability to befriend these men and leave me unable to build the rapport that is essential to my anthropological research. After a heavy volley of verbal taunts attacking my manliness, I decide to share in the beer and marijuana. This is not a simple capitulation to peer pressure; instead it is a decision made with the future of my project on my mind. As I will explain later, I was already suspected as a narc and I felt that further refusal to join in their lifestyle and expectations would damage my ability to gain their confidence. Yet, I couldn't help but think, "Is this the way fieldwork is supposed to be?"

The party continues for the next two hours as the little 23-foot fiberglass *lancha* (boat) with no radio, life jackets, or first aid kit, jumped through the waves of the Caribbean. I marvel at the ability of my companions to stay fixed to the bench without holding on, while I, out of both fear and inexperience, grip the gunwale of the boat to keep myself from bouncing out. About halfway through the voyage we stop to admire a pod of dolphins that has approached the boat, and my companions chide me into clambering up front to snap pictures of the curious animals. The only other pause in our journey comes when a piece of flotsam warrants a u-turn to inspect whether it was *un paquete* (a package) of cocaine, a rare but possible occurrence. We "unfortunately" have no "luck" today and quickly return to our voyage.

Finally, we arrive within eyesight of our destination, crack another celebratory beer, and set out a trolling line to fish barracuda for dinner as we cruise towards land. "*Ponte verga, David!*" (Put your mast/penis) was the call as I put out the line, a skill I had learned only the week before. They all hooted and hollered as a barracuda struck, but then groaned at me when I lost it. "*Fallaste, David!*" (You failed), they shouted at me accusingly. My luck, or perhaps inability to complete the job, meant we would eat canned pork with eggs instead of fresh barracuda steaks, a disappointment to everyone including me.

We soon pull up to a one-room house built on stilts above the water (*una palofita*) located just to the side of a mangrove island, our home base for this venture. Alas, I survived the crossing, but my mind raced with doubts of my ability to relate to their lives, to adopt their ways, to show that I am not afraid and that I am willing to lay it on the line in order to gain their trust and confidence.

The goal of this trip was to fish as much Caribbean Spiny Lobster in the next month as was possible. At around $250 pesos ($23 U.S. dollars) a kilogram, and with a goal of 100 kilos for the month, these fishermen were looking to earn around $600 each; a healthy sum by rural Mexican standards. Our first day at the house was spent recovering from the voyage, looking for paquetes that may have washed up in the local mangrove, and snorkeling for our dinner of fish and lobster. It seemed like this wasn't going to be such a hard thing after all. However, early on the second morning it became clear that the vacation was over and it was now time to work. Fishing that morning began with a few words of instruction from Jose,[1] the patron of the crew. He said, "David, everything here is fast, so keep up." In the next instant Jose was ready and plunged into the water, spear gun and gaffing hook in hand. Instantly my heart began to race; I didn't want to disappoint. I fumbled to get my snorkel and mask positioned correctly while the other two fishermen aboard impatiently waited for me to plunge into the warm waters of the Caribbean. I entered the water and was immediately distracted by the myriad of coral structures and tropical fishes; but this was not a snorkel trip, this was work. I looked around to find Jose, who had entered the water only a few seconds before me, but I couldn't seem to find him. He was already a good 20 yards away, legs churning, and the space between us was rapidly widening. I swam as hard as I

Lobster fishing crew.

could to catch up with him, and luckily he had encountered a *piedra* (coral structure) in which several lobsters were holed up. This gave me just enough time to close the gap between us and catch my breath. I watched and counted the seconds as he gracefully descended, approached the caves, hooked a lobster, and then casually floated back to the surface where he killed the lobster with the same hook. "Forty-five seconds," I noted. Jose worked the whole set of caves and tossed five mostly dead lobsters to me with a warning to hold them by their antennae to avoid their sharp spines. Thus it became my job to hold on to the product and transfer it to the boat while he continued to dive.

Over the next several hours, I lamely tried to imitate Jose's diving technique in an attempt to help him locate more lobsters. I had no real luck at imitating him, or in finding lobsters, and only managed to nearly crack my head on the bottom of the boat. "Watch out David, always look up before surfacing!" was the warning given to me behind thinly veiled expressions of both laughter and incredulity at my amateurism. I even had difficulty with the "easy" task of getting myself in the boat when it was time to be transported to the next spot. My companions hopped into the boat as if they had springs in their feet, while I gripped the edge and tried desperately to haul myself in. They all yelled at me to kick and laughed at my inability. I finally got myself in the boat and was given a ribbing for being *la hija* (the daughter) and then chided for being too slow. My apparent inability is excused through a well-placed joke about how I really came along on this adventure so that I could experience "the big size" of the fishermen in my "tight little asshole." After some weak attempts to deflect these verbal assaults (the vocabulary of Mexican cursing was never taught to me in my university or high school Spanish classes), we arrived at the next set of coral and returned to the "solace" of the water. Again I attempted to keep up with the knowledge and conditioning of these fishermen, but already I was worrying about their frustration with the fact that I was more of a hindrance than a help.

This process continued for six days while I joined this lobster fishing crew at their camp. We were up at the crack of dawn, out diving by seven or eight in the morning, swimming constantly for five hours, relaxing in our hammocks by mid-afternoon, eating a huge meal, and having a *cafecito* (little coffee) along with our game of cards or dice before we passed out into our hammocks shortly after nightfall. We showered with a cupfuls of rain water collected in a giant barrel, threw our garbage straight into the ocean, and rinsed our plates with ocean water hauled a few feet away from a latrine that was little more than a plank over the water, sheltered by walls of roofing material. The solar panel on the roof of the place afforded enough power for a CD/radio and a single light bulb. We ate a variety of seafood cooked on a propane stove, and I was told that nearly every single one has aphrodisiac effects. This was always followed by another crack regarding whose hammock I'd be sleeping in that night!

Scattered throughout the day were copious amounts of marijuana smoking. Through the haze of the day, and the fast pace of the actual work, I tried to remain focused on my "job" as an anthropologist. I snuck in questions about their positions on conservation and got replies such as "I agree with it, but not in the way the government just comes and takes away what has been only ours for so long." I spent part of each day writing in my small field notebook, much to the curiosity of the fishermen. "What are you writing in there, David?" "I am writing about what we did today and some of what you said to me," I replied. "Read it to us. We want to know what you are saying," Jose asked. I was surprised by this request. I was not expecting to share my notes, let alone translate them into Spanish but quickly realized that I owed it to them to be honest. I read directly from what I wrote, "We fished 12 kilos of lobster today, which Jose says is a good day." They quickly lost interest in the rather mundane collection of facts that I had written down, and went back to their individual tasks of cooking, repairing gear, or reading the three-day-old newspapers we brought with us.

Throughout these six days I was constantly tested. My body was tested; it ached from the continuous swimming. I gained impressive wounds on my feet from my flippers, and the spines of the lobsters pulped my soft academic's hands. My mind and tolerance were also tested. I was constantly berated verbally, beat up linguistically as the butt of all jokes. I was interrogated about my research and my presence both here with the fishermen and in their hometown. The actions of my companions also tested my conscience. I was obligated to participate in their lifestyle of looking for washed up packets of drugs, highly illegal fishing activities, and drug consumption. Yet all of this testing brought me to the realization that this was the work I had to do to gain the confidence of my subjects. I was building the sort of trust essential to the anthropological endeavor.

Welcome to the life of a budding anthropologist working in the Mexican Caribbean. This was my first big fishing adventure after waiting nearly two months for someone to take me out with them. I was the source of intrigue like a new toy, the subject of harassment as the most inexperienced, and generally suspect for my inability to verbally defend myself against their taunting. At the same time as they pushed and pressured me, these men were the most generous hosts. They fed me, checked to make sure I hadn't been too cold in my hammock, and made sure to find me a ride back to land after my six days were up. What I have described here is only a fraction of what I experienced on this first big adventure of my fieldwork. Clearly, it was not only a learning experience, but it was also a test of my own ability to adapt to a situation, to drop my preconceived notions about right and wrong behavior, and to be (for the first time in my anthropological career) really confronted with what are my own limits of cultural relativism. I realized that to both survive and do anthropological research in this place I must take on their rules of the game, their way of seeing things, and their ways of acting in the world. Therefore, getting to my anthropological agenda necessitated that I undergo, at least partially, a personal transformation from academic to fisherman.

In this essay, I want to discuss the process of early fieldwork as I have experienced it. Mostly, I hope to focus on the issue of gaining trust and confidence, as well as the personal changes that are inherently linked to this process. These issues are ostensibly engaged with during graduate training in anthropology, but become strikingly real and challenging while in the field. In other words, I will describe the transformation of fieldwork from an intellectual and theoretical exercise to that of a lived experience; from the classroom to the streets and the boats! While fieldwork was much as I had expected it to be, many surprises were in store for me that have not only impacted my proposed project, but my own personality.

The Research Plan

While I drove the nearly 3,000 miles from Boulder, Colorado, to the state of Quintana Roo, Mexico, I had plenty of time to stew over the pending year of anthropological research to which I had voluntarily subjected myself. I was taking on an intellectual project that a granting institution, Fulbright, had deemed important enough to warrant funding. I not only had the stamp of approval from the decision makers from the Institute of International Education, but also had passed the scrutiny of those Mexican intellectuals that had reviewed my proposal. Thus, I am currently funded for 10 months to investigate the impacts that differences in the management structure of marine protected areas (MPAs) have for the actions, thoughts, and livelihoods of the fishing communities that are impacted by the conservation project. The original plan was to "test" whether the assumed benefits of community-based resource management (CBM), as discussed in anthropological and conservation literature, can be seen. By recording and comparing the actions, comportment, and livelihood choices of two communities in Quintana Roo, one with and one without community-based decision making, I hoped to either support or negate what I have intellectually felt were assumed and unproven results of CBM.

I chose the Quintana Roo coast of Mexico for both of my intended field sites because it was in some ways convenient. It is close to the United States, the people speak a language in which I had training, and it had several MPAs with varying types of management structure. I was also attracted to the intrigue associated with international tourism development in the region. Oh yes, I can't deny the fact that during my first two pre-fieldwork visits I fell prey to the aura of tropical paradise and tranquility that I thought characterized the region.

It is a well-known part of anthropological folklore that the best laid research plans will be spoiled by unexpected situations, and it is the job of the anthropologist to follow the courses that arise. While this is often addressed intellectually before entering into the field, it is another thing to experience the emotional, theoretical, and logistical changes created by encounters with the unexpected. In addition, despite the nauseating repetition of "building rapport" heard in my methods courses, I never seriously considered that a large part of my job as an anthropologist would be to gain the trust and acceptance of my informants. Both of these issues became especially salient in the first few weeks of my fieldwork due to extraordinary circumstances in the community that I first entered.

As I will explain below, early in my fieldwork I encountered many obstacles and unknown factors that endangered not only my project but also my personal safety. More importantly, these issues hammered home the anthropological reality that fieldwork is more than just research, it is about establishing oneself as both trustworthy and a friend. In my case, establishing trust and "rapport" has meant taking on roles and adjusting to field situations that I never expected. At the same time, unforeseen events in the field have forced me to abandon the neatly packaged research plan that I had spent so much time and energy developing for both my committee and my own intellectual interests.

Building Trust Despite the Square Groupers

Upon arrival to my first field site my research plan was left half-paralyzed and the feasibility of gaining trust, confidence, and access to the community was seriously encumbered. A few short days into my fieldwork I learned that a number of the fisherman had won what a local ex-patriot Gringo affectionately called "the square grouper lottery." About a six weeks earlier, a majority of the town's fishermen had the luck (or was it planned?) of coming across more than a metric ton of cocaine that washed up on the beaches in and around town. A Colombian speedboat dumped several paquetes of 100 percent pure cocaine overboard because it had been detected by the Mexican military. This tactic enables drug transporters to escape Mexican justice and also guarantees that at least some of their product will be washed ashore and make it to its destination. Needless to say, there is a substantial economic reward for those who are daring enough to connect the product with its owners. While I had heard rumors prior to my fieldwork of this sort of activity existing up and down the coast of Quintana Roo, I had never really contemplated the impact that this might have upon my own investigations. This blissful naivety was quickly shattered.

My original plans to complete the "participant observation of fishing activities phase" of my research in the first month and a half were dashed by cocaine. With the fishermen instantly enriched, there was no real need to go fishing. For weeks the fleet of lanchas sat idle on the beach, there was nary a movement. I woke up early every morning and walked the beachfront in the hope of finding someone to take me out fishing, but had very little luck. Instead, the fishermen were zipping through town on their brand new motorcycles and scooters and happily imbibing for weeks on end. When I explained my project to a British woman working at a local dive shop, she told me, "It's too bad you showed up when you did. Normally the fishermen would be going out every day, but these days no one is. They are too busy celebrating."

My frustration began to build. How could I investigate the political ecology of fishing and conservation management without completing the "participant observation" that was to frame my understanding of local livelihood production? Thus, within my first weeks of field-work my plan for investigating the resource use of local fishermen was turned upside-down by a stroke of "luck." What does one do when this happens?

My curiosity, desire for a good story, and the realization that drugs are part of the eco-nomics here made me want to dig up every detail of this cocaine networking. Yet, I had to remind myself of the warning I had received at a Fulbright cocktail party only two weeks before my arrival here. A Mexican political scientist and journalist sternly advised me, "Keep yourself out of the drug trafficking in Quintana Roo. The Mexican mafia isn't kidding around."

So, what could I do? My first reaction was to panic because I was already behind my schedule. I e-mailed my advisor for some sagely wisdom from the experienced. He told me to relax, soak it in, read a good novel or some ethnography, and don't worry about it so much. He also assured me that my committee would understand that things change, and that I may not be able to complete all of the promised field methods that had been so care-fully thought out for my research prospectus. Of course this was perfectly practical advice, but it did little to quell my anxiety about being behind. Ultimately, what he advised me to do was to forget about my research proposal, my agenda, and live life in this community. While this sounds extremely liberating, my emotions ran wild with confusion and bewilderment. I had been focusing on this research design for nearly three years of my life and I felt as if my per-fected plan was now useless. Would I ever be able to recuperate and resuscitate my project?

I ended up following his advice. I forced myself to take it easy and introduce both my project and myself to as many people as possible. Some community members were quite gracious in these first few weeks, willing to talk to me and tell me the basics about the town and its people. However, this seemingly simple task was also severely hampered by the cocaine bonanza, which made many others seriously paranoid about unfamiliar faces. In fact, the timing of my arrival coincided with the first investigations carried out by federal police forces. Several of the young men in town were questioned and purportedly abused by these police. It should be no surprise that, as a stranger suddenly waltzing into town and asking lots of questions about the jobs, relationships, and changes that are happening in town, I was received with caution and reserve. At one point a relatively well-connected non-local bluntly stated to me that I had the perfect cover for a CIA or DEA agent! I had heard of other anthropologists having this problem, but had no ready response that could defuse sus-picion in total. Thus, my visions of the grand public reception of the anthropologist, or at least the public's willingness to talk openly with me in the first weeks of my fieldwork, quickly evaporated. I was seriously struggling to build rapport and to get my research back on track, and it quickly became clear that I was going to have to *work* to gain the trust of this community.

Keeping Secrets and Encounters with Trust

Trust and confidence are two-way streets, and in these first few months they were not only preoccupations of mine, but were also concerns of several fishermen that had been bold enough to talk with me. This was made blatantly obvious through my interactions with a particularly gregarious fisherman named Enrique. One afternoon about three months into my work, an obviously drunk Enrique came to my house to have a chat with me. We talked about his fishing experiences, and without solicitation, he told me about his involvement in drug trafficking and illegal fishing. I found the incredible stories to be very informative, and I was sincerely grateful for his willingness to talk honestly with me. All the while the warnings of the political scientist in Mexico City were ringing in my ears. At the end of our conversation I tried to make it clear that what he told me would remain confidential. I thanked him for the much-needed vision into the rationales behind drug trafficking and illegal fishing that he had provided, and he left my house apparently unconcerned.

Over the next few weeks I wasn't too preoccupied with the information I had gained from Enrique. While it was important to the overall story of the town, it was clearly something I would keep to myself. Yet, unbeknownst to me, Enrique was very preoccupied with the security of the information he had given me. One night a few weeks after our initial encounter, he and several friends came to my house for some cold beers. In the course of the conversation I was asked by a curious fishermen, "Do you work?" I explained that my job was to talk to people, that I write daily about my experiences and knowledge gained, and eventually I would publish a dissertation about what I had learned. Everyone seemed fine with this explanation, the party ended when the town's generator-run electricity cut out, and my guests went their separate ways. I thought nothing of this conversation or how it could be interpreted until several days later, when Enrique visited me again.

In an alcohol and cocaine-fueled stupor, Enrique came to my door and asked me why I had tricked him and lied to him. He was obviously angry, so I invited him in and asked him to sit down and explain to me what the problem was. I didn't really understand what the issue was until he related several stories regarding people who had met unfortunate ends for knowing too much. I then realized that he was worried about the confidentiality of our conversations. I explained to him that I was using coded names and that my investigation was not focused on the confidential details he had shared with me. He regarded me with skepticism, got right into my face, and very bluntly told me that I was never to share the information with anyone, especially people in town because they talk too much. He then laid it out very clearly by telling me that it was all right if I was FBI or DEA, but he wanted to know the truth. I had to reassure him that I was neither, that all would be kept in the strictest confidence, and that I would never intentionally cross him. After about an hour defending myself and my research methods, his mistrust was apparently quelled. Enrique, finally satisfied, then proceeded to invite me to his house (a first) for beers and to listen to Los Tigres del Norte (a musical group famous for their songs about drugs, immigration, and life on the U.S.–Mexico border).

Thus, the issue of drug trafficking preoccupied my first few months in this community: It was a source of personal danger (if I had gotten to know too much) and fear and also had seriously altered my research plan. Eventually, some of the fishermen have been forced to go back to fishing, although I heard it is still on a much lower scale than in the past. As is obvious from the introduction to this essay, I have even managed to get myself out there with some of them. While I fretted that I would never get to my participant observation, I was barely aware of the fact that by just being in this community I was getting it done and that I had learned a considerable amount about how things work in town. More importantly, while hanging out I learned about and participated in illicit behaviors, all of which proved that I was not going to betray my informants.

Teamwork and Confidence

Building confidence and rapport in this community was not only created by my participation in illegal activities, but also by my involvement in a daily ritual among the men in town. During my first weeks of fieldwork, I rediscovered a personal passion and at the same time encountered an absolutely fantastic (and unsuspected) route of gaining entry and respect in this community—playing *futbol* (soccer). Every day at about five o'clock in the evening most of the men, ranging in age from late teens to early 40s, gather on a crude soccer field carved out of the brushlike forest that characterizes this coastal region. The pressure to do well starts as everyone is warming up and taking shots on goal. The cockier players declare that they will score a *golazo* (a great goal) while the others standby ready either to ridicule them for missing the shot or to congratulate them on a promise made good. The warm-up always seems to last forever as people exchange comments, talk about gossip, and generally concentrate on making fun of one another through a slew of curses and sexual innuendo. After some time and a declaration that it is getting late, two people are cajoled into selecting teams, and then everyone finds their respective betting partner on the opposite team.

The stakes are not monetarily high, the normal bet being a soda after the game, but winning or losing matters for each person's own personal status among the men. During the game, play is generally aggressive yet fair, but the criticism is sharp and biting. Missed scoring opportunities, flubbed passes, and poor defensive coverage are always met with a comment. This is just local pickup soccer, but any controversial foul or goal is met with a "world cup" cacophony of curses and complaints. It is clear that the game does mean more than just the score at the end of the day. The games usually last about 40 minutes and are punctuated by the setting of the sun and the ferocious attack of hordes of mosquitoes and sand flies. Afterwards, everyone rides to the center of town to pay their debts and enjoy a refreshment. As the electricity of the town turns on, we all sit discussing the game, reviewing the day's activities, and continue to give one another a hard time.

It is into this scene that I threw myself after a six-year hiatus from playing the game that was essential to my youth. Soon after my arrival I made a habit of going and playing in the daily game, and now it is expected that I will show up and play. If I don't, I better have a good excuse. When I first began to play, I barely understood a single thing that was going on. The Spanish was filled with slang, double meaning, and curses of which I had no clue. I was instantly the source of ridicule (although at the time I didn't know it), being told I was a *cangrejo* (literally crab, but insinuating I was homosexual), a *puto* (male whore), and a *pinche gringo* (damn gringo). Though I didn't always comprehend what they were saying to me, I did understand was that the soccer field is a place of machismo, where you are expected to have no fear and go all out. Simply by showing up, I put my personal reputation and machismo on the line.

Thus, unwittingly soccer became a significant factor in building rapport with the men of the community. It enabled me to quickly meet many of the younger men, some of them fishermen, and separated myself from the tourists that simply snap photos of the local guys playing their favorite sport. Joining in sporting activities was never mentioned in my methods books and courses, and I never thought soccer would figure in my participant-observation, but many days I have learned more on the field than I did trolling through town talking to people. Soccer gave me an opportunity to pick up on the local slang, learn everyone's nicknames, listen to the local gossip before and after the game, and observe the social interaction among a significant proportion of the adult men in town. In addition, it provided me with another opportunity to prove that I am not afraid, that I am willing to mix it up with these guys, and that I wanted to learn what it means to be a man in this town. Amazingly, despite the fact that I was always the target of insults as the "gringo," I was asked to play for the town team (second string of course) when they play against other communities. Soccer helped me integrate into the town, and everyone came to know the *guerito* (little white guy) who plays "futbol." Ultimately, it provided an unpredicted opportunity to build trust, confidence, and rapport in this community.

Staying Connected: Home or Away?

At the same time as I was struggling to find an entrance into community life here, I was also trying to cope with some of the expectations of modern fieldwork. In contrast to the more isolated fieldwork of the generation before us, anthropologists today face a much higher expectation of continued contact with their career and lives at home. In my first weeks of the field experience, I was both blessed and frustrated by the ways in which the Internet has reframed the anthropological experience. It was a wondrous miracle that there was Internet access in this town that lacks 24-hour electricity, land-based phone connections, and even the most basic mail service. E-mail was the most effective way to contact the outside world, but due to the isolation and tourist economy, my initial connection at a local dive shop was an extremely expensive hourly rate of $10. The system here was set up for tourists wishing to send a message or two, not for a researcher who is trying to communicate with academics and bureaucrats here, and maintain various projects that continued on the home front. Thus, I was faced with an unexpected dilemma of sacrificing money out of my limited budget in order to stay in touch with list servs, friends, and family or severing the ties. Ultimately, I chose the second option, and was forced to deal with the emotional and career consequences of infrequent contact with my known world.

Eventually I struck a deal with the local Internet network run by the gringo hotel owners to pay by the month for unlimited connection time. However, all the time that I struggled with this connection dilemma, I couldn't help but think how modern communication technologies have changed the world of anthropology. While we often talk about the impacts of technology on our subjects, we rarely reflect on how it has changed the anthropological experience in itself. Perhaps I am naïve about the amount of communication that existed in the past, but I can't help but presume that earlier anthropologists (even those who did their fieldwork in the 1980s) had no choice but to forsake their connections with home, to drop all those projects they were working on, forget about conferences and papers, and solely focus on the field context in which they found themselves. In contrast, today's anthropologists are expected to maintain an interest and involvement in their academic lives at home while they are in the field. In my own experience, I am communicating about the American Anthropological Association (AAA) meetings in the U.S., editing papers for a book project, and even answering questions e-mailed to me about my former part-time job at CU-Boulder! Of course I can drop all of these to focus on my surroundings, but in the race for a job in the anthropological world, abandoning communication could severely damage my employment chances.

Modern communication technologies also had impacts upon the issues of confidence and trust. The more time I spend e-mailing necessarily means that I am spending less time "being" in the community. In contrast to some other regions of the world, in the region where I am located, simply connecting to the Internet differentiates me from the local people. The majority of people in town do not know how to run a computer and have only a slight idea of what the Internet is. My use of the Internet, especially because my connection exists at a gringo hotel outside of town, separates me economically, culturally, and physically from the town in which I am living. My laptop itself is a direct symbol of my affluence and the unintentional but real separation between these people and myself.

Clearly I am struggling with the dilemma that the Internet presents. First, it is necessarily time away from town and daily fishing and subsistence activities. Second, it aligns me with the outside world of gringos and academics. Third, it is a symbol of status that few locals are likely to achieve barring major changes in the economics of the town. I have heard from other anthropologists that using Internet cafes has been a vital part of their fieldwork and helped them connect to the lives of their subjects. While this may be true for those of us working with urban, multi- and transnational populations, in some ways I feel that my time spent e-mailing and looking up information online is detrimental to giving my complete attention to the local context. At the same time, my time at a gringo hotel provides me the opportunity to see the work lives of their employees, gives me a sense of the tourists that come to the region, and provides insight into the difficulties faced by foreign entrepreneurs in town. Thus, while there are significant downsides to the modern fieldwork addiction to the Internet, it has its benefits. Besides, it keeps me both sane and connected to events in the wider world (there is no newspaper delivery here either!).

Multi-Sited Ethnography

Originally, I had planned on spending five months in each of the two communities. However, the fact that it took time to gain access to the first community, prove I wasn't going to report their activities to the authorities, and get my language skills up to speed led to a new stress in my anthropological quest. After three months there, I realized that I had little to no "data." My research was delayed due to the cocaine impacts on fishing activities and the implications this had for my planned participant observation. My gut feeling that there was still significant mistrust in my presence and project contributed to my lack of data. For example, I didn't even feel comfortable starting my recorded interviews until four months into my project, and I struggled over the feasibility of my research design and the realities of multi-sited ethnography.

Clearly multi-sited ethnography gives the researcher powerful tools for comparison and contrast, and the ability to follow flows of goods, people, or ideas. Back in the world of graduate school I was enamored with these potentials and decided that in order to produce a quality dissertation I needed to include a multi-sited component. The fact that I took for granted the time needed to gain entrance and acceptance into small, isolated communities has made me doubt whether the multi-sited approach is feasible in my case. I have hemmed and hawed about dropping my visit to the second research site. I have thought to myself, "What in the world will another single community study prove? I still have so much to learn here in my first community. How can I go through the lengthy introduction and confidence-building process again?" Ultimately, I decided to drop the comparative angle and to remain in a single community for the rest of my grant period. Why am I doing this? I feel that I still have so much to learn here and that gaining detail and depth in one place is much better than having a superficial knowledge of two.

Advocacy and Guilt

My experience of early fieldwork has also been infused with an overwhelming feeling of inability, paralysis, and guilt over the fact that I have very little to offer in return for the generosity of the people here. I have always felt that anthropology should be more than an intellectual or descriptive exercise and that it can be a method, which can help communities achieve their desired goals. Thus, I have felt that the practice of anthropology should involve some sort of advocacy, but I am frustrated by the difficulty in achieving this dynamic role.

In my early fieldwork I am repeatedly struck by the fact that I know so little; it seems impossible for me to have any role in creating change here. In addition, I question my ability to do what is right. Who am I to say what is right or wrong for the people? I am not from their community, and will be lucky if I return on later research trips. Although I may be better educated than nearly everyone in this community, does this give me the right to interject my opinion? How much does my own cultural baggage interfere with understanding what is desired by community members? How do I balance between the needs and desires of different factions within the community? These questions have been mulling around in my head for the last six months and unfortunately are still not (and may not be) answered.

I discussed my dilemma with several informants, and many said that I just need to offer my friendship, that is all they ask. At the same time, they have told me that the community is wary of anyone who wants to "help" since that was ostensibly the goal of the conservation NGO (nongovernment organization) that came to protect both the environment and the community's right to the fruits of conservation-based tourism development. Instead of feeling grateful about the NGO's objectives, a considerable portion of the townspeople now feels that this NGO fooled them into giving up many of their subsistence rights for a future that doesn't offer much for them: tourism. Thus, there is a negative track record of outsiders coming in with the aim of helping the community. How can I avoid this trap? In addition, this negative image of outside researchers has been exacerbated by the fact that none have returned to follow up on their work. I am constantly asked, "When are you leaving? Are you going to come back?" I always try to let the skeptics know that I want to come back, that I want to continue my connection here, but that funds and life might get in the way. To this they usually reply, "You'll be just like the rest; you won't come back."

Ultimately, I have decided that my advocacy at this point can only be small-scale. I am offering a free English course; I have brought some supplies to the local schools, and I patiently listen to the stories that the people tell me. I still feel as though I am taking away much more than I am giving back, and I have no idea how to remedy this situation. I now finally know why anthropology has been perceived as a tool of colonialism, and I am often wracked with guilt over the inequality created by difference between what I take and what I give back. At the same time, I think perhaps I am helping to reverse the colonial process; in many ways these people have more to teach me than I have to teach them. If I can give a fair and accurate account of what I have learned here, give back on some small scale, and maintain my relationship with this community, I will have done something that has—albeit minor—impact. Finally, knowing I still have much more time here, I hope at the end of my stay I will have much more to say—perhaps some solid suggestions, and an informative description of people's lives.

Returning to the Water: Researcher or Fisherman?

Fast forward to month six of my fieldwork. Again, I am at the fishing camps of the local cooperative, but this time we are here to fish the *caracol* (conch) quota. This is my third trip to the area, and my second time for the quota. While the ocean crossing still makes me nervous, I do not let these fears overwhelm me. I join the six-man team in taking out their quota of just over 300 kilos of caracol in four days of very hard work. In a relaxed manner I slip into the water, despite the dangers that certainly exist. I pull out four to six conch, wait for the

Crew processing caracol aboard lancha.

boat, and toss them in to the affirmation of *"eso"* (like that) from the boat captain. I shrug off the fact that our motor breaks while the sun is setting, we have no tools to fix it, and there is no flashlight. Luckily we are only about a mile from home and on the lee side of an island that gives us ground to pole our ways home and save ourselves from drifting off to sea. *"Una aventura mas"* (one more adventure), is my reaction while I secretly count my blessings. As we process the catch on board, I react and deflect their accusations of being a *marido* (husband) or puto with my own verbal taunts. I certainly do not have the linguistic skill to retaliate in an equally verbose manner, but the men are impressed with the fact that I try and have some success. At one point, I am even branded with the positive image among the crew that I am a *desmadre* (a disgrace), just like all the other fishermen. During this trip the conversation is not guarded regarding what I do and do not know or what they should and should not tell me. Instead, we talk openly about both legal and illegal behavior, and they know that I will not get them in trouble.

Author throwing caracol into lancha.

Finally, after months of struggling I have gained the confidence, trust, and rapport that are essential to the anthropological endeavor. It has not always been easy, and it has often involved taking on a personality that would never manifest itself in my life at home. In many ways, I have taken on the outlook and actions of these verbally crude, yet beautifully loyal and friendly fishermen. I find myself swearing all the time. I have a serious affinity for seafood. As I cruise through town I shout out unsolicited and meaningless insults that are traded between *cuates* (friends). I even find myself wondering what I would do if I ran across a paquete floating in the ocean. Of course, when I really think it through, my "normal" self takes over and chides me for even thinking about this possibility. This rational brain also enables me to avoid the daily drug and alcohol abuse that is a significant fact of life here. Thus, the researcher still exists within me, but as time moves on I realize and embody the fact that rapport is not just about getting along with people; it is also about gaining trust by taking on their realities as your own. Am I a Mexican fishermen? No, most definitely not, but I am finally beginning to learn what it means to be one.

Note

[1] All names are pseudonyms to protect the identities of my informants.

Sleeping with One Eye Open:
The Perils of Fieldwork in a Brazilian Juvenile Prison

Kristen Drybread
Columbia University

Deviance

"**F**ieldwork never turns out like you plan." Several professors told me this as I crafted my dissertation proposal and prepared for extended field research. I acknowledged their wisdom, and accepted that I would be in for some unexpected experiences while in the field. Still, I was certain that at least the focus of my project would remain stable throughout my field research. After all, I had decided to study adults who work with "children at risk" in northeastern Brazil precisely to avoid the trap that other ethnographers dealing with such children usually fall into: namely, anthropologists who set out to work with children on the streets or in reforming institutions usually end up writing about the adult advocates who facilitate and mediate their relationships with the children they originally proposed to study. Assuming in advance the problems of mediation, authority, and age that have made adults the focus of child-centered research in Brazil, I decided to intentionally study adult advocates—in particular, their discourse about "children at risk" and their practice of children's rights advocacy.

My strategy backfired. Advocates for children are perfectly willing to let foreign scholars examine and write about the kids they work with. Most, however, are unwilling to have the researcher's gaze turn upon their professional practice, and her tape recorder turned on during their conversations. The adult advocates I tried to study kept me at arm's length, paradoxically pushing me towards the kids who I had assumed I would not be able to approach. And, as my rapport developed with the kids particularly feared by local child savers, I began to also bear the mark of the kids' stigma: inside of my principal research site, a juvenile prison called the CASA, administrators and experts began to treat me like a criminal.

Ethnographic literature often tells the story of fledgling anthropologists who enter into their field sites and quickly fall into relationships with local leaders or power brokers who see in the fieldworker—among other things—an opportunity for status, knowledge, and, perhaps, foreign goods. In some instances, these types of relationships take longer to form than in others, and in some cases the anthropologist has to suffer a certain degree of humiliation or discomfort in order to gain access to the place and the people she intends to study. Still, the general formula is that, despite inevitable gaffs, misunderstandings, and discomforts that come with trying to enter another culture as a participant observer, the fieldworker is ultimately accepted into her host community and respected as a scholar who is endeavoring to conduct important research. In my case, this never happened. My research has never been respected as such by the administrators of the CASA. And, the more time I spend in my field site, the more suspect my research—and I—become.

Strange Methods

"What she's doing is not research," I overheard a social worker gripe to the director of the CASA as I was using the restroom next door to his office. "All she does is sit around all day talking to the boys. That's not research. All of the other students who have come here from *our* University have collected data: they have used our records and talked with the professional staff to collect statistics on the origins, crimes, and tendencies of our boys. What statistics is she collecting? Have you ever asked? None. You see, what she is doing is not research. She's putting her nose where she shouldn't . . . and who knows what she does in there with the boys!" There was a heavy pause, rife with insinuation. "All I know is that it's not Research. She's not collecting data that other Researchers—*real* Researchers—have collected here." Another, lighter pause. "You want to know something? I don't think she even knows what Research is."

Self-styled Brazilian intellectuals speak of Research with a capital "R." It is an activity reserved for the elite, and immediately confers status upon anyone who publicly claims to be performing Research. That is, if the research being undertaken is considered legitimate.

In the far reaches of Northeastern Brazil, anthropological fieldwork is not a recognizable method of research. Here in the badlands, the local branch of the Federal University does not yet have a full Professor of Anthropology on staff and—with the exception of a few professors who are cloistered in their offices on campus—most (self-proclaimed) intellectuals in the region have no notion of cultural anthropology as a branch of study. Consequently, when I tell "educated" people that I am conducting an anthropological investigation, they assume that I have come to excavate the ruins of a former community of runaway, rebel slaves. In their minds archaeology and anthropology are synonymous; the former encompasses the latter. Therefore, it is little surprise that no one in this town can understand what the local juvenile prison can possibly have to do with anthropology.

My academic claims have generated two responses: Some self-styled intellectuals chuckle at my having misnamed my sociological project a work of "anthropology." This group takes my age (I am a twenty-something who can pass for an adolescent, and I am at least 10 years younger than any local intellectual attempting individual research), my style of dress (particularly my nose ring), and my imagined confusion about the discipline of anthropology as signs of incompetence. They consider me a ditzy *gringa* who is neither intelligent nor serious enough to deserve their respect. And, my ethnographic methods only strengthen their perceptions of my ineptitude; they do not recognize my work as Research. This is annoying. The other popular local interpretation of my motivations for frequenting an all-male juvenile prison are, however, much more offensive. The local "intellectuals" who do not judge me incompetent, have deemed me suspect. They insinuate—some have been so bold as to say outright—that my claim to be conducting research is a pretext: a lie told in order to gain (primarily sexual) access to incarcerated adolescent boys. The women who seem to entertain this belief treat me as though I am some kind of lecher; the men treat me like a whore. My motives, my qualifications, and my methods (of research) are the subject of constant scrutiny, gossip, and reproach.

"Who did you say is sponsoring your research?" an administrator asked, returning my passport. He had confiscated it when I entered the institution today in order to call the Federal Police to see if he could discover a reason to have me deported.

"A couple of foundations: the Wenner-Gren Foundation for Anthropological Research, the Institute of Latin American and Iberian Studies at my university, Columbia University, and The Fulbright-Hays Foundation. You've probably at least heard of the Fulbright Foundation—it's international."

He tried to look pensive. "Fulbright? No. Never heard of it. Are you sure it exists?" He threatened, "I am going to have to call and confirm that."

"Go right ahead," I told him. He wouldn't be the first. Several of the adults implicated in my research have made similar phone calls in the past few months. They leave no room for doubt: I have worn out my welcome.

Blind Spots

Most "fact-finding" missions conducted in Brazilian penal institutions are accomplished in less than a month—generally in a period of days. When they agreed to let me study the

CASA, the institution's administrators assumed I would be able to collect sufficient data in a day or two; they could give me some numbers and send me packing. Even though I explained my intentions to conduct extended field research at the outset, it seems that no one actually believed I would dedicate more than a year to collecting information about the institution and its inmates. My continued presence seems to have gotten some people worried. I think they are anxious about what I might see (and what I might report afterwards).

Now, while I would like to consider myself a diligent, incisively observant (albeit tender-footed) anthropologist, I know that much of what actually takes place within the CASA escapes my attention. Even in an atmosphere that is not self-consciously one of "high-security," it is impossible to apprehend *everything*. We all go through life with blinders on, and during fieldwork those blinders become (or ideally, should become?) painfully patent. Theory, culture, gender . . . all prohibit—and conversely enable—a fieldworker's limited and situated perceptions, as do her contacts with the people in the community where she is studying. Like it or not, she becomes involved—embedded, even—in local politics and struggles and cannot befriend everyone. Establishing one contact often means precluding another. Furthermore, relying on friendly, helpful locals to mediate situations with people often means trusting certain people to provide her with a reasonably representative view of the community and its culture.

Fieldwork demands a certain amount of trust. In my case, I have come to count on supportive locals and inmates and to believe that the information they make available to me, while inevitably partial, is genuine (notice I am not using the word true). I know that they make choices—conscious or otherwise—in deciding which stories, beliefs, practices, and rules they share with me. Since they are entrusting me with their constructions of the CASA and of themselves, I accept what they have decided is important for me to know and record, and I do not pry (too much) into the aspects of institutional and personal life that they choose not to share. People share so much information that I am not able to comprehend it all, much less continually question the motives for its revelation. Besides, I inevitably hear multiple accounts of the stories I am told and am, therefore, able to learn a great deal from the details particular individuals choose to withhold and to reveal in their own tellings. Consequently, in *most* cases I do not set out to investigate the things that may have been omitted, or purposefully hidden from me. I believe that even when particular people distort information or tell me boldfaced lies, this too is meaningful and can contribute to my analysis: I have not set out to find Truth, but to collect stories.

Granted, sometimes information I receive is so obviously skewed that I search out other versions in order to be able to evaluate and analyze what has been passed on to me, as well as the possible reasons why it was given a particular slant when presented. In most cases I do not assume deliberate duplicity; I trust the people who willingly participate in my research and I sense that they trust me to portray them in the most honest (and sympathetic) manner possible. My ethical stance demands that I not betray this trust; therefore, I do not set out to find what the people who *help* me might be hiding from me.

On days when I am feeling particularly cynical, I entertain the thought that the people who have decided to help me in my fieldwork—particularly the adults—might be engaging in illegal or unethical behavior and, in order to keep my attention from this, they show me only the positive aspects of their work and their discourse. I hope not. But, since it has always been my intention to seek out the positive aspects of the Brazilian juvenile justice system in order to challenge negative stereotypes of juvenile offenders and to critique the current movement of juvenile justice from reform and towards punishment,[1] I am not likely to assume that the inspiring information people share with me is merely a smokescreen, designed to blind me to sinister aspects of life in the CASA. The institution is dangerous. It is filled with teenagers who have been convicted of violent crimes and always teeters on the brink of lawlessness. I do not need to seek out horror stories here; it is almost impossible to avoid them. I appreciate that many, many people in the institution—particularly the inmates—have set out to show me another, less obvious and much more sympathetic side of the facility.

I willingly admit that, as a foreigner conducting fieldwork in an unfamiliar place, it would not be incredibly difficult to manipulate my vision. With kindness, candor, and responsiveness, an administrator or inmate could quite easily limit my gaze to aspects of life at the CASA that he or she personally considers appropriate for me to (re)present and analyze in my work. Many of the people who have been reasonably forthcoming when talking with me, I am certain, have done so. This is, in part, why I am having trouble understanding the hostility the administration of the institution harbors toward me and my work. If they had been helpful, they would not have had much difficulty controlling my research and I most likely would not have been led to question the ethics, foibles, and failures of their practices and discourse.

The obvious discomfort my presence provokes among most of the administrators of the CASA makes me question: Why do I make them so uncomfortable? What might these people be trying to hide?

Indiscipline and Punishment

I am finding that Brazilian policing—especially within the realm of incarceration—operates according to a strange mixture of secrecy, intimidation, and freedom. Rapid fact-finding missions may detect, or even glimpse, the strategies of silence and coercion that allow prison administrators to maintain a façade of control over their facilities. Reports commonly indicate that torture—or at least the threat of torture—is a common tactic used by Brazilian prison officials to keep inmates reigned in. I do not want to suggest that practices that could

be construed as torture are absent from the disciplinary regime of Brazilian penal institutions. I have experienced firsthand the physical and verbal abuses administrators dole out to
intimidate prisoners—and anyone else who could potentially challenge their authority or
publicly critique their practices. However, I am starting to think that such practices of overt
dominance point not to sadistic authority but to a perilous lack of control.

In my experience it is, in fact, the inmates who seem to dictate the order of the yard of
the CASA. Their codes of honor, respect, and silence determine the status and security of
each inmate. Fights, rebellions, escapes, and murders are common means of social control
within the prison yard. And although an atmosphere of constant fear pervades the CASA,
the boys also have the satisfaction of knowing that they, and not the administration, are in
control of the institution. "If we wanted to, we could take this place over and kill every last
one of them," Carlos told me one day, after suffering a particularly humiliating confrontation
with a guard. "They know that. They shit on themselves every time we have a little rebellion."

"Why don't you just take the place over then?" I asked, challenging him slightly, but not
too much—I wouldn't want to be around in the event of a full-blown takeover.

"Because of us. You take them out, and there'd be only us. It'd be worse. It's already
hell here. Imagine if it was everyone for himself. It'd be shit. Nobody'd survive. It'd be escape
or die."

"If they're so horrible, why do you guys have so many rebellions, then?" I retorted. (I tend
to be a bit cheeky when I talk to the guys; I don't want to them to think that I am scared, that
I am motherly, or that they pull one over on me. I've worked out a tone for my conversations
that is somewhere between friendly and snide—and it's almost always a bit acerbic.) "Since I
showed up here, there have been—what?—six? Why do you do it, if it's so dangerous?"

Carlos didn't reply immediately. He seemed to be measuring his response. He couldn't
come up with just one, so he gave me a carefully thought out list: "Vengeance, to teach the
cabuetas [squealers] to keep their mouths shut, to have something to do . . . who knows?
Maybe it's to scare the administration—I don't know. They happen because they just happen—I don't know." He shook his head in silence for a moment. With dead seriousness he
added, "There are rebellions here because it's hell. It's a prison, dude; rebellions happen. No
prisoner is gonna have his liberty taken away and not do anything. He has to rebel."

I took a deep breath, letting his words sink in. Then, I questioned, "Yeah? Has to? Are
you sure?" Carlos looked confused. I continued; steering our conversation towards what I
thought might be a philosophical discussion of the nature of the prisoner and the meanings
of confinement. "Is there a way it could be prevented? Do you rebel because you have to, or
because there's nothing better to do?"

I was searching for an existential response, but Carlos gave me a much more concrete
and, perhaps, more political one: "Damn, this Kris." He shook his head. "You're sharp. Yeah.

There's not a fuckin' thing to do around here. A guy's already in crime. What's he gonna do? You start thinking of the bad shit you could do, the people who've pissed you off. You can't give a criminal too much time to think. You've got to keep him busy. That's why it's the administration's own fault. If they had stuff for us to do—a school, activities, sports and all that shit they say we have a right to—a guy wouldn't have time to think about crime. You're right on there. We rebel because they must want us to; if they wanted this place to be calm, they'd fill it with activity. You gotta keep a criminal's mind busy."

Signs of Suffering and Solidarity

The fact that the inmates of the CASA have very few activities available to fill the endless hours of waiting for freedom has been an asset to my research. I may not be a particularly entertaining individual, but talking to me gives the boys something to do. I listen, I respond, and I don't threaten to kill them or punish them if they say something I find offensive. I know that some of the boys genuinely enjoy talking with me. Others seek me out for conversation simply because they are bored. In either case, I feel that the inmates generally accept me as someone they can talk to and someone they can trust.

Establishing trust was time consuming, and it was not particularly easy. A few accidents, however, helped. In fact, I unwittingly managed to get on the good side of some of the inmates of the juvenile detention center before I actually began my fieldwork. In the summer prior to my qualifying exams, I was conducting preliminary research among institutions working with street children of the city. I accepted an invitation from a social worker from one such institution to visit the CASA, to check on one of her former clients, and to see for myself what happens to teens who, she told me, "aren't lucky enough to be saved by the social projects of our city."

On the day of our visit, I brought a notebook and a pen with me: the rudimentary equipment of a fledgling anthropologist wanting to record her thoughts and observations during a whirlwind tour of a potential field site. The pen allowed me to capture some of the images that, nonetheless, became imprinted in my memory: the competing smells of rotting chicken and stale urine, the damp slabs of concrete intended to serve the boys as beds, the crushing silence—save periodic outbursts of what I assume were inmates banging on closed iron doors. Even if I had not written about them in my notebook, I would never be able to wipe from my memory the faces of the seven hollow-eyed boys who had been locked inside a tiny cage euphemistically called "The Room of Reflection" for eight consecutive days in punishment for a failed attempt at escape. I would also never forget the psychologist who used my presence as a visitor from the United States to tell the incarcerated teens they were lucky to have been sentenced under Brazilian law: "In her country," she repeated to each of them in a tone that seemed to contain both regret and glee, "a boy like you would be in prison for life. Or he'd be sent to the electric chair."

When I returned to the CASA to collect descriptive details of the facility for a chapter about juvenile crime in my doctoral dissertation, I had long forgotten about the pen. I didn't remember that I had left it behind inside "The Room of Reflection," with a lanky, pimple-faced boy named Rubens. Almost as soon as I entered the blue iron door separating the inside of the CASA from the outside world for the second time, he called me over to thank me.

An inveterate troublemaker, Rubens was now locked—by choice—inside a small, windowless dorm across the yard from the entrance. He is marked for death by his fellow inmates and prefers the dreary security of his dorm to the perilous freedom of the courtyard. The front door of the compound is not visible from his dorm, yet with a sixth sense developed in confinement Rubens knew that someone unexpected had entered. Somehow he immediately recognized me from afar and sent word through other detainees, asking me to come and talk to him.

As I stepped onto the porch of his dorm, Rubens greeted me like a familiar friend. Through the small slats in the wall of his locked dorm, he told me that my pen had become the instrument for a number of tattoos covering the arms and backs of the young prisoners. This made me their instant ally—not only because I provided quality ink for the boys to make "killer" tattoos but, especially, because the gift offered them a proof of my solidarity. I did not know it at the time, but pens are among the legion of items forbidden inside the yard of the CASA. Like forks, shoelaces, and eyeglasses, pens are seemingly benign objects that can be

A place of reflection or space of fear?

used as lethal weapons—if there is someone around who needs to be killed. By giving Rubens a pen, I inadvertently broke one of the cardinal rules of prison security: I not only brought a weapon into the prison yard, I passed it on to an inmate. Through this innocent gift, I unwittingly began to form an alliance with the world of crime and with the inmates and against the law and the administration of the CASA. And I hadn't even begun my formal research at the institution!

Despite the favor I had won among the inmates prior to beginning extended fieldwork, they did not immediately trust me or accept me as a virtual colleague. Suspicion pervades the institution, and all relationships within it are hedged with misgivings. It took time, patience, and good fortune to establish the mutual trust that obtains between me and the inmates who have become my principle informants. I must admit that it also required considerable obstinacy on my part, as well. I often wonder if anyone else would have the fortitude—or the foolishness—to endure the trials I have passed through in establishing my own peculiar place within the CASA.

My acceptance among the inmates has passed through several phases. When I first arrived, I was a welcome novelty for inmates and administrators alike—a stranger to show off to. Everyone wanted to be around me, to touch me, and to tell me their story. The boys who had heard the story of the pen approached me with the hopes of gaining an equally valuable gift, and thereby increasing their own status within the institution. This lasted three days. For the next two weeks of my research, I was given an office in a room shrouded in ill augury, where the then-administration decided I was to call individual inmates in for interviews. This situation cast me in a role similar to that played by the psychologists and social workers who evaluate the "progress" of inmates and make recommendations for their continued internment or their release. During this phase, I was generally considered an ally of the administration. I was treated as a staff member, which meant that the adults regarded me as an equal worthy of respect and the boys kept their distance from me, reluctantly approaching only when I requested to speak with them in my temporary "office." Thankfully, this uncomfortable stage of my research was short-lived. The next phase of my research began after I returned from an unplanned, extended hiatus. I came back to the institution with a reinvigorated resolve to learn about the lives of the institution's inmates. I had gotten a reputation among them for integrity and I possessed a mark that earned me status among—and a measure of solidarity with—them: the scar from a nearly-fatal knife wound.

Confinement in a "high-security" penal institution does not mean isolation from external networks of information. Sometimes inmates know more about the sagas unfolding outside of their prison house than they know of the conflicts brewing within. And, conversely, mothers, lovers, and friends of prisoners oftentimes know more about the dramas inside of penal institutions than do the inmates themselves. Words move with relative freedom through prison walls. So, before I had a chance to tell them about it myself, the inmates of the CASA knew that I had been knifed. And, as they told the story among themselves, they supplied me with the reputation of a badass.

My wounding was not nearly as glamorous as the stories that were invented by the boys about it. On the Sunday prior to what was to be my third week of research at the institution, I suffered a knife wound while buying groceries at the supermarket. Passing by the supermarket's display of knives, I remembered that I had been intending to buy one I could reserve for cutting nonmeat items (I am a vegetarian and was living with a carnivore). Serrated kitchen knives are commonly sold without packaging in Brazil, presumably to reduce costs for the customer; and price is what led me to buy one without packaging. I included the knife in my purchase without reflecting too much on the potential hazards it posed, assuming that the store would not sell unpackaged knives if they presented a significant danger to customers. The supermarket checker presumably did not consider the knife a particularly threatening object either, because he put it in a white plastic sack without covering the blade—as store policy requires he should. He treated it as any other innocuous item for sale at the grocery.

I only began to realize how dangerous a table knife is when I suddenly felt a warm, wet sensation in the region of my appendix as I picked up my bags and began to exit the supermarket. I looked down to see that the simple act of walking had set my grocery bags in motion, and that with the momentum created by one or two steps, the bags had swung against my stomach, providing the knife blade with enough force to pass through the layers of skin and muscle that make up my abdomen. The handle of the knife was sticking out of my midsection, but the blade was nowhere to be seen. Blood and blubbery white tissue—intestines?—were sneaking out of the sides of the wound, pooling around the handle of the knife. I pulled the weapon out in a panic, sure that I was soon to die.

Fortunately, I survived—but with no thanks to the supermarket, which refused to assist me, or the private hospitals, which refused to accept my medical insurance. I was saved by an emergency operation performed at the State-funded hospital, generally reserved for the indigent. Following surgery, I was held in the hospital for several days of monitored recovery. The hospital was unbearably hot, dangerously overcrowded, and in a dubious state of hygiene. It rang with the cries of relatives whose loved ones had recently departed. Its corridors were filled with patients forced to lie on the hallway floors because no spaces remained in the bedrooms, and the hospital did not have enough mattresses to go around. I was lucky: my condition was sufficiently dire to qualify me for a mattress. It was not, however, severe enough to earn me a permanent bed inside of a recovery room. I was placed on a rolling cot in the hallway of a female ward, where fresh air and hospital visitors were able to circulate around me.

I was not the victim of a teenaged mugger or a potential rapist, but the hospital records hanging above my bed did not say this. They told the story of the wound itself, not of its cause. So, the visitors who read about the treatment of my knife wound in my hospital charts all drew their own conclusions—or, rather, causes; they invented the story of the wounding for themselves. Female strangers who dared to speak to me about the wound assumed that it was the outcome of a domestic skirmish, and urged me to forgive the boyfriend or husband they imagined to have inflicted the wound. Most men assumed that I was the hapless victim of a purse snatching and urged me to use more caution. Though none of them ever spoke to me in the hospital, the relatives of the inmates of the CASA must have imagined that my wound was the outcome of a run in with outlaws whom I was tough enough to have confronted, but from whom I was strong and savvy enough to have escaped. This is the story that arrived at the CASA. In the eyes of its inmates, the three-inch scar on my abdomen is a mark of confrontation—of fearlessness and attempted self-defense. Having survived a knife wound and experienced the pain, fear, and adrenaline rush of a confrontation with death gave me status among the inmates. It also gave us an impetus to talk about danger, suffering, and survival; for the first few days following my return to the institution to continue research, we all sat around the prison yard telling each other the stories of our scars.

An Observer Is Not a Witness

When I resumed my daily visits to the institution, my place within the CASA had been tacitly, yet resolutely, (re)defined. For reasons that were never made clear to me, I was told that I was now to stay inside the prison yard with the inmates, and out of the Administrative building. No longer was I allowed to take my lunch with the administrative and professional staff of the institution, eating a well-seasoned meal from glass plates and using silverware. Instead, I was told to eat with the boys, in the yard, using whatever plastic or paper container I could find to hold my food (usually something well-used and borrowed from one of the boys), and like the inmates I ate without using utensils; I used my hands to convey the cold, insipid, and invariably watery food we were hastily served to my mouth. I was forbidden to use the institution's only female restroom, and had to either go home or crouch above the filthy toilet in the security office whenever I had to pee. I was also lectured and punished as if I were one of the boys every time a minor disciplinary infraction occurred, or was rumored to be in the works. Every day I spent at the institution, I was treated more and more like a criminal.

Considering the work of the ethnographer as situated participant observation, it seems that one of the principle dangers of conducting ethnographic research among convicts might be the potential of unintentionally slipping into too active participation. While I have found other aspects of my research to be far more hazardous, I have also found it impossible to set myself completely apart from illicit activities. I have had to silently witness activities like drug deals, prostitution, and the hatching of escape plans in order to establish credibility among the inmates of the institution (all the while struggling with my conscience and with my desire to lecture the boys on the morality and safety of their actions). The boys very purposefully put on displays of rule breaking and criminality in front of me, to test my ability to keep my mouth shut. The infractions I was made to witness were relatively minor and would not have led to excessive punishments had I squealed, precisely because the boys did not know whether I would narc on them or not. By silently witnessing minor crimes, I established myself as a *chegada*, a woman who can be reasonably trusted.

Cabuetagem, or narcing, is an offense punishable by death inside the CASA. Since I began research, inmates have staged upwards of six rebellions and put to death seven of their peers for disrespecting the unwritten code of silence that permits them to establish and enforce their own hierarchies, codes of conduct, disciplinary procedures, and economic relations within the institution. Stepping inside the yard of the CASA is a bit like visiting the island in *Lord of the Flies*. The boys are in a constant struggle for power, and they fight according to their own rules; dominant society's normative expectations and regulations do not govern conduct within the institution—unless someone squeals, thereby inviting adult authority to assume control in a particular situation. In order to gain the confidence of the inmates, I had to demonstrate that I respected *their* rules and would not seek the intervention of adult authorities if they broke institutional regulations, or if they disrespected me personally. Hence, I was put through a series of minor trials in order to prove that I could keep my mouth shut. As I passed each test, I was made aware that I was being assessed and that, through my behavior, I was gaining their confidence, and respect. I used these moments of spoken evaluation to communicate to the boys that I would not release information that joints are being sold clandestinely throughout the institution and would not reveal to authorities that guards and inmates arrange for girls to make "intimate" visits with inmates in exchange for a fee (although authorities suspected that both activities were occurring, but had no concrete proof). I assured the inmates that I would not turn my observations or their words over to authorities as evidence to be used against them—even if I did not personally condone their actions. I also assured inmates that I would not pass on the rumors I heard brewing in the institution about possible escape attempts and fights—guards get paid to collect and disseminate such information. However, I also told the inmates that I could not lie about observed acts of physical violence; if someone were attacked in my presence, I would have to bear witness. Hence, I only ever saw one inmate get hit by his peers during the entire time I was in the institution, and his beating was a disciplinary measure taken by inmates who (wrongly) accused him of stealing from me.

I always brought my bag with me into the yard of the CASA. At first, this was because I wanted to have my notebook and sound-recording device with me in case I needed either one of them for my research. In time, the practice took on an additional purpose. Staff members lock their belongings away before entering the yard because they consider the boys to be inveterate criminals; they are certain that to enter the yard with a bag is to invite theft. After receiving several suggestions from staff members to guard my belongings in the administrative building, I realized that I was the only adult who brought anything with her into the prison yard. From that moment of epiphany on, I began to deliberately carry my bag in the yard with me as a display of trust. By entering the yard with my bag, I hoped to demonstrate to the boys that I did not presume their criminality. It was my way of allowing our encounter to begin with the presumed trust that underlies—and perhaps makes possible—friendly relationships between equals.

My bag became an incredibly important symbol in the institution. Each day inmates would ritually take their turn looking through its contents, commenting upon the items that had been included or excluded from one day to the next. Some of the boys told me that they felt proud when they were looking though my bag; it was the only experience they had of feeling trusted. One day I entered the institution with R$25. A few hours later I was called into the administrative building and asked to make a contribution to a party that was being planned for the inmates; I gave R$5. When I returned to the yard with my bag, the absence of R$5 was noticed. Without consulting me, the boys decided that the money had been stolen, and that the thief had to be punished. While I was sitting on the porch of one of the dorms talking to a new inmate, a group of boys brought the individual they decided was the culprit over and put on a visible demonstration of punishing him in front of me. As soon as I was able to understand what was going on, I put a stop to the beating and explained the reason for the missing money. With my prompting, the aggressors apologized to their victim. However, they insisted that, as far as they were concerned, the beating had been necessary. "Now everyone knows what will happen if they disrespect you," Pequeno, one of the punishers, explained.

Months later, I still think about the beating and wish that it had never happened. However, I feel that it would be dishonest to—by omission—pretend that it never took place. It did. And it was a meaningful event—principally because it was both so common and, yet, so exceptional.

Given the status of the CASA as one of the most violent juvenile detention centers in Brazil (if not *the* most violent), it is remarkable that I have only witnessed one act of physical aggression inside of the institution during all these months of research. Several rebellions—a few of which were fatal—have occurred since I began fieldwork, but I have not been present at a single one; they always occur on the days I am working at a secondary research site (the juvenile court, for example). Hence, I have difficulty reconciling the violence I hear about with my experiences in the institution. That is why this one beating is so significant: it proves to me

He who breaks the law of CASA gets a slap in the face and a bullet in the head.

that the violence I hear about is real, and that it never occurs when I am in the institution is remarkable. Without deliberately setting out to alter the institution, I have somehow intervened to make it less violent—at least temporarily. Perhaps fieldwork is not just about observing culture but, whether we are aware of it or not, the practice is also about creating culture?

"Our job has been a whole lot easier since you came," the head Monitor (security guard) was fond of telling me. He and his team of 10 men are responsible for preventing escapes, controlling violence between inmates, and maintaining order within the yard of the CASA. Unlike administrators, they are in constant daily contact with the institution's inmates. And, unlike administrators, they seemed to genuinely appreciate my presence inside of the CASA. The head Monitor repeatedly assured me, "None of them would dream of doing something that would hurt you or get you kicked out; the others would kill anyone who did. We can relax when you're here because we know nothing is going to happen—or at least it's a whole lot less likely something major is going to happen."

Invasions of Privacy

Ironically, nine months into my research at the institution, the administration suddenly decided to block my access to the yard of the CASA, claiming that it was a measure taken for my own protection. "Those kids are dangerous," the woman who informed me that my access was being terminated explained. "You think you are safe but you never know when they are going to turn on you. They could take you hostage. They could rape you. We can't let that happen. It would be an international scandal. So, we can't allow you unlimited access any longer. Your research is over."

She politely told me that I could return to ask administrators questions and to interview them—at their convenience (a polite way of warning me that I would be turned away if I showed up at the door of the CASA again). When I asked her how she and the other administrators suddenly came to the conclusion that I was in personal danger after having passed nine months inside of the institution, in close contact with the inmates, and without ever having been publicly threatened or endangered, she simply replied, "You have been here long enough. You have seen all you need to see. Your presence inside is dangerous." After a brief pause she added—in what seemed to me to be an afterthought, "There's always the threat of rape."

Anyone who knows *anything* about life inside Brazilian prisons would know that rape is one of the least possible dangers faced by a woman inside a male penal institution. One of the key tenants of the unwritten code of conduct among Brazilian convicts is that rape is an unpardonable offense, punishable by sodomy and summary execution. In most Brazilian correctional facilities, administrators have taken to secluding convicted rapists in special, secure wings, in order to prevent other convicts from enforcing the extrajudicial punishments demanded by their own codes of honor. The CASA is no exception. Imagining themselves as hardened criminals and the CASA as a prison, the inmates have internalized the rules of conduct within adult prisons and unanimously maintain that, "The destiny of a rapist is to get fucked and dance"—the latter a polite way of saying "to die." Boys sentenced to confinement in the CASA for having committed acts of rape are either secluded from other prisoners, or strict secrecy and silence are maintained about their actual infractions by juvenile justice professionals who encourage teens convicted of rape to manufacture alternate explanations when telling peers about the acts that lead to their internment. Word of a rape conviction would mean death.

Being taken hostage, suffering injury in a rebellion, falling victim to theft: all of these are possible, but unlikely, hazards I admittedly face upon entering the CASA. Rape, however, is not a danger. Despite the fact that I periodically receive love notes and invitations to "feel what it's like to *trepar com um bandido*" (fuck a gangster), I have always been able to deflect such overtures with candor or laughter—as the situation requires. The boys outwardly respect my "No." Not one of them has made me fear the danger of sexual assault. I am reasonably certain that several of them *thought* about having sex with me, but I firmly believe that there is not a single one who would actually rape me. And even *if* (and I do mean *if*) an inmate entertained the thought of rape, I am certain that he would not hazard it inside the CASA; to rape a woman in the institution would mean death—and all inmates know it. In my opinion, the threat of rape is an excuse fabricated by the administration to remove me from the CASA. They want me to stop "snooping around," but they are not willing to say this outright. So, they have invented a convenient excuse: rape.

Rape is about sex, but it is mostly about power. This case is no exception. When my permission to enter the CASA was suspended by the administration, I went over their heads and obtained judicial authorization to continue my work, since the Judge of the local juvenile court has ultimate legal control over the facility and its inmates. He is responsible for the welfare of the inmates and the execution of their sentences, while the administration of the CASA facilitates the execution of these sentences and maintains responsibility for inmate security (mainly for keeping inmates under lock and key). In cases of conflict between the two branches of power—the Judicial and Security—the Judge always has the last word. After listening to me explain my research, its methods, progress, and goals, the Judge ordered the administrators of the CASA to allow me to resume fieldwork at the institution.

In order to soften the blow to the authority of the institution's administrators that consent for my research would constitute, the Judge allowed the administrators to impose "necessary" security measures to protect me and the inmates during my research, without interfering in the research itself. The measure that the administration implemented was that of the "intimate search." The director of the institution rationalized the procedure as follows: "To make sure you are not bringing in substances that are dangerous to your own safety or the safety of the institution, we have to do an intimate search. If you bring something illicit in it increases your danger of rape. We have to search you completely. The boys we have here—I don't know if you know what they've been involved in: rape, homicide, rape, assault—everything that is evil. There are rapists being held here and we can't guarantee your safety. It would be an international scandal if you got raped in here and we said that we gave you permission to be alone with these boys when we already know what they're capable of. It would be better if you did not continue your research here. But, since you insist, we have to search you. The search is necessary for your own protection."

Perhaps I am daft, but even after a great deal of reflection I am still unable to understand how someone searching the cavities of my body is going to protect me from (an imagined) rape. In my way of thinking, the procedure itself can be construed as an act of rape, since it is a forcible violation of (the "intimate" regions of) my body. As a security measure, it is completely absurd. As a technique of intimidation, however, it borders on brilliance. Undoubtedly, it would be highly effective if I agreed with the analogy man:mind::woman:body and considered a violation of my bodily integrity to be the most degrading insult I could possibly suffer; the proposed search would have led me to "voluntarily" terminate my study. However, the offense to my intelligence and professionalism that the administration's hostile practices constitute is much more insulting to me than is a latex covered finger probing my vagina.

Reflecting upon recent events, I am led to the conclusion that the new "security measures" implemented to control my visits are not about sex at all but are about access to intimate information and about the violation of privacy. I was banned when I refused to allow the CASA's "technical team" (its staff of psychologists and social workers) to listen to personal interviews I had taped with some of the boys. The inmates granted me permission to tape life-history interviews because I promised that I would not let anyone else in the institution hear what they had allowed me to record. To surrender the recordings would be a violation of privacy, not to mention professional ethics. When the technical team called me in to demand to hear the tapes, I refused; I was punished. I was banned. When the judge overturned the ban, the intimate search was implemented, I presume to teach me that it is much less inconvenient to disrespect the privacy of the less powerful than to have the more powerful invade my own. The searches have been a perverse lesson about power, access, and violation—and about Brazilian history. The country's 25-year military dictatorship ended in 1989 and is seldom discussed in the open, but the techniques of power and intimidation it relied upon for maintenance have not been forgotten—or consigned to obsolescence.

Being Toyed With

At times, I think that the administrators of the CASA are hostile to my presence inside of the institution because they do not want me to document their use of disciplinary practices that do not fall in line with legal mandates for "humanized" treatment of juvenile offenders. In other moments I wonder: Could it be that the administrators of the CASA are uncomfortable with my presence because they are worried that I might see too much? Are they afraid I might discover that the institution is not under their control? Are they afraid I will see them be brutal in the exercise of power? Or, are they afraid that I will see their powerlessness? As my research develops, all I can be certain of is that the administration clearly does not want me around.

The CASA administration's support for my fieldwork has been in inverse proportion to the amount of time I spend at the institution. On my first visit, I was treated with the utmost attention and respect. When I came back asking to conduct more intensive research, I was greeted with friendly reserve. As my visits continued, their welcome cooled. The past four months of my research have been conducted within a climate of open hostility.

First, I was banned. Then there were the cavity searches. Now my presence has been restricted to the administrative building, where I can be monitored. And, I am rarely allowed to meet with the boys who have agreed to let me conduct recorded life-history interviews with them. Though I have made arrangements to hold one-on-one interviews with inmates in the morning hours when only half of them are in school (if the school is actually operating; it wasn't during the nine continuous months I spent in the yard, and there is little to make me believe that it is actually functioning now), each time I ask for a specific inmate to come in and speak with me, I am told either, "He said no" or "He's in an activity." Since the implementation of this procedure, the only inmates I have been able to interview are those who have happened to be in (or extremely near) the administration building at the time of my arrival and invited themselves to participate in an interview.

When I asked one of these chance interviewees, Ronaldo, why some of his associates who had agreed to talk to me were suddenly backing out, he responded with a look of incomprehension. I clarified: "They tell me no one wants to talk to me; that people say 'no' when I call them. Why? What'd I do?"

"Nothing," he said. "Shit. Reginaldo was even complaining yesterday that you'd forgotten about us. He was all mad that you promised you'd put us in your book and then you stopped showin' up."

"What? I called for him last week and they told me he said he didn't want to come in and talk to me."

"That's not it. They call and he thinks it's to talk to one of these cows on the technical team [of social workers and psychologists]. Of course he's gonna say 'no.' But if he knew it was you, he woulda come. They didn't say it was *you*. If I was in there and they called me I wouldn't come either—unless I *knew* it was you."

I was angry, so I decided to find out: "Tell me: Is it true that the school's working now? That you guys are just full of activities? Or is it like always, and they're pulling my leg?"

"More or less. They've added a band thing and the soccer guy is actually coming now. But school? It's like always: nothing. It's just empty talk—pure bullshit."

"I thought so. Thanks." The administration is clearly at war with me, but they have not yet figured out that I am not a gracious loser. Without skipping a beat, I immediately employed the only tactic I could think of to counter their strategy for denying me contact with the inmates: I asked Ronaldo to pass the word around that I was coming every morning and that whoever wanted to could ask to come in and talk to me. That was last week. Since then, I have not been turned away with an excuse that no one is available or no one wants to speak to me. On the contrary, there has been a small crowd awaiting my arrival.

I can tell that the efforts of the boys to ensure that I am able to record their stories for a book infuriates the administrators. One even said to me, "Why do you waste your time with this trash? Do you think they're going live to see it in print? I doubt it. And do you think it's worth writing down? Most of what they say is just lies."

"Really?" I shot back. "And I guess you never lie." I raised my eyebrow for emphasis: "Right?" He stormed away. I felt a guilty pleasure in attacking him. Perhaps the hostile conditions of my fieldwork are turning me into a vindictive bitch? More likely, the disrespect I have suffered at the hands of administrators allows me a certain freedom: I can now dispense with the pretense of having to treat them with regard. One thing I am certain of, however, is the fact that my treatment at their hands has made me more prone to certain expressions—and sentiments—of violence.

Rising Hostility

Before coming to Brazil I was, in general, a very calm individual. I had never been in a fight. I rarely argued. Force was not part of my education. My political heroes and role models were men and women who consciously avoided physical force in fighting for their ideals: practitioners of civil disobedience, not soldiers or militant rebels. To me, violence was never a viable solution to conflict.

After spending over a year in the company of teenaged convicts and Brazilian bureaucrats educated in "diplomacy" during the country's military dictatorship, I now have a hard time fathoming nonviolence as a viable strategy of political action or self-preservation—at least in Brazil. In the first place, this is because, after hearing story upon story of murder and blood-vengeance, such actions have become frighteningly mundane to me. At the very least, I no longer categorically consider murder and severe beatings to be excessive reactions to perceived disrespect; such actions are too common among inmates of the CASA to be extraordinary.

In trying to understand the violent acts committed by the inmates of the CASA it is crucial to observe that whenever the boys participate in deliberate violence, they do so in order to seek retribution for a perceived wrong. Although a handful of the institution's inmates have been convicted of unwittingly or accidentally participating in violent crimes, the vast majority of CASA inmates have killed, maimed, or wounded their victims intentionally, as a means of exacting vengeance or righting perceived wrongs. In their view, murder and violence are viable procedures for executing justice.

Murder as justice? Murder as the imposition of respect? This may sound incredible—even contradictory—to those who do not hold a Hobbesian view of human nature. But, in the context of northeastern Brazil violence is often the only course the poor and disenfranchised can take to gain recognition; it is often the most effective means they have for demanding to be respected and treated as human beings. It is common for Brazilians in positions of power—or those who aspire to power—to treat their social and economic inferiors as if they simply do not exist. When dealing with authority figures or wealthy citizens, the poor and powerless are supposed to *baixar a cabeça*, to lower their heads and silently accept the orders or abuse that are piled upon them. When the weak lift their heads or raise their voices, they are generally ignored—treated as though they do not exist. The inmates of the CASA tell me that suffering such treatment is infuriating. I agree. After being thus treated by the administrators and politicians who wanted to stifle my research, I have a sense of exactly how galling such deliberately affected disdain can be. (Admittedly, I have had to control my urge to punch snide administrators). And, after witnessing several confrontations between inmates and administrators, I have learned that the boys are only given attention—albeit negative attention—when they become violent. Often, their violence is not a statement of some inveterate criminality, but rather it is a last ditch attempt to be reckoned with, to be treated with at least a modicum of respect.

In northeastern Brazil, men who murder are respected. And almost everyone, it seems, does it: rich, poor, marginalized, influential; it is not only the "criminals" who kill. Here, murder is almost mundane. In fact, common lore and local newspapers reveal that it is clearly a tool used by the powerful to maintain power, command respect, enforce "justice," and preserve order. Its deployment is so common, in fact, that not one of my friends found it strange or extraordinary that, just before I was banned from entering the CASA, I began receiving anonymous phone calls warning: "Be careful where you stick your nose, *Americana*, your Mom wouldn't want you to return to the United States in a coffin." They took the threats seriously and encouraged me to do so as well. Like the boys of the CASA, I have taken to sleeping with one eye open.

Note

[1] In the nineteenth century the U.S. founded the first ever juvenile court. It was built upon the notion that children are persons in development who cannot be held responsible for their actions to the same extent as adults. The court assumed that children commit crimes because of some lack in their education or personal history of socialization; therefore, it was believed that, through education, the juvenile offender could be reformed into a law-abiding citizen. Reform, not punishment was the goal of the juvenile justice system. The U.S. is slowly dismantling its juvenile court, popular opinion and the media insisting that evil children who kill are beyond reform and need to be locked up permanently. Brazil holds to the model of the juvenile court and has what is arguably the most comprehensive system of legal protections for children—and juvenile offenders—in the world. The relationship between the law and ideas of childhood innocence are, in part, why the violences Brazilian children participate in are given a lot of attention. Its why my project is set in Brazil.

Pangs of Guilt:
Transnational Ethnography, Motherhood, and Moral Dilemmas in Central America

Kate Goldade
University of Arizona

Baby Steps

"**B**abies open doors!" my advisor enthused upon hearing the news that I would be taking my three-month old baby daughter to the field. Just two months into my dissertation research, my experience already resonates with his insight. We are living in the foothills of one of Costa Rica's most popular tourist-destination volcanoes. My husband, my baby daughter, Sonia, and I have come to this region so that I may conduct a transnational ethnography with people who are not from here: the Nicaraguan labor migrant women working as harvesters in the coffee and ornamental flower industries. My advisor was not the only one to comment on Sonia's influence on the research. In academic circles, colleagues predicted that she would ease recruitment challenges and knock down trust barriers, thus smoothing the work of eliciting narratives on sensitive, yet pertinent topics confronting my informants around reproduction, reproductive health, and motherhood. On the other hand, a fellow Central Americanist lamented that she could never take a child to the field lest some harm were to come for which she could never forgive herself.

I could anticipate the benefits of a baby's disarming presence to the research but did not understand the nuanced personal challenges of being a parent while doing fieldwork. By her mere presence, Sonia regularly invokes interactions to be considered rich data. Being a mother helps me to see important themes and has even led me to refashion my original research proposal. Most significantly, having Sonia brings me a deeper understanding of working motherhood, the situation many of my informants face.

Also, I am beginning to learn what it means to be a transnational mother, one whose work involves traversing national and cultural boundaries yet remains at odds with the close proximity required of caring for one's children. I am one too. I face corresponding dilemmas on a daily basis, which brings me closer to an insider's perspective. Trade-offs, weighing health risks for Sonia against getting my work done, and negotiating the ethical dilemmas of motherhood are now a way of life. Yet, at two months time, I am cautious not to overestimate the congruence of my situation with that of my informants. I am beginning to understand how our unequal positions of power work and how I am privileged in my own negotiations, even if they often cause me personal distress. In this initial phase of research, intellectual confusion and emotional guilt prevail, as I delicately dance around moral dilemmas as both a new mother and a new ethnographer. I am forced to proceed with caution. I am taking baby steps. In my case, the rewards of motherhood are both personal and intellectual. Sonia has undoubtedly enriched my research experience and findings, but I continually fear the answer to the question, at what cost?

Sonia's Smile

Like the way that my own mother's visit did during my Peace Corps service in Nicaragua five years ago, being a mother myself has made me more human in the view of Central Americans. As is the case across the globe, kinship ties are powerful humanizers here. However, ideas of the life course speed up the process of childbearing by about 10 years, commonly spawning suspicions of birth control or even rumors of infertility when one is childless beyond the age of 25. To return as a married mother at the age of 30 brings me closer to that ethnographer's manna, cultural congruence. My age and marital status no longer provoke probing. They make sense. To study matters of fertility, reproduction, and transnational motherhood, the core of my dissertation, does not seem odd. In the eyes of my informants, I am a mother first, a curious North American doctoral student/researcher second. Having Sonia here certainly speeds up trust-building processes that are often the principal source of frustration in these initial stages of fieldwork.

For example: The other day, I was excited to be interviewing a newly recruited informant after an extended game of phone tag and one cancellation on her part. She was shy. Her answers were not forthcoming. As I asked her my carefully crafted interview questions I

Author (left) interviews a Nicaraguan labor migrant as she makes small repairs to the basket she uses while picking coffee.

constantly engaged in self-analysis to make her feel more comfortable. I checked my own temperament and posture, the setting, and my volume, all in an effort to convey understanding and to smooth the clearly choppy interview dynamic. Nothing worked. As we wrapped it up, I assessed my failings and felt reassured by the fact that I would be doing several more interviews with her. I closed the notebook and signaled that I was finishing up to my husband who was walking Sonia through a nearby row of coffee plants. He came over and I introduced him to the informant as he handed me Sonia, at which point she exclaimed, "She's yours?!" In an instant, her entire demeanor shifted. She swiftly assumed that cross-cultural high pitched baby talk and began to interact with Sonia. A willing conversationalist, Sonia eagerly offered her a big, drooly open-mouthed smile, topped off with a full-body shudder, her newest way of communicating excitement. Immediately, the informant returned to the topic I'd been trying to get at earlier (with little success)—her feelings of isolation as a migrant. My position as a transnational ethnographer helped in this regard. She commiserated; "Isn't it hard to be in a country that isn't your own?" We talked for awhile longer. She invited me to her home the following day and offered to introduce me to another migrant, all with Sonia smiling away in my arms. Undoubtedly, the data that followed were the products of Sonia's smile.

Transnational Motherhood, Transnational Ethnography

In another initial interview, a recently recruited informant was explaining how she made the difficult decision to bring her five children with her, to expose them to the dangers of the journey and the instability of labor migrant living. She does not trust her own mother or mother-in-law back in Nicaragua to care for them in the way that she would. She moved her eyes to Sonia, nursing in my arms, as she commented, "As you know, nobody takes care of one's children like their mother."

So far it appears that being a mother and having faced the dilemmas of ensuring Sonia's safety at the same time that I continue my work, which requires much travel, has already facilitated my efforts to gain trust with my informants. However, social perceptions of an ethnographer are never neutral. Previous experience has taught me that seeing Sonia and me together could just as well prompt shame or jealousy in a future informant who has decided to leave her children behind in Nicaragua.

To date, all of the labor migrants recruited for the study are mothers. In their process of migration from Nicaragua they faced the excruciatingly difficult decision of what to do with their children. Taking them to Costa Rica means subjecting them to many hardships, including the dangers of crossing the border on foot, crowded and transient living conditions, fear of deportation, and social isolation. Once the children arrive there is the problem of who will care for them while both of their parents work, now that they are out of reach of kinship and social networks of support that provide childcare. In the case of one informant, her children—ages three and seven—trail behind her while she picks coffee. She fears for their safety as they risk snake bites and the slippery hillsides. However, leaving them in Nicaragua would mean enduring the guilt and emotional pain of separation. In addition, in some cases, it means more worry about the child's well-being depending on the faith in the caregiver—usually a grandmother or aunt. These mothers must call home often and negotiate tough decisions regarding their children's care over the phone.

An informant shares that she often cries herself to sleep while looking at a photo of her six-year-old son whom she left when he was three. Another has not seen her two daughters in seven years. Such periods of separation are unfathomable to me. I am struggling to move Sonia out of our room at night, the next step in improving her (and our) sleep. The contrast between these experiences prompts me to ponder who gets to mother their children in this transnational world. Transnationalism is the idea that human actors have agency and wield it to assert themselves in the face of that giant steam-rolling force of globalization, often through movement and migration previously unimaginable. My experience so far shows that it works in gendered ways. Whereas labor migration may be an attractive option for those parents (usually fathers) assured the good care of their children in their absence, transnational motherhood appears to present more challenges than benefits—

that is, unless you are a Fulbright-Hays-funded transnational mother with a full-time Dad at your side. Like running my tongue over a loose tooth, my mind returns to consider the extent to which transnationalism involves a shift in power relations, or if they are simply enacted over longer distances.

When it comes to transnational ethnography, on the other hand, shifts in power relations between the informant and ethnographer seem clearer. In classic ethnography an anthropologist departs from his privileged position as an extra-educated person studying in a Western university to land in a small, usually very poor, village characterized by traditional systems of economic and cultural exchange. Thanks to the massive movements of people around the globe, part and parcel of transnationalism, an ethnographer can meet her informants on territories unfamiliar to both parties. Although it does not completely erase the struggles of power differences, being foreigners in a strange land serves as a common touchstone.

Moreover, ethnographers are particularly well-suited to understanding transnationalism. For instance, in my case, my nationality enhances my ability to evaluate the dynamic between Costa Ricans and Nicaraguans. Being from neither place makes me more neutral to both parties, giving me a unique view into the situation. Holism is a hallmark of the ethnographic method. Using it, researchers can provide insights on the fast-moving human side of this transnational world, a side that often slips past statistical studies. It is the job of ethnographers to understand the new and complex social arrangements made possible by increased global movement and communications.

However, the dilemmas presented by transnational ethnography involve the work of understanding multiple "insider perspectives." Although Costa Ricans are not my primary informants I rely on them for everyday advice ranging from small lessons like bus etiquette to weightier matters like the best-educated pediatrician in town. Plus, they are my principal research collaborators. Indeed, one of the greatest surprises in fieldwork has been the discomfort and daily work of negotiating the moral politics of parenting among Costa Ricans, and specifically, our closest friends here.

The Moral Dance of Mothering

Often times, I feel as if I'm engaged in a moral dance with locals over the ways that we parent Sonia. Everything from ear-piercing, dress patterns, feeding and sleep habits, and pain-alleviation techniques are up for debate. My observation must resonate with other new parents. The onslaught of unsolicited advice associated with the transition to parenthood and accompanying identity shifts is arguably a universal cultural phenomenon. Indeed, after giving birth to Sonia in Arizona my impressions of new motherhood involved the confusing mix of opinions regarding her eating and sleeping habits. In the social context of ethnography, however, the symbolic stakes have changed. How I care for her reflects the degree to which I condone or contest Costa Rican ways of mothering, a touchy subject. After stepping on toes in these symbolically loaded conversations I have found myself seeking graceful resolve, or fumbling for pardon.

A few weeks before our departure, amidst the frenzy of packing up and storing our household's belongings except for the items we had selected through foggy, sleep-deprived deliberations, I called our local host, Doña Blanca. I wanted to allay at least one of my several fears as a new mother taking her newborn to another country: the risk of malaria and other mosquito-borne illnesses in the area. To my questions, Doña Blanca responded that malaria does not exist in this region nor did she know of any local cases of dengue fever. Did not know? What does that mean? "But, *in general*, is there dengue fever in the area," I urged, nervously. Transmitted by a bite from an *Aedes agypti,* a class of mosquito that feeds around the twilight hours of dusk, dengue is an extremely painful and temporarily debilitating viral illness that can be hemorrhagic in subsequent incidences and, in extreme cases, lead to death. Preventive measures are to try to limit the breeding grounds of *Aedes agypti,* which are pools of stagnant water, an overwhelmingly difficult task in the tropics.

Brusquely, she explained that she had not seen any mosquitoes in her house and she was always careful to keep her house and patio clean. I wondered what cleanliness had to do with it. And, from her defensive tone, I could tell that I had offended her. She followed her response with an offer to find us a crib and to hire us a local nanny, both of which I gently refused. It occurred to me that she was assuring me in other ways that she would be providing Sonia a safe place to live. Compounded by my rebuffs to her generosity, it seemed that she interpreted my questioning of dengue as a lack of her consideration for Sonia's well-being. I had to convey my trust in her. Delicately, I retraced my steps and explained, half-truthfully, that Sonia's grandparents were very concerned and had asked me to clarify the risk of dengue. "You have to ensure Sonia's grandparents that plenty of Costa Rican children grow up safely here," she responded.

On our very first morning at Doña Blanca's, we awoke to national newspaper headlines bemoaning this year's exceptionally high rate of dengue. On the second day we read that dengue had claimed its first deaths, about half of whom were children under the age of one. My concern elevated to fear. Knowing that I could not bring it up with Doña Blanca, I turned to her daughter who works in the local hospital for reassurance. She explained that all cases of dengue were the result of lack of "self-care," that the inflicted were only those people who did not keep their patios free of garbage and their yards well-manicured, and that for this reason, we were safe. To this day I'm still not sure how garbage translates into increased risk for dengue. You're *fine,* she said in a patronizing tone.

I did not feel any better. I considered the screenless windows right next to Sonia's crib, the house's surrounding gardens with shallow flooding from the afternoon rains, and the fact that I had had dengue five years prior, despite the utmost "self-care." Intellectually, I could understand her reasoning as a cultural logic for making sense of the omnipresent risk of contracting a serious disease for no better reason than being in the unfortunate position of mosquito landing pad. Personally, however, I was very worried about the risk of Sonia contracting dengue and wanted to share this with someone, a fellow mother, who would lend a sympathetic ear, not a demeaning rebuke. Doña Blanca's daughter's response not only left me feeling the loneliness familiar to ethnographers in the first months of fieldwork, but frustrated with the moral dance. How could I ever express worry if it was always to be construed as a moral questioning of Costa Rican way of life?

In what felt like a personal compromise, I joked that I am a nervous first-time mother with tendencies toward overprotection, a concept that has taken hold with this country's plentiful interaction with U.S. media and culture. We both laughed. In this instance laughing at my worries with her communicated that my concerns were not meant to cast ambiguous blame but simply convey a human feeling. In general, making myself the subject of jokes has been a useful move in the moral dance. It can feel self-defeating, particularly since a foremost task of the first months of fieldwork is to establish the research as respectable and worthwhile. However, laughing can help to ease cross-cultural tensions. Sometimes, it's just the most logical option.

On another occasion, a friend blatantly disregarded the way we had decided to introduce Sonia to solid foods. One weekend our friend generously invited us to her family's home to collect some of their citrus fruit harvests. We were strolling through her lush back yard as her husband picked us a bag full of mandarin oranges and lemons. I had just finished explaining to her that we were starting Sonia on vegetables and brown rice cereal in order to encourage her taste for these things rather than the sweetness of fruit. I turned around to see Sonia delightedly sucking on a mandarin orange, at the hand of our friend. My husband and I caught one another's eye, shared a worried glance, followed by a knowing smile, and ultimately we both started to laugh.

Besides some personal discomfort such interactions are giving me a better understanding of the politics of mothering—that is, the meaning behind moral judgments regarding parenting (especially mothering), attitudes, and decisions. From my privileged stance as Western researcher I have the luxury of understanding interactions for what they are: a caring show of concern for Sonia and the defense of her safety in Costa Rica. In contrast, Costa Ricans level harsh scrutiny toward Nicaraguan mothers and mothering practices with blatant utter disdain. Guiltily, in light of Costa Ricans' perceptions of Nicaraguans, I come to understand that teasing criticisms of our worries for Sonia are meant caringly and that to be engaged in the moral dance is a privilege, not a burden.

Pangs of a Researcher's Guilt

In daily interactions, Costa Ricans regularly and unabashedly articulate their contempt for Nicaraguans. Often, they direct their scorn at migrant women's reproduction and make moral judgments of their ability to mother. Although this issue is not at the heart of my original dissertation proposal, it is what I hear most on a regular basis. While grasping at thematic threads during this exploratory phase of the research I am still trying to make sense of whether being a mother prompts them to share these prejudices with me, makes me more sensitive to them, or if they constitute a regularly occurring social phenomenon. However, from our very first day here, an interaction repeated over and over again goes like this: A national asks what we are doing here; we answer that we are here so that I can conduct a study on Nicaraguan migration; and the national responds by rattling off a litany of Costa Rica's social problems for which migrants are to blame and that oftentimes includes at least one discriminatory joke. As I grapple with a dizzying slew of prejudices against Nicaraguans, I am flooded with guilt for being a U.S. citizen, for being a mother from the U.S., and for the way that my original research question may inadvertently support these prejudices.

Most commonly the complaints circulating involve migrant mothers, my informants. One complaint is that Nicaraguan women migrate when pregnant simply in order to access superior health care services; another is that they become pregnant with the intention of garnering the newborn's legal entitlements to education and health care until age 18. Most extremely, there is the belief that Nicaraguan women come here with the sole purpose to steal a husband, in order to have Costa Rican babies and thus ensure their own legal status. In all accounts, Nicaraguan (over) reproduction is to blame for dwindling state resources in the health care and education sectors.

Not only do they overreproduce, their mothering capacities are considered suspect, as several nationals have already shared with me. In a recent exploratory interview, a local doctor bemoans the cold and uncaring attitude that Nicaraguan mothers display for their children. A teacher complains that their lack of parenting skills leaves their children undisciplined, and their laziness leads them to overrely on the education system for caring for children. An acquaintance tells us a story in which she pulled over to the side of the road to berate a Nicaraguan mother for carrying her baby in the rain without using an umbrella. Before peeling away, she warned the aberrant mother that she would be subject to police fines for doing so. In these interactions, I don't know how to react. Usually, I put my head down, take a note or two and try to keep a straight face, not letting the person see my shock at their gall. Usually, I leave the interaction feeling guilty, both as a Western mother and as a Western researcher.

First, I would never be the target of the kind of disdainful scrutiny turned on Nicaraguan mothers and mothering practices, simply due to my status as a U.S. citizen. Facing such judgments in my own life presents me with unpredictable and uncomfortable dilemmas, but it does not make me the target of discrimination. Costa Ricans respond to my concerns for Sonia with teasing but not hostility. Moreover, the dwindling state resources have more to do with cutbacks associated with structural adjustment programs initiated by policy makers working for the U.S. over the past 20 years, as a local scholar has demonstrated (Sandoval 2004). That is, while migrants (i.e., my informants) and their children take the blame, North Americans (i.e., Sonia and I) may be at greater fault.

Second, as I consider my original research objective, which is to understand the sociocultural side of the demographically puzzling trend of Nicaraguan migrants' elevated fertility in comparison to Nicaraguan nationals, I experience researcher's guilt. It occurs to me that my study's results could bolster anxieties over migrants' rate of reproduction and serve as a kind of handmaiden to related tensions. Being a mother myself and in light of the discrimination migrants already face, I cannot stand this thought.

I'm not surprised by the realization that my study's objective is neither politically or morally neutral. The challenge has been to figure out how to handle this heavy feeling of guilt associated with my intellectual understanding of the moral politics of transnational motherhood. Guilt can be paralyzing for ethnographers (and mothers too). It is our responsibility to face it, understand it, and incorporate it into the research somehow. Upon much reflection, I have decided to alter my research's objectives and methods somewhat by adding a sample of health care personnel in order to present a more holistic picture of the moral politics surrounding migrants' reproduction. Although it may extend my time here, it will give a better sense of the challenges migrants face in seeking reproductive health services, an important consideration for understanding fertility outcomes.

Undoubtedly, dealing with guilty feelings will be an ongoing project this year, I am sure, for I have already caught glimpses of the trade-offs and the ethical dilemmas inherent in balancing new ethnography with new motherhood.

Negotiating Maternal Guilt

Deciding to bring Sonia to a developing country at the tender age of three months required a lot of confidence. In the face of questioning from family and friends we had to defend Costa Rica's safety and emphasize its peaceful history, the field site's clean water supply, and its proximity to the capital. Mixed with our confidence was nervousness, but as former Peace Corps volunteers, my husband and I felt prepared to handle any of the challenges moving here would hold. After all, millions of Costa Rican children have survived just fine. Two months into life here, I realize that it was not possible to fully prepare ourselves for negotiating a whole host of new risks to Sonia's health. Nor could we estimate the tricky ethical dilemmas of balancing the research with ensuring Sonia's safety.

Recruitment for my study has occurred in spurts, so far, and generally seems to move slower than I was hoping. It has required the physical work of hiking up and down these beautiful hills, hills cloaked in a quilt stitched of dark green coffee patches and bright green sugarcane fields, to my informants' homes flung far across the territory. The vast majority of Nicaraguan migrants in this region are undocumented. As agricultural laborers they live on the geographic and social margins in old dilapidated farm houses in exchange for their work in the surrounding fields. To avert their suspicion of strangers and their fear of deportation, I prefer to accompany a local nurse on her house visits in order to explain my study and ask permission to return on my own to conduct a series of interviews. Although the nurse is Costa Rican, she appears to be accepted by the local migrant population. Importantly, she has kindly agreed to collaborate with me despite a lack of apparent personal benefit to her. However, her ethics depart significantly from my own as was painfully clear on a recent house visit.

With Sonia in his arms, my husband, the nurse, and I were hiking to a home inaccessible by road. She warned us of the poor hygienic conditions of the home and complained that the children were so covered in lice it was possible to see them jumping off their heads. Upon learning of the reported symptom of an unyielding cough had by one of the home's residents, local health officials feared a case of tuberculosis (TB) in this household, particularly since it fit the risk profile: crowded living quarters; home to three families; all Nicaraguans, who are often considered harbingers of communicable diseases. The case was unconfirmed. I felt pangs of maternal guilt for potentially exposing Sonia to these health risks. Yet, I marched on with the prospect of recruiting another informant. One of the women in the house had recently given birth and I was eager to talk to her about her experience of prenatal care as an undocumented migrant, among other things.

During the visit I felt my eagerness wane as the nurse took the opportunity to deliver several scoldings to the potential informant before the subject of my study was even mentioned. *You need to bathe these children more often! Why aren't they in school?* And finally, as I resisted the urge to run and hide, *Why haven't you had a tubal ligation?* The recently born baby was the informant's third, the point at which the nurse feels compelled to suggest that women undergo permanent sterilization, she shared with me later. I clenched my teeth, smiled uncomfortably, and silently vowed to return on my own. At the informant's impressionably confident response that the procedure scares her and she is not ready to end her reproductive life, the nurse looked directly at me as she scoffed. Costa Ricans' blatant disdain for Nicaraguans was not anything new, but this was the first time I could be associated with it, an uncomfortable yet common situation in ethnography: dependency on collaborators with disagreeable ethics.

The very next day, I felt like I *had* to return to this house for several reasons: to clarify my work as researcher, not as moral police, as empathetic to the migrants' situation, and as a fellow new mother. I worried that the nurse had compromised my trust with the informant, critical for eliciting narratives on sensitive topics I was hoping to address in my interview series. However, Sonia was still at an age when she could not go very long without nursing so we would have to bring her along again. When we reached the house, one of the household's several young children stopped playing in the yard to welcome us by pulling out two chairs for my husband and me to sit on. As they stood staring at us the children scratched at a full body rash, perhaps scabies. Dirty foam poked out from the torn seat covers and I scanned the yard for flea-carrying animals as I sat down with Sonia. Flies swarmed all over, landing freely on the faces, feet, and hands of everyone present. My husband and I did our best not to notice and to appear comfortable so as to set the tone for a fluid and dynamic interview. Although we are both familiar with the discomfort of observing poverty, with Sonia it is now much harder to disregard the health risks.

I immediately started nursing her. I was comforting myself as much as I was comforting her. With the benefit of hindsight I can laugh as I reflect upon my thinking, but in the moment I felt better knowing that she was getting the immunological properties in breast milk. Plus, at least then the flies could not land on her mouth. At one point I started to cough and couldn't stop without taking a sip of water. The grandmother present at the interview shared that she'd had a similar cough that they couldn't diagnose. My mind flashed to the nurse's fear of a case of TB. Transmission of TB is through airborne contact, although usually prolonged contact. *What are we doing here?* I thought to myself. I remembered the subtly admonishing tone of our dear friend, a pediatrician and fellow international traveler, when he told us that he was shocked by our decision to take Sonia to Costa Rica for her first year of life.

In the interview, the new mother was very open and articulate despite my questionable association with the nurse. She would make an excellent informant. My ethnography was not compromised after all. As we hiked away from the house I felt absolved of my researcher's guilt, but my maternal guilt lingered. In my mind I tabled the decision of whether or not to return and include the mother in the study, despite her experiences' obvious resonance with my research proposal. Before motherhood, deciding to risk TB for the research would have required little deliberation. With Sonia, it has changed. Weighing the ethical dilemmas of ethnography against those of motherhood will be a common situation this year, I am sure.

Maternal guilt, particularly as it is related to weighing the trade-offs of working parenthood, is nothing new. My sisters and friends have articulated it well for me before. I anticipate that with more time and more trust, my informants will provide me with further understanding. For the sake of the research, I am trying to comprehend whether transnational working conditions make this guilt a unique feeling at all. Although I have felt maternal guilt related to working across transnational boundaries, I also know that my own situation is so very different from that of my informants. For starters, I have to keep in mind the huge measure of support that I receive from my husband who has relegated his own career trajectory to be a full-time father for the year. This too shapes my experience and benefits the research, even if it has also been the source of personal discomfort.

Mr. Mom's Wife

Unlike my own status as mother and wife, which make me more human, for his "non-traditional" role as Sonia's principal caregiver, my husband's status is a constant matter of question. Our arrangement is not a familiar one here, or anywhere for that matter. We are charting new territory, and this brings us some uncomfortable moments. As we prepared to leave for Costa Rica, to the news that Eric would be devoting most of his time to taking care of Sonia so that I could complete the research, several people smiled and commented, "Oh! He's going to be Mr. Mom." If a little sexist, such reactions usually only annoyed me slightly. To my own surprise, on a day not too long ago, recent similar comments from the local health workers tipped my annoyance to anger.

After deliberate consideration of Sonia's eating and sleeping schedule my husband and I had managed to arrange a three-hour window for me to leave. I left them to walk to a health center, about 20 minutes up the mountain on foot, where a nurse had offered to assist me with study recruitment. Earnestly, I arrived at the exact time she proposed that we meet. She was on her way into the kitchen and instructed me to follow her. I was surprised to see the entire staff, including several nurses, a doctor, and a pharmacist, packed into a room not much bigger than a walk-in closet, huddled around an electric skillet. They watched as the center's cleaning person prepared them a pancake breakfast. As I entered, I caught the looks of the patients waiting in the lobby. Just a month into life here, I had not fully shaken my Western concepts of time, work, and productivity—I had to keep my judgments in check.

Their apparent camaraderie impressed me. Social interaction was predominated by laughter and joking, one of the most nuanced forms of communication, and one of the trickiest to comprehend in one's second language. Shortly after we entered, all eyes were on me as I accepted their generosity: a spot at the tiny crowded table, a cup of coffee, and a pancake. After lobbing familiar initial questions at me one of the nurses asked who was taking care of my baby daughter so that I could work. When I told them that my husband was at home with Sonia her response slipped past me as the room erupted in laughter. I had gathered that her joke referred to the fact that I was working outside of the house while Eric cared for Sonia.

Compounded by my annoyance that we were wasting time and their disregard for the patients waiting to be seen, I felt myself turn red with anger. Still, I was trying to establish a relationship of collaboration and gain their respect so I attempted to change the tone of the conversation. I claimed innocence: I did not understand the joke, perhaps my Spanish comprehension was to blame, or was it because I was unfamiliar with local TV shows? My approach backfired. The nurse's explanation gave everyone another opportunity to laugh at her joke—a derogatory label applied to men who do housework. The doctor followed it up with a teasing question in which he asked whether Eric prepared my lunch and had it waiting for me when I returned to the house. To save face I had to laugh, but inside my blood was boiling. I was seeking professional collaboration and felt like their jokes were a sign of disrespect. Plus, if only they knew how much consideration we'd put into making such a solo outing work.

In two short months of fieldwork it is clear that collaboration is a bonus, not a given. Transnational ethnography adds some unique challenges insofar as it must take into account the dynamic between informants and nationals. For me, aforementioned prejudices among the national population makes finding collaborators a thorny process. Balancing the logistical challenges of transnational motherhood makes it even harder, as this example further illustrates.

The pancake breakfast stretched out into more unexplained waiting. The nurse had not prioritized recruitment for the study. It was secondary to her regular day's work. I waited patiently. I checked my watch. Sonia is probably taking her bottle right now, I thought. I have a couple more hours to spare.

We were eating fruit at a local stand, a pit stop on the way to do the house visits before the recruitment visits, when my cell phone rang. It was my husband calling from one of our neighbor's homes—our nearest landline. Sonia had not taken the bottle and was very upset. He had tried all of our tricks so nursing her would be the only solution. I could hear her panicked crying in the background. The nurse and medical student had moved on. It was going to be a while before we could do the recruitment visits; perhaps hours at this rate, I thought. I was 20 minutes away on foot and had just missed the local bus—the next one would not pass for another half hour. I had to go. I yelled to the nurse that Sonia was sick, that I needed to go, that I would be in touch. She was very understanding. When I arrived, Sonia was crying so hard that her whole body shuddered, a new parent's most frightening sight.

That was the day that we decided they would accompany me on recruitment and interview outings until Sonia was more comfortable with bottle-feeding. Fortunately, this has only enhanced interview dynamics, as previous examples show. Even with a fully supportive partner the dilemmas of working motherhood are quite challenging, although in my case they add to the research since they help me to gain an "insider's perspective"; indeed, they are a way of life for my informants. However, my informants do not have the full-time support of a coparent, nor often do they have the ability to bring their children to work, or the luxury of gathering valuable data from such struggles. Once again, being Sonia's mom enhances my research. In light of the particular health risks she faces in Costa Rica, I feel those now familiar feelings of maternal guilt. Although, just as all ethnographers must assess the personal benefits of completing field research, I ask myself, how does this experience benefit Sonia?

Sonia's Stardom

"This is the best place to be a baby. People love babies here," the friendly American recently commented from the table next to ours in a nearby coffee shop. Some days, and some babies, I thought as I bounced my bright-eyed and smiley Sonia on my knee. Keeping in mind the anxieties over Nicaraguans' reproduction, it is clear that not all babies are valued alike. However, Sonia is definitely loved here. If she is a local star, my husband and I are merely her roadies.

Total strangers and recent acquaintances greet Sonia with affectionate caresses and words wherever we go. Women squeal with delight to hold her. She melts stoic elderly men into grinning baby-talk babblers. As we walk the region's hills to do our shopping, to conduct interviews, children of all ages yell out to her *Hola chiquita!* (Hello little baby girl!) and when I am moving around on my own, unknowns from across the demographic spectrum constantly ask me, "*Y como está la niña?*" (And how is the girl?). For instance, after a moment on our recent bus ride to the nearest town, it struck me as strange that the woman sitting next to Sonia and me had not uttered the commonplace croonings of endearment—*preciooooosa, muuuuñeeeeeca* (precious, doll). I glanced over to see that instead, she and Sonia were quietly holding hands. Offers to babysit from practical strangers are common—jokes abound that we ought to leave her in Costa Rica when we go. At local stores and eateries, clerks and cooks reach out and grab Sonia, holding her to free our hands for eating or shopping. On several occasions I have been called Sonia by mistake.

My husband and I enjoy the affection she receives, knowing it would be so different in the United States. We hope that Sonia is absorbing this feeling of cherishment and can hold on to it for years to come. In spite of all of the numerous dilemmas, all ethnographers enjoy the reality that fieldwork brings plenty of personal benefits on top of the anticipated intellectual contributions. Certainly, having her here has enhanced my research findings, yet there is personal fulfillment for us in this experience too. In addition to getting one step closer to having that doctoral degree completed, for me it is sharing the joy and pride of my daughter within a cultural setting where (many, if not all) babies and children are explicitly treasured in all realms of life. When we consider the sense of care she must feel, even with such nascent cognitive development, we feel justified in our decision to have her here. To consider these benefits makes the health risks and spending her first year separated from her grandparents and other extended family seem minor in comparison. She is not simply opening doors for the research but gaining a unique and special introductory chapter in her personal story. At least, to think of it in these terms lessens pangs of guilt for this new transnational mother.

Reference

Sandoval Garcia, Carlos. 2004. *Threatening Others: Nicaraguans and the Formation of National Identities in Costa Rica.* Athens: Ohio University Press.

The Unwelcome Guest:
Episodes from a Year in Bahrain

Andrew M. Gardner
University of Puget Sound

Paper Tigers

In the earliest hours of the morning, just as the sun creeps to the horizon, the wailing of the prayer call echoes through the caverns of this modern Arab city. The temperature begins to rise, and the streets spring to life. By eight o'clock, the boulevard in front of the glistening urban mall two blocks away is packed with automobiles, and it is in that busiest hour that I depart for one of my various destinations on the island. I am in my sixth month of fieldwork in Manama, Bahrain, just south of the conflict in Iraq, and these prayer calls—booming from loudspeakers atop the minarets of mosques both large and small—mark my days. My watch is still essential, as I am very much enmeshed in "first-world" fieldwork. I find myself interviewing people in busy offices, coffee shops, and in their homes. As I race back and forth across the city to meet the various demands of my schedule, these prayer calls serve as the slow beat of the city's heart. They mark the passage of time and bring me ever closer to my imminent departure.

The continuity of my days, and the occasionally furious activity of my fieldwork here on the island, contrast with the intellectual confusion underlying my work. Six months from now, perhaps, I'll have identified the central thread that connects my interviews, observations, and experiences, but for now, I am adrift. The dilemmas of fieldwork, some general enough to resonate with the sort of things I remember from graduate school seminars, others new and specific to my work in Bahrain, continue to buffet me to and fro. There are times, usually late at night as I'm about to drift off to sleep, that the overarching purpose of my work here seems clear. At those moments, I can see how all of this weaves together, but that feeling is usually gone by the morning, and I am again cast into the confusion of the day. I move from one interview to the next. I just keep moving, and hope that I can sort all this out later in the comforts of my office in Arizona.

I have an easier time describing the problems I've encountered. In the simplest sense, I'm studying the Indian diaspora in Bahrain. Yet from every angle this neat category of "Indianness" breaks down into smaller and smaller fragments, each defined by linguistic, cultural, ethnic, geographical, and religious heritage. Despite tracing their history to the subcontinent, many of my informants have never lived in India. Some tell me they "aren't even Indian, really." These sorts of individuals have lives spread across the globe. Perhaps they support a wife or parents in India; perhaps they've become citizens in Canada, New Zealand, or Australia, and are waiting another year or two to save enough money to start anew. They may have relatives in other parts of the globe, and many of them move between Gulf States as work contracts expire. Holding an Indian passport—an object that confers at least some sliver of identity to some portion of the Indian community in Bahrain—masks hundreds of different livelihood configurations that reach to the corners of the globe.

In a country where nearly half the populace comprises foreign-born noncitizens, any portrayal of the Indian diaspora must incorporate an understanding of the society that plays host to them. So my focus has expanded, and I find myself straddling the ethnographic fence between these groups, between citizen and noncitizen. In the process, I've come to focus on the interactions that shape the lives of both communities, hard as it may be to actually define the boundaries and inner cohesion of these groups. Anthropological training is tailored to finding the "insider's view" of a community or people—in the anthropological jargon, we call this the *emic* perspective. But here's the crux of my dilemma: in the charged and problematic space where these groups meet, I find myself torn between vastly different emic worlds. It's this dilemma that underpins the many hurdles and problems I've encountered during my short stay in Bahrain, and it's the subject to which I'll return at the conclusion of this essay.

Languages of a Community

"What language are they speaking?" I asked. "Kannada," the person sitting next to me replied, "but the singing is in Hindi. This is a song from a very famous Indian film. Everybody knows this song, no matter where in India they are from." I thanked him for the tip. As a white face in a large crowd of Indians, this wasn't an unusual question, but as an anthropologist I was embarrassed. Not that he would notice, for the Indian community in Bahrain isn't accustomed to anthropologists poking about. I'm embarrassed because I've had to ask these sorts of questions time and time again in my fieldwork. I set out to Bahrain for my dissertation fieldwork in November of 2002 under the Fulbright Program, with some additional support from Wenner-Gren for equipment and field assistants. My proposal suggested I would be collecting data for an ethnography of guestworkers in the Gulf as part of the growing interest in transnational movement of people, capital, and culture.

And so here I was, with Malinowski's proscription to "learn the language" still rattling about in my head. But which language? Once I got to Bahrain and muddled through four or five days of jet lag, I began to explore my neighborhood. Indians run the deli down the street, one of the countless "cold stores," as they are known here, that dot the urban portions of the island. Filipinos seem to be coming in and out of buildings all up and down the block. There's a Pakistani construction crew working on a new apartment building across the street, and I talked with Sri Lankans, Indonesians, Brits, Afghanis, and South Africans in that first week. I noticed a lot of Ethiopian women coming and going from the building next door, but they keep to themselves. Where do they work? I arrived on the island speaking English, of course, and I can get by in Arabic. My French is useless here.

None of these ethnic identities were clear to me when I got off the plane, but sorting them out is the first skill one is taught in Bahrain—who comes from where? On an island where every second person is a foreigner, your citizenship is your identity. People on the

A street scene from Manama's central souk on a Friday afternoon. From their attire, it would appear that all the men in the photograph are South Asian guestworkers. (© Kristin Giordano 2003.)

street or in the stores take a look at you and venture a guess, sometimes by the language of their greeting, other times with an explicit question like "British?" The local newspaper sets the tone. A Bengali is robbed by two Bahrainis in the souk, the old central market in the center of town. A Bahraini teenager runs over a Pakistani man near the port. Two Indian store-keepers go at each other with knives in the island suburb of Muharraq. A Sri Lankan housemaid falls to her death after attempting to rappel to freedom from a third-story window on a rope made of bedsheets. Nationality is always noted, and one quickly learns the subtle semiotics of dress and habitus, useful tools for interacting in the transnational and culturally heterogeneous context of contemporary Bahrain.

I had some help. Another U.S. anthropologist working in Bahrain met with me shortly after I arrived. She too works under the theoretical umbrella of transnationalism, and it's a small island. As we sipped on our coffee, the conversation slowly wound its way around to a discussion of how we might divide the transnational community in Bahrain—who would do what? I didn't want to step on her toes. I suppose it seems academically mercenary to the outsider, but I wanted to draw a line between our research topics. She had been working with the Filipinos, and she suggested I work with the Indian community. This made sense to me—they are the largest expatriate group on the small island and they have a history here that goes back centuries. And so there it was: an on-the-fly decision on my part, one that would determine the entire terrain of my dissertation, produced in a half-hour over a cup of coffee . . . at Starbucks, no less.

So began my forays into the Indian community. While visiting an Indian social club for men and women from the southern Indian state of Kerala, everyone stared at me like I'd forgotten my pants. I met one of the club secretaries. He gave me a phone number and put me back on the sidewalk. I joined the Toastmasters, and had better luck there. An Indian colleague from the institution sponsoring my research took me for drinks at the India Club, and I chatted with a few men as we watched the teenagers play cricket on the tennis court. In all these initial attempts, most of the Indians I met spoke English, but as I discussed the community with the gatekeepers—those individuals who come out of the woodwork in the first, nervous days of fieldwork, introducing themselves as representatives of the community one wishes to study—I quickly discovered that the majority of Indians on the island were destitute laborers, and most were from South India, from classes and regions where Hindi, much less English, has little currency. Malayalam, Tamil, Telugu, Konkani, Kannada: these are languages that the comprehensive ethnographer of the Indian community here ought to speak. And with much deliberation, I decided to give up on attempting to learn the rudiments of any of these languages—to trade knowing any one of these subcommunities well for an ethnographic vantage point from which I might survey all of them. As a result, I use English to explore the relationships between these various groups and translators when visiting the labor camps.

To the Labor Camps

It's Sunday evening. I'm jetting down the "Corniche," the waterfront highway that weaves along the urban northern shore of the island, in the back seat of a 2002 BMW 740i. Although the car is nearly a year old, plastic still covers the leather seats, as is the custom in Bahrain. It's a beautiful car. The city lights shimmer on our left, the Gulf waters are to the right, and we're racing a gold Lexus with Saudi plates. It's both breakneck and casual, also seemingly the custom in Bahrain. Our speakers are bumping to Camron's "Hey Ma"—*I drink, I smoke, me too, we gonna get it on tonight*. Ahead is the Pearl Roundabout, a concrete sculpture some five stories tall in the center of a gargantuan traffic circle upon which 18 lanes converge from all directions. Scaffolding surrounds the sculpture, and yesterday, through my windshield, I watched a crew of south Asian men repainting the smooth cement faces of the gently curving structure. Today, traffic is backed up for a half kilometer, and we eventually yield to the Saudi teenagers in the other car. We lose the race, but my friend Abdullah cackles with delight anyway. We're headed to the mall.

For the Saudis, Kuwaitis, and Qataris, Bahrain is sometimes seen as an island of sin— pubs, clubs, prostitutes, unveiled women, sheesha smoke, and plenty more. In 1985, Bahrain and the Saudi mainland were finally connected by a bridge, or rather, a causeway. Tourists, many of them from the wealthier nations nearby, began to come on the weekends. Hotels sprang up all over the island. Clubs opened, prostitution rings began to grow, and new sources of money began to flow on the island. Despite a conservative Islamic current in the Bahraini population, the island's people are widely recognized as the most culturally accommodative in the region, a sentiment that Bahrainis themselves noted frequently in our conversations. Several of the men I got to know noted that "we have Jews here!" They pointed to the Hindu temples discretely located in a few places on the island. And they have an uneasy alliance with the plethora of bars and clubs that have sprung up around the island. This accommodative attitude has allowed the island to evolve into the Ft. Lauderdale of the Gulf; it's also made the island one of the most desirable destinations for foreign laborers of all classes.

European nightclubs, weekends at the horse track, shopping malls polished by an army of custodians, marble mansions in the peripheral suburbs, drinks tonight at Trader Vic's—for the newcomer, Bahrain appears to serve the wealthy locals and the even wealthier visitors that stream across this causeway in shiny new cars. Beyond the pathways traveled by the tourists, however, is the other face of Bahrain. These are the domiciles of the disenfranchised Shi'a majority on the island and the reason Bahrainis are referred to as the "beggars of the Gulf" by other, wealthier Gulf Arabs. Great numbers of the Shi'a majority dwell in "villages" peripheral to the urban hub of Manama. Teenage Bahrainis linger in groups on the street, aimlessly passing time in front of walls covered in anti-American, or, more frequently, anti-Israeli graffiti. Intermingled in these peripheral neighborhoods are the labor camps that house the great majority of the foreign laborers on the island. These camps are tucked at the end of dirt roads, in the middle of an industrial area, behind a tall cement wall, invisible from the nearby road.

On this same Sunday, I spent the afternoon at one of these labor camps. "Camp" is probably not the appropriate word, as this dwelling was really nothing more than their current boss's unfinished cinder block garage, now divided into four rooms. All but the two bedrooms had a dirt floor. The men were heating water in five gallon buckets when I arrived, using those electric wands designed for igniting charcoal briquettes. Rats ran about the rafters over my head. Six men slept in each bedroom, the floors of which were covered in a surreal and garish linoleum with giant clown faces printed at odd angles.

The men at this camp were excited to have a visitor, and our conversation went on for several hours. A friend helped me translate difficult portions of the conversation, as their English was minimal, and I can't even say hello in Tamil. At the labor camps, the interviews "feel" like the anthropology I heard so much about in my coursework. The men talk about wells drying up, unproductive paddy land, the dowry system, unemployment, extended households, and remittances. They talk about the lure of the Gulf. They talk about dreams dashed by four months of hard labor in the hot summer sun, of four months for which they were never paid. They stopped going to that construction site, and now they are "illegal" workers, piecing together short stretches of work wherever they can.

On leaving, they admired the small car I rented from Avis, and they asked me how much I paid per month. I told them the truth—about $400. Driving away, my friend noted that $400 is more than they make in four months of work.

The author (second from left), S. Kumar (third from left), and a group of Indian construction workers in their labor camp. (© Andrew Gardner 2003.)

The Geographies of Transnationalism

How does one study transnationalism? I had spent some time on a project in Saudi Arabia, and I spent last summer in the United Arab Emirates, but Bahrain was new to me. In the five months between the day when I received sponsorship to conduct my research in Bahrain and my actual departure, I had been completely enmeshed in my comprehensive exams, so in anthropological terms, I was hardly prepared for fieldwork in Bahrain. I was familiar with the Gulf, and I knew the literature on transnationalism and migration. But the anthropologist's job as I saw it—to deeply explore the local culture and then work outward, contextualizing that culture in increasingly larger political, economic, and social arenas—posed a particularly fearsome set of difficulties.

Take the geographies of these transnational families: I interviewed a woman last week—I'll call her Reena. She was born in Goa, India, when it was still a Portuguese colony. She learned Portuguese in school, then moved to Uganda when she was still young. The family shuttled back and forth between India and Uganda during her childhood, and after years of service for the British colonial bureaucracy, they became naturalized citizens of the U.K. She married in Goa, which had since reverted back to India. After her husband passed away, she joined her sister in Bahrain. Her sister went back to India. One brother lives in Uganda, and several other siblings now live in Canada, which in many ways is the family's new home. Her new husband in Bahrain still has family in Goa, and their daughter is in school at the American University in Dubai. When their daughter finishes school she would like to work in the United States. And for two decades, Reena and her husband have made their home in Bahrain.

I heard some version of this story over and over again in the first six months of fieldwork. For the lowest class of laborers, the transnational connections are usually just to India, or perhaps include a brother or relative in some other part of the Gulf. But for the middle class, these are lives strung around the globe—relatives in India, relatives to the west, dreams leading back to India, dreams leading away from this small island to New Zealand, Australia, Canada, or the U.S. For many migrants, Bahrain is a waypoint to the globe.

As social anthropology, these complex geographies are a fascinating by-product of globalization. Yet they also pose a confounding and formidable hurdle for the budding anthropologist. As I've been trained, understanding the historical political economy of the community you study is of vital importance, and these forces—the political economy of oil, the British Empire, population growth in India, like great icebergs nudging against one another—are the forces that bound and shape the possibilities in the world of the Indian diaspora in Bahrain. But people in this community, the Indians in Bahrain, speak a dozen different languages. They come from varied cultural backgrounds. British colonialism, amongst other factors, shaped their national history, and in some ways this fact explains the contemporary factors driving outmigration. But one mustn't forget the Portuguese colonies on the subcontinent, and none of this talk about colonialism should eclipse the 50 years of rapid postindependence change, wrought by the capable hands of the Indians themselves. Or what of Kerala, the state from which the great majority of Gulf laborers come, and its continuing penchant for Communism? The localities from which the Indian population comes, I've found, are a complex and varied social tapestry, shaped by a global political economy that eludes any simplistic reduction.

Yet this is only half the picture. These Indians, complex as their cultures may be, now live and work on an island that has its own long history at the crossroads of global trade. From a sociocultural perspective, it is complexity projected upon complexity, a labyrinth that often seems too formidable to traverse.

I Am an American

Last week, a string of attacks against Westerners culminated with the bombing of a Riyadh housing complex, killing 34. The bomb was supposedly the handiwork of Al Qaeda, and as I write, the suspects are on the run. One of the places they could run to is Bahrain. Riyadh isn't too far from here, and Bahrain is a popular weekend destination for Saudis. Nor does the causeway between the mainland and the island offer any particular security for me. In the course of my six months here, a variety of destabilizing events have occurred. On New Year's Eve, a large crowd of Bahraini teenagers went on a rampage on the avenue one block from my flat. Hotels were ransacked, cars burned and destroyed. The police arrested dozens of the teenagers who were subsequently pardoned by the king. A few months later, security forces disrupted a "terrorist cell." They found a cache of weapons in a predominantly Shi'a area but puzzlingly arrested five Sunni "terrorists." And at the beginning of the conflict in Iraq, a bomb was detonated near the U.S. Navy base.

However, any perceptions the reader might have about "wartime ethnography" would probably not apply here. I've had no confrontations with Bahrainis, Saudis, Pakistanis, Afghanis, or any other individuals during my stay here, and the war never directly infringed on my daily activities. But working in an area of conflict has certainly impacted my research, and negotiating the complexities produced by the U.S. attack underpins all aspects of my fieldwork to some degree. While the current U.S. administration has effectively obliterated any cultural credibility we had in the region, I continue to struggle with the ramifications of conducting my research project in a vaguely hostile environment.

Most of my problems have revolved around the high degree of uncertainty in my life. In recent months, it was never clear if I was about to be evacuated, or if the social conditions on the island would suddenly become so tenuous that I would be unable to continue my work. Under the Fulbright program, I am under the guardianship of the American Embassy, and as early as November of 2002 the Embassy began to issue a series of warnings to the

Fulbright students. "Information sources" would indicate that a rally would be at such and such a location on such and such a day, and that all American citizens ought to "remain vigilantly aware of surroundings, avoid crowds and demonstrations, keep a low profile, vary times and routes for all travel, and ensure travel documents are current." As the American battle cry in Iraq reached its crescendo, the Embassy began a "voluntary evacuation" through which all nonessential personnel, including Fulbrighters, could leave on the State Department's tab. One Fulbright researcher left, and the various red/orange/yellow alerts issued by the Embassy had us convinced we would be shortly be forced to evacuate, even if we wished to stay.

This didn't happen, largely due to the particularly intrepid attitude of the Embassy's public affairs officer in whose care the Fulbrighters are entrusted. However, we were repeatedly summoned to one of the most dangerous locations on the island: the American Embassy. Already it had been the focus of several demonstrations, one of which resulted in the death of a Bahraini protestor. Passing through the high first gate, the undercarriage of my car is checked for bombs by the Ghurka regiment. The Bahraini regiment has a permanent shade tent erected in the empty lot outside, but they don't come on the Embassy grounds from what I've seen. Passing the sandbagged defense points, I park and cross two additional checkpoints on foot. In the cool environs of the Embassy, I sit with the other Fulbrighters and a handful of Embassy personnel. We learn how to alter our driving routes, detect surveillance, survive chemical attacks, and avoid confrontation with potential terrorists. They've issued Embassy personnel gas masks, and they might have some for us if

Graffiti in an upscale Bahraini neighborhood. Note that this photo predated the conflict in Iraq.
(© Andrew Gardner 2002.)

things get worse. For a week after this particular meeting, I kept a close eye on my rearview mirror, ever-vigilant for a motorcycle-terrorist making his approach.

This close relationship with the Embassy, my constant access to information, the badge that allows me to enter the Navy base to purchase cheap booze, and my American citizenship are constant factors in my interviews and interactions in the field. All my acquaintances in the Indian community knew of my ongoing visa problems during my first months on the island, and the fact that a high-placed official at the Embassy finally intervened on my behalf only compounded my image as an American insider. Some of my Indian acquaintances joke that I am "obviously a CIA agent," and in line with my access to fresh (albeit unclassified) information, these are really more than jokes. In the months leading up to the war, I was repeatedly plied with questions about the date of President Bush's intended invasion, as if we Americans were keeping some common knowledge a secret. My Bahraini friends believe the same, but they don't joke about it.

For the Indian community, my U.S. citizenship isn't an insurmountable problem in establishing friendships and finding informants for my project. In fact, my experience suggests that the Indian community is studiously divided on the issue of the war. From my perspective, they have a nuanced understanding of democracy, the variability it can accommodate, and the ways that it can be abused. A significant number of them have relatives or children in the United States, increasing the flow of information regarding the process by which this calamitous war came about. My citizenship has been more of a problem in establishing connections with Bahraini citizens. I had come to the island with hopes of working intensely in both the guestworker and Bahraini communities, seeking to unravel the complexities of their often-problematic relationship. But for many of the poorer Bahrainis— those without experience abroad and without the ability to parse the English media—we are a single force: Christian, anti-Islamic, and imperialistic—qualities that seem increasingly apt characterizations of the American stance. We are here to steal Arab oil, we are here to change their traditions, and I am the point man in the attack.

Negotiating Culture

In the six months I've been on the island, I've come to realize that my project's approval was an anomaly. Years ago, I spent two months in Saudi Arabia, and the project I'm currently conducting was originally designed to be implemented in Jeddah, Saudi Arabia's cosmopolitan hub perched on the shores of the Red Sea. As I put the finishing touches on my proposal, my contacts in Saudi assured me that the project would never be approved. I retailored my proposals at the last minute for the United Arab Emirates and Oman; Oman refused the project, but the proposal itself had a second life. It bounced around the Gulf, and finally found a home in Bahrain. I discovered this some five months before departure, and although my proposal would work as well in Bahrain as any of the other Gulf nations, I lacked the sort of detailed knowledge of Bahrain's history that one might assume is necessary for a project of this sort.

Even the project's reception in Bahrain was ambivalent. The University of Bahrain, a typical host for Fulbright scholars, declined my application, and I instead received approval and sponsorship at a local vocational institute. The director of this institute, a man with a personal interest in ethnographic methods and the foreign populations in Bahrain, was released from his post in the week prior to my arrival after a political maelstrom at one of the ministries, and the current administration of the vocational unit has seemed puzzled at best by my presence. At the American Embassy, the staff of the Public Affairs office—both American and Bahraini—continues to refer to my project as an "exposé." For months now, I've found that if I describe my project to a Bahraini as a "study of the Indian community," the almost-immediate response is, "But why don't you want to study us, the Bahrainis? We have a very wonderful culture!"

And what is culture? It is one of the most difficult notions for me to describe to the undergraduates I have instructed. They are perplexed that even we cultural anthropologists have a hard time with the concept! But for the Bahrainis—and I suspect for many people outside of the discipline—it's not such a difficult task. Culture is something described in the feature section of the newspaper, reiterated in festivals and school plays and on permanent display at the national museum. It's also something that is marketed, something that will draw tourists to the island. It's something old, and it's something that needs to be protected. And it's something to be celebrated, not something to be critiqued.

Yet, while many of my Bahraini friends and acquaintances I've come to know well have digested the fact that I'm not here to study Bahraini culture *per se*, many also realize that the difficult relations between citizens and noncitizens are best hidden from prying, Western eyes. Many are keenly aware of the "culture war" being conjured up by conservative pundits on both continents, and many assume I'm gathering ammunition for this battle. For some, the sooner I leave the island, the better. On a practical level, this context has an impact on the tenor of my interviews. Most of the Indians here—and nearly all of the manual laborers—do not possess their passport. Their local sponsor illegally holds the passport, and as a result, the laborers cannot leave the island at will. For Bahrainis, this is insurance that the laborers they sponsor will honor their contractual commitment to work, no matter what the conditions might be. Conversely, the laborers can be forced to leave at the sponsor's whim. It's an extremely tenuous situation for Indian men who have mortgaged family landholdings, borrowed money at exorbitant interest rates, and sold precious possessions for the brokerage and visa fees entailed in finding work in the Gulf. Their first two years' wages—and sometimes more—simply pay off these debts. Talking to me, especially about these very issues, is a difficult and dangerous proposition: it's not something they'd like their sponsor to know about, because in the final accounting they depend on his goodwill. Hence, many of my interviews often have a clandestine feel to them. Confidentiality and anonymity is discussed at length. The men look over their shoulders before they respond. Who else is in the room? Are there any Bahrainis around?

In a sense, they are always around. Photographs of the royal family—the king, the prime minister, and the crown prince—look down upon me from the billboards on the highway. They stare from the walls of restaurants and cafes, and they gaze at me from the walls of the classroom in which I teach English to interested Indian laborers. All three of the rulers are always seen together, and always in the same order, left to right. They look benevolent, or rather look like they want to look benevolent. They are about to smile. They watch me traveling back and forth on the island, and my interviews are never far from their gaze.

Activism and Anthropology

So I try to live in the Indian community. I go to meetings, to parties, to clubs. I've become good friends with some of the people that I've met, and my social calendar is full. I suppose I'm somewhere close to being able to portray the "insider's view" that is the goal of many anthropologists. More importantly, in the context of my research, I've learned enough to challenge the neat boundaries drawn by nationality—to portray the diversity of people that fall under the category of "Indian" in Bahrain.

But as I noted early on, the social topography of Indian life—of all expatriate life, for that matter—cannot be separated from the culture and system that plays host to the foreigners on the island. They coexist, and there is no way to unravel the symbiosis between citizen and noncitizen in contemporary Bahrain. And I've struggled with this other half of the equation: I don't know if I'll leave the island with the emic perspective on Bahraini culture.

Some months ago, I went to the villa of an American expat for a party. It was a casual affair, and a group of Bahraini men and women mingled with the Americans in the backyard. The host of the party, an American, complained that the Indian maid never cleaned the playroom in the back of the house, as she had been told. A young Bahraini said he'd take care of it. He called the woman out from the kitchen where she had been washing dishes, and in a combination of Arabic and English, he angrily berated her for poor performance, showed her the room, and told her she had to clean it every day. She looked frightened, nodded her head, and scampered back into the kitchen as the guest smiled to the host.

This discourse is common on the island. I hear it all the time—at restaurants, in offices, in stores, in homes. I literally hear this sort of thing every day. It's a tone that, as an American, grates on my ears. Of course we have similar divisions in our society—different classes, different ethnicities. But, for the most part, we abstain from expressing ourselves in this manner and hide deep-seated animosities behind a façade of politesse. That façade, part of the cultural baggage that I bring with me to Bahrain, doesn't exist here. At its extreme, I find this Bahraini discourse on race almost unbearable. For example, one of my good Bahraini friends noted that "fucking a Filipino guy doesn't really count as sex because they're not really men." And when I asked another man why I hear he and his friends calling each other "Hindi" all the time, he noted that, "it's like calling someone a nigger in the States, man." At my tour of the Grand Mosque, our guide mocked Indians for "worshipping monkeys," and another acquaintance told me that we shouldn't eat at an Indian restaurant because "they are a dirty people."

The Bahrainis I spend the most time with are educated and worldly. Most of them are Sunni. For the most part, they don't say things like this, at least not around me, and for the most part, I believe they don't think like this. But these attitudes prevail outside the erudite circles I've described, and the further I go in that direction, the more I hear. What am I supposed to do with these attitudes? How do I find the path to an emic view that includes this sort of material? How do I account for the vast superiority complex that characterizes citizens' interactions with guestworkers? How do I see beyond my personal contempt for racism and view this situation dispassionately?

I've been turning this over and over in my mind. And these issues have made their way into the theoretical foundations of my work here: these attitudes, I've come to hypothesize, are a reaction to the predominance of foreigners in their midst. The Bahrainis live their days in a sea of foreigners, most of whom are better educated and better trained to manage the bureaucracies and businesses that are part and parcel of the Bahraini vision of modernity. And like the illegal migrants who stream across the borders of my own country, the guestworkers here are willing to work much, much harder than the typical Bahraini citizen. The distance citizens establish with this racist discourse is, I think, a strategic way to preserve their hegemony in the multicultural environment on the island. It's a product of three decades in which every piece of trash that's thrown on the ground is picked up by a foreign janitor, where food is served almost entirely by foreign staffs, and where even the corporations and businesses that fill the skyscrapers on the island depend upon trained and educated guestworkers from India and other points abroad. No matter what capacities they bring to the island, foreigners serve—a fact that is reiterated constantly in the interactions between citizen and guestworker.

The Bahraini people have experienced sweeping social, political, and economic changes in the past century. Over the past 50 years, great amounts of wealth flowed to the island, and both state and citizenry have struggled to negotiate the fallout of these rapid changes with their traditions. In a more material sense, the Bahrainis continue to struggle with the new inequities these capital flows have structured. There is much in these intertwined processes that is of great interest to anthropology, I suspect. But like many anthropologists, I am drawn to the oppressed, and my intellectual acrobatics are, in the final accounting, scant sympathy for the Bahraini people. There are reasons for the troubling character of these relations between citizen and noncitizen—probably good reasons that I haven't considered. But balancing these two emic perspectives is often too taxing, and I find myself pulled to the Indian cause. When an Indian laborer borrows two years' wages to come to the Gulf, receives no pay for four months, desperately (and illegally) searches for another job, is thrown in jail and then deported, I feel an immediate sympathy. I care, and I want to help. I want this to stop. I want to stand up for his rights, to raise the alarm.

How do I untangle my notion of appropriate human rights, deserved by all individuals, from the specificities of my American upbringing? What portion of these "inalienable" rights belongs in the ethnocentric, American baggage of my Western enculturation? In the past, I've been comfortable with activism to secure individuals' rights or freedom when the target was a corporation, or even a government. For the most part, these are faceless institutions—in my imagination, when I envision the culprits, I see white men on a golf course or in a boardroom. But their faces are blank. Here on the island, the Bahrainis have faces. They are people, some rich, many just barely getting by. Some say things I would never say, and do things I would never do. Can I say more than that?

Acknowledgements

The research described in this essay was made possible by the generous support of the U.S. Fulbright Program and the Wenner-Gren Foundation. In Bahrain I received institutional support and found many friends at the Bahrain Training Institute. I would also like to thank Erin Dean, Rylan Higgins, Mary K. Good, Jennifer Shepherd, and the many other friends and colleagues who read early versions of this essay for their insightful comments and critiques.

Of Goats and Foreigners:
Research Lessons on Soqotra Island, Yemen

Nathalie Peutz
Princeton University

Soqotra Entries

It is three o'clock in the morning and I am waiting to check in for my return flight to Soqotra island after a weeklong visit to the Yemeni mainland. This is not an "arrival story"; rather, it is a familiar procedure now routinized by at least five such previous arrivals to my field site. As I stand amidst the Soqotrans and their boxes of vegetables, auto parts, satellite dishes, and even a full-sized refrigerator, however, my so-called ethnographer's eye is blinded by a sudden panic. Instead of contemplating all of the various household items and appliances that pass here for a passenger's luggage, I become a loud American. I find myself berating the manager of Yemenia Airlines about weight limits and airline safety codes; I argue that surely a large refrigerator should not be allowed on such a small aircraft; I advise him that Yemenia should schedule more than a once-weekly flight from Yemen's capital, San'a, to Soqotra's capital, Hadiboh, and that passengers and cargo should be separated. My expression of alarm is both obnoxious and banal, and the manager laughs at me. Later, however, our flight was grounded for "engine trouble" while the flight attendant tried to reassure me: "Don't worry, August is now over and all the crashes happened in August."

It is only after our safe landing and a night's sleep that I start to appreciate this scene with the detachment that ethnographic observation often requires—the overloaded plane, for example, is an apt reminder of both the relative isolation of Soqotra island and of its rapid "development." With schools now in session and the month of Ramadan soon to begin, many Soqotrans are returning from their "summer" (to them, autumn) family visits to the Gulf countries. The twice-weekly flights to the island (one from San'a, one from Aden) remain fully booked. Moreover, Soqotra has been closed to all maritime traffic for the past five months due to strong winds, and basic supplies on the island, most of which come from mainland Yemen, are running low. There is no butane gas left for sale, for instance, and even some of the urban residents will make do with cooking fires until the sea "opens up" again, hopefully in 10-days time. It was only six years ago that the runway expansion enabled civilian flights to land here during the monsoon season. Before that, Soqotrans had to rely primarily on their own production for staples such as local dates, goat milk and dried fish, and the storage of imported corn, rice, sugar, and tea. Nowadays, the satellite dishes and modern conveniences service not only the growing class of urban, salaried Soqotrans, but also the community of mainlander Yemenis who are moving to Soqotra to open businesses and stay.

Although in many ethnographies anthropologists now seek to avoid telling the once-standard story of first arrival and "entry" into the communities they studied, in Soqotra—and this is probably true for many islands—arrival stories are crucial markers of identity and change. "First, there were the Sultans," Soqotrans will tell you, "although they too came from outside, from Mahra [a province in eastern Yemen]." Then came the British, then the Party, and then the Republic," the story continues, referring to the three different political regimes to have governed Soqotra in the past four decades: the British, administering through a protectorate ending in 1967; the socialist People's Democratic Republic of Yemen that ruled South Yemen until 1990; and now, the Republic of Yemen, unifying the former North Yemen and South Yemen.

It is not only political regimes that metaphorically "enter" Soqotra, but also religious, social, and environmental ones as well. "When the *mutaTawwi'in* [the pious] entered," many say, "people drummed less" or "women stopped surrogate breast-feeding" or "we learned more about our religion." Indeed, during the first months of my fieldwork, I imagined these mutaTawwi'in as an identifiable group arriving, much as I did and still do, among the parcels of *qat* leaves also new to this island.[1] Only later, did it become clear to me that these pious mutaTawwi'in were mainly local Soqotrans—men and women who had become more vocal regarding their devotion in the period of religious opening that ensued after the mere tolerance toward Islam displayed by "the [socialist] Party."

Finally, the establishment of the UNDP-funded Soqotra Conservation and Development Programme (SCDP) in 2002, following on the heels of the Soqotra Biodiversity Project launched in 1997, brought with it a new regime of international monitoring and expert control. Some Soqotrans talk about the "entry of the *bi'a* [environment]" as a turning point in their relationship to their own surroundings as well as the outside world. "Before the bi'a project came, we didn't even know what protection, or the environment, or tourism were," a middle-aged man told me during a community meeting. Along with having "entered" Soqotra, the bi'a (really an abbreviation for *mashru' al-bi'a*, or the environmental project, but used habitually as a metonymy in which the multimillion-dollar SCDP project and its funds becomes the primary environment worth caring about) facilitates the entry of a steady parade of foreign visitors, experts, and tourists, most of whom stay for one to two weeks. Like these outsiders, the bi'a was my initial gateway to Soqotra.

Put simply, I had aimed to study the consequences of Soqotra's ever-increasing incorporation into the Yemeni nation-state after a long period of relative "isolation," a characteristic that is always highlighted in any literature concerning Soqotra. Specifically, I imagined I would trace the emergence of an environmental citizenship, its relationship to the UNDP project, and the concurrent construction of a specifically Soqotri heritage as part of and perhaps also in reaction to the increasing Yemenification of the island.

Not knowing where I would situate myself in Soqotra, I approached the SCDP managers in San'a and suggested that we help each other. I would volunteer for the bi'a project if, in turn, I could have their backing and also benefit from their support structure, including Internet access and transportation. Although my official research sponsorship came through the Yemen Center for Study and Research in San'a, the SCDP administers all scientific research on the island, and thus most, if not all, researchers pass through its doors. The SCDP managers suggested that I live in one of the newly created Protected Areas so that I could support the activities of its Association, especially their newly established "ecotourism" campsite that aims to generate income for the community. Generously, the SCDP office in San'a purchased a solar panel for my house in the village so that I could use my laptop computer. "We are in the twenty-first century, after all," an administrator remarked.

From the viewpoint of many mainlander Yemenis, Soqotra is a distant and backward place, only vaguely connected to Yemen, and beloved by European tourists for its bizarre trees. Indeed, a telling and true story concerns a San'ani who flew to Soqotra but did not realize that he had been traveling for some 300 kilometers over the Arabian Sea. Shortly after landing in Hadiboh, he stole a Toyota Landcruiser and tried to drive back to San'a, stopping only for directions. The amused Soqotrans directed him all over the island until the befuddled thief was finally arrested and deported. In the course of my fieldwork, I have often watched Soqotrans ridicule the "dim-witted" and "uncivilized" San'anis. Once, while we were resting on a rocky outcrop in one of the mountain plateaus, pastoralists who live in modest stone houses mimicked their urban compatriots by feigning to walk bow-legged, hands grasping an imaginary *jambiyya* (a curved dagger worn at the waist), and cheeks puffed out as if storing large wads of qat. "How backward!" a Soqotran observer replied. Later, these same men invited me to join them in what became an evening of mock tourism. We walked the 10 minutes from the village to the new SCDP-supported campsite and proceeded to take our meals and our tea on schedule, while being "guided" in our activities and, ultimately, adding a Soqotri entry to the multilingual guestbook: "We came here and enjoyed the food and hope to return again someday, for the rest of our lives." A week later, the entry had been ripped-out by a local teacher who disapproved of the Soqotri "dialect" taking its place amidst the English, French, Italian, German, and Arabic.[2] It would make Soqotrans look stupid, some reasoned.

These moments during which the peripheral and "relatively isolated" Soqotrans parody the envoys of power—the citizens of the (Yemeni) center and the wealthy tourists from afar—are frequent, but not nearly as recurrent as the expressions of self-disparagement I usually hear. "We are beasts [*baha'im*]; we don't know anything; we are Bedouin; we are like goats," the adults in the village tell me again and again. Consequently, much of my enquiry here has been focused on the relationship between globalization and self-worth, or, in the question posed by Michael Herzfeld, "What hegemony has this power to make people so despise themselves?"[3] And how and when did this "regime" (of self-deprecation) enter the island?

These are questions that I shall attempt to address in the course of writing up my dissertation, albeit from the privileged position of a U.S. graduate student with virtually unlimited access to resource material and material resources. Nevertheless, these questions are more than just academic. I had arrived in Soqotra with an acute awareness of my relative wealth in relation to that of my research subjects and of the power I have to define them (in writing). Idealistically, I had hoped that by being sensitive, working transparently with my interlocutors, and giving back to the community in which I lived these disparities might be mitigated. The longer I'm here, however, the more I recognize how my own presence serves both to validate and contest my interlocutors' "worth"—as they see it.

As a foreigner living on this small, remote island, I hold up a mirror to the Soqotrans' own insecurities regarding their place in this rapidly changing world. Thus, I find myself needing to grapple with this question of self-worth on a daily, practical level. How do I contribute to making Soqotrans feel "inferior"? At the same time, the Soqotrans have seen the likes of me before and have strong ideas about researchers and their research. I am evaluated by the Soqotrans I know in multiple ways: according to the work they see me doing, according to the research they think I ought to be doing and the ways in which I should be doing it, and according to the degree to which I am able or attempt to live in their world. This essay is about my efforts as an anthropologist to "fit in" in Soqotra and the Soqotrans' attempts to teach me how.

Foreigners and Funding

Rewind 11 months. I have arrived at my research site, surprised to discover that only 75 people live here and, moreover, and that the village consists essentially of one extended family. Although the entire Protected Area contains about nine small villages—hamlets, really—none of them are larger than the one I've been assigned to by the local Association. The people of this hamlet—I'll call it Qayher—are perturbed by my intentions to live with them for a year. Foreigners, and even mainlander Yemenis, for that matter, do not reside outside of Hadiboh, although three prior researchers with long-term experience in Soqotra have spent considerable periods of time in adoptive villages around the island. Currently, Qayher hosts three male (Soqotran) teachers for the Protected Area's one primary school. These "outsiders" live together in a one-room house that they share with the local assistant teachers. There are no other accommodations available in Qayher, but for a derelict room left vacant after a widow's death. So the cows were kicked out, the walls have been replastered, and once the mud dries, I'll move in.

Meanwhile, it rains torrentially. Here, in the mountains, we receive word of two shipwrecks near Soqotra's eastern cape. One ship en route from the United Arab Emirates to Somalia lost six Indian crew members, maybe nine. From within the Protected Area, several goats and sheep were caught in the flooded wadis and washed out to sea, as were a few cows. This morning, I heard a shout from the open plain and watched as my host ran over to lift a fallen cow, too weak from the previous season's drought to stand. When the rains let up, I sit in the yard with a group of young boys and ask them the Soqotri names of various household and personal items nearby. They get the hang of this game and tell me to wait. Then, each boy runs off separately and returns after some minutes with tree sprigs and plant leaves. Excitedly, they hold up each leaf-sample and enunciate the Soqotri name of its source. I dutifully trace each leaf on a piece of paper and record the plant's name: *sibra, tayf, imta'a, emeeru, qamhin, tareemu, mitrir, raheeni, eukshe.* Personally, I don't consider plant names to be the vocabulary most essential for basic communication, but these boys proceed as if they are right on the mark. Are the Soqotrans really this nature-conscious, I ask myself? Or have other (foreign) researchers, passing through here, set the tone for what is nature, what is knowledge, what is research, and what is important?

As a fragile ecosystem with high levels of plant and animal endemism, the Soqotra archipelago is vulnerable to invasion by foreign species. As a metaphor, this works for people as well as plants, and it is not too much a stretch to state that the Soqotrans are worried about their own possible (cultural) extinction at the hands of "invading" outsiders. To understand the Soqotrans' relationship to their immediate environment and to the outside world, I realized that it would be necessary to examine their attitude toward "foreigners" entering the island: tourists, development workers, conservationists, and researchers, as well as mainland soldiers, bureaucrats, and merchants.

"Soqotri" identity itself is contested as Soqotrans are divided over who, of the islanders, is and is not an outsider.[4] Yet, almost all Soqotrans share a resentment towards the mainlanders who, for the past decade, have been migrating to Soqotra in search of economic opportunity. Soqotrans see them as profiting from their natural resources while diluting their cultural identity, especially their language. Foreigners, in contrast, tend to present themselves as donors wishing to help Soqotra and its people. Conservation, development, tourism, and even research are depicted uncritically by their (foreign) proponents as the key to the Soqotrans' future welfare. Consequently, a discourse has emerged among both foreign expatriates and Soqotrans by which the legitimacy of foreigners here is determined according to the degree to which they can argue that they are aiding the island and its inhabitants.

For foreign researchers, including anthropologists, this is a difficult question. As foreigners with presumably substantial funding, it is often expected that our actual research practices—and not only the results—will benefit local communities. This may be due to the precedent set by UN-contracted research teams who paid relatively large sums for interviews and for the logistical support that facilitated their work. As researchers, however, our professional interests do not always align with the Soqotrans' basic needs: improved food security, health care, and education. Research-weary (and wary) Soqotrans everywhere have made it clear to me that they have seen too many researchers with too few results. Although Soqotrans were included as stakeholders in lengthy decision-making processes concerning the island's zoning plan, conservation goals, and potential growth industries, the majority of this funded research has ended up as "expert" reports and recommendations, or as catalogues of existing practices—all largely inaccessible and irrelevant to the Soqotrans who took part in them. Soqotrans are told repeatedly that they will benefit from this production of knowledge, as they are told that they will benefit from tourism, but except for the few who are remunerated directly for their services (guides, drivers, translators, and assistants), most Soqotrans have yet to "taste it."

Some Soqotrans have become skeptical of the anthropologists, conservationists, botanists, zoologists, economists, and linguists who move around their island-laboratory. Recently, a Hadiboh-based researcher asked me to distribute an economic survey to the villages in the Protected Area, including Qayher. I approached one of Qayher's leading women, "Halima," and explained to her the purpose of this survey: to collect comprehensive data on the island's economic activities that would facilitate the planning of future projects and interventions. "So what they want to know is how many children you have, how many goats, how many kilos of dates you produce each year, like this," I glossed. "What's the point?" Halima replied. "If I tell them how many children, will they give me aid? Will they give me 1,000 riyal

[$5] for each one? If I tell them I have only two goats, will they give me more? If I tell them I have a lot of goats, will they take some away?" No, no, I laughed, knowing that Halima, my friend, was also partially joking with me. "What, are my words not okay? Can I not say this?" she asked. "I think your words are fine," I assured her. I could laugh with Halima then because I had no personal investment in these results. Moreover, I could fill in the majority of the survey myself, although I would not distribute this information without the villagers' explicit consent.

At home in a Soqotri house: a girl agitates buttermilk in a hollow goatskin.

It has not been so easy to ward off frustration when it is my own questions that are being dismissed. However, by observing how other researchers' motives are placed in question when the benefits to local people remain illusory, I have learned to check my portrayal of the Soqotrans' attitude toward foreigners. In this, or a similar exchange, Halima is not simply being uncooperative or opportunistic as many foreign development workers and researchers (including myself) might believe. She is posing a serious question. "What is my 'worth' worth to you?" Halima asks of us. If I am willing to share the intimate details of my life with you, then what are you willing to render in return? And will it make a difference?

Being a Bricoleur

I came to Soqotra determined to find some direct and immediate way to "give back" to the community in which I lived and learned. The notion of advocacy has held its sway over me, although during a preliminary attempt at fieldwork—within the Somali refugee community in San'a—I learned that one is not always so "lucky" as to step into this role. In San'a, I was constantly disappointing the refugees who thought that my status and work as an American researcher might procure them a visa to the United States, if not an airlift for an entire minority tribe. Not only was my access to the United Nations High Commission for Refugees (UNHCR) office thwarted by the same guards who restricted refugees from entering, but even the doors of the U.S. embassy were closed to me, an American citizen, during this period of heightened security. Trying to assure these desperate refugees that my future publications would broadcast their struggles and desires revealed me to be a poor advocate.

During my fieldwork in Soqotra, then, I knew to avoid suggesting to people that my research would "help" them in the future, especially given the prevailing skepticism toward the benefits of research. Instead, I aimed to disassociate the results of my research (a dissertation) from the consequences of my being here (mutual assistance). In other words, I wanted my interlocutors and friends to feel that I had been engaged in positive interactions during my time here, and not just delivering empty promises of some future return.

While I remain drawn to the ideal of effective advocacy, I had thought that in Soqotra I might fashion myself as a "translator" between the people of the Protected Area and the SCDP project. But translators, like advocates, cannot be self-appointed. Even though communication between the "bi'a" and its beneficiaries is often muddled, the people here do not need me to voice their concerns; they articulate them quite frequently. Conversely, the SCDP management in Soqotra is not all that interested in my feedback or suggestions, nor do I wish to be construed as their mouthpiece in the Protected Area. Meanwhile, and despite the fact that I had been introduced to the village as an anthropologist ("researcher"), my primary identity as understood by its inhabitants is that of a bi'a-volunteer placed by the SCDP to help in the campsite.

At first, I welcomed this role for it seemed to make sense locally and it gave me a concrete sense of what to do, where to start. Later, as I began to see more clearly how projects and developments are placed upon people in Soqotra, I started to regret my emplacement by the SCDP (another "project" of sorts) into their lives. It is possible that the village may not have accepted me otherwise (recently I heard recounted people's first and horrified reactions to the thought of "a nonpraying *kafir* [unbeliever]" and single [even though married] woman living in their midst), but I feel uncomfortable with the fact that they were probably not given much of a choice in the matter. Perhaps I sensed this tension even before I could articulate it, for I plunged into the task of trying to make myself actively useful.

What have I been doing for Soqotra? I often find it difficult to explain to others how my days in this small village can be so busy. Usually, I awaken as the children head off toward school; they leave early in order to complete their homework along the way. It is sobering to watch them walk from one side of the plateau to the other wearing their official school uniforms, one of the foremost signs in this remote place of their inclusion within the Yemen nation-state. The boys wear black trousers and a white shirt while the girls wear black coats and a white headscarf imprinted with "Alkuds Lena [Jerusalem is Ours]" or "Christian Dior"—both slogans in what is to them an illegible script. Women have already walked up the escarpment to bring water to their grazing cows and to collect firewood for the day's meals. Men herd the goats or tend their date palms.

I eat breakfast with the male teachers and then walk to the local government school where I teach a half-hour period of textbook English to the seventh grade. This is my "service" to the community. From the schoolyard it is possible to notice almost immediately when a vehicle enters the plateau. If a car turns toward the campsite, then I walk there after finishing the lesson and help the young men set up cushions, cook meals, and interact with the tourists. It is here that I act as a translator, literally and metaphorically, for Soqotrans who had never encountered groups of Italian vacationers in beachwear before and for the tourists who have come to Soqotra seeking "pristine" landscapes and an "isolated" culture. This is my "assistance" to the Qayher families who run the campsite.

I spent the better part of today, for instance, helping the guard organize the campsite's kitchen. We erected a sink by pounding metal piping into cement floors and walls; we hung shelves and cleaned out spice-strewn cabinets; we salvaged bottles of water not yet nibbled through by mice, and then tried to seal up the stone house against further raids. I had resolved just weeks ago that I would no longer take on the responsibilities of the Protected Area Association, especially since most of its members (the male inhabitants of the area) have little interest in running this venture. Funded by a foreign embassy, the campsite was conceived of as a way for this community to profit from "ecotourism." For the majority, however, any investment in tourism—time, effort, let alone money—is simply a risk they are not willing to take. And so, here I (still) am. I suppose I have adopted an attitude of "if you build it they will come." As a result, I've spent hours working here, hoping to encourage the youth stuck with this job. Sometimes I think it is a minor miracle that this campsite exists at all—not only because of the community's reluctance to accept this externally conceived project, but also simply because of the "modernity" of its facilities. Here, in the midst of this remote and arid plateau, where the inhabitants must bathe in the stream and collect their water from a communal storage tank, are a running shower, a porcelain toilet, and a kitchen sink!

So forget advocate or mediator . . . in reality, I spend a great deal of time performing odd jobs and filling a variety of roles: English-teacher, driver, first-aid provider, electrician (my solar panel is now wired to power an electric bulb in nearly all the Qayher homes, but this requires constant tinkering), campsite overseer, and, in frenzied times, assistant cook. I can't pretend that I don't get frustrated when I "lose" a day to what feels like (social) bricolage: repairing this, providing that . . . all in an effort to play an active part in this community. At times, I worry about having set the wrong priorities and I pull back, hoping to refashion myself as a researcher. Then, armed with pen and notebook, I visit different families in the Protected Area and attempt to conduct informal interviews about people's feelings toward the environment, tourism, the state, and Soqotra. But many people react indifferently to such an artificial encounter.

Instead, it is during my work with others that these conversations often transpire; or as I sit with the men gathered in the teachers' house: my "right" as a "teacher," even though no other women enter; or as I relax with the women—drinking tea, listening to cassettes, and applying makeup (a serious pastime)—after they, too, have completed their chores. Other times, I may feel as if I am doing too much and that my efforts are not reciprocated by either information or true "inclusion." But this is also false. There is a not a day that goes by, literally, that for each of my meals I find myself a guest of a family. I spend my time in other people's intimate, domestic spaces (with husbands and wives) and this may well be because of my active involvement in their daily lives. Ironically, it is not my SCDP-designed position as a campsite assistant that has earned me this respect—although most of my "work" takes place there—but my meager efforts to teach seventh-grade English a few hours a week. Being their children's "teacher" is far more valuable to the adults of Qayher than would be any of the loftier roles I had first hoped to fill.

Still, I struggle with other dilemmas that emerge from this desire to "give back." In many cases, my usefulness here is simply the result of the wealth and power differential between the Protected Area inhabitants and myself. For example, after seven months of having to wait, like my neighbors, for a private car to periodically enter this area in order to have transportation to Hadiboh or elsewhere, I finally decided to buy my own. Having a car would allow me to interact with more people during my limited stay here, I reasoned, and my neighbors were pleased that there would be a vehicle available in case of medical emergencies. Not a bad decision, except that this 20-year-old Toyota Landcruiser remains a glaring symbol of my radical affluence and mobility. Even though the car will have cost me "only" $500 after its sale, this is the very amount that would allow some people on this island to fly to the mainland for urgent medical care. Additionally, my "knowledge"—my ability to drive, read, use a computer, speak foreign languages, fiddle with electrical wiring, and so forth— is held up by the older generation as proof that they themselves "are like goats who don't know anything." This self-deprecation is learned early. One morning, an eight-year-old girl walked into my house and said, in Arabic, "We are Bedouin. We don't know English, we are just Bedouin." "Well, I don't speak Soqotri," I replied. "Yes, you do," she insisted. "You speak English, Arabic, and Soqotri, everything. We are just Bedouin."

So what am I giving back, really, if not a reflection of their own "lack"? I am a woman who has more education and resources than do any of the village men. I am a foreigner—I am a resource—and I am perhaps part of the problem.

Dressing the Part

"That's it! You are Soqotran!" I am often told. This is meant as a compliment for having learned to eat rice and even porridge with my fingers and for wearing "Soqotri" clothing: a colorful long-sleeved satin dress over trousers and a slip, a headscarf (*hijab*), and, when leaving my house, a black overcoat ('*abaya*) pulled over everything else. When I am frustrated or tired, I hear these recurrent compliments as condescension. By making it so easy to "be Soqotri," are these Soqotrans not in fact intimating that I will never progress beyond an external grasp of their lives? After all, Soqotri women's clothing today is really Arabian-style "Islamic" clothing. The essential items are the 'abaya and hijab, which, imported from mainland Yemen, reflect the trends emerging from the Gulf States and Saudi Arabia. I am not Muslim, but now I dress as if I am.

The secular expatriates working for the SCDP consider me strange, although some "understand" this to be an "instrument" for my research. Foreign women are the most perturbed by this, I think, because as Westerners with feminist upbringings they feel that we (Westerners) should exhibit "freedom" and "choice." It is presumed that this particular clothing, especially the hijab, nullifies both, but try telling that to the young women in Hadiboh who follow the latest fashions as shown on satellite television, young women who now wear black gloves with fur-trimmed cuffs in the hot weather of the city. Nevertheless, an Italian couple that visited Soqotra in February and again in August was alarmed to notice the "increasing" prevalence of black overcoats on the island and asked one of their compatriots working here if I might have been the trendsetter! Exactly why I dress like the women in my village is not the most interesting question to me. Whether it is an "instrument" for research, a symbol of "rapport," a utilitarian garment (given the dust and the measured use of water), or even something more, like a preference, a headscarf is just a piece of cloth, after all, that can be as political or as neutral, as religious or as fashionable (or both) as the wearer herself.

What I do find intriguing is how my gradual "inclusion" in the lives of my neighbors, interlocutors, and friends is occasioning its own exclusions. Commended by Soqotran women for dressing "like us," I am also expected to behave more and more in accordance with their norms, meaning that my interaction with "unrelated" men is slowly diminishing. Women expect this of me; men treat me with growing reserve; and I feel a little uneasy now when in all male company. Of course, this determines my avenues of research. Six months ago, I was attending the all-male Protected Area Association meetings: my privilege as a foreigner with UN-project ties. Now, my sensibilities have shifted and I am no longer so assured of my place between cultures. Will I boldly insert myself into future meetings? Or will I rely on other ways of knowing what had been discussed (men inform their wives and sisters who then compare "notes")? Presumably, as someone of the self-styled "Third Sex"—the foreign female advantageously positioned to move between male and female "spheres"—I can do either. But what would be the consequences? Would my inclusion be as superficial as my attire?

I am not suggesting that clothing choices do not carry deep significance. My image and my reputation are deeply interlocked and it is on my reputation, ultimately, that my "acceptance" here is based. Even when I traveled to the United Arab Emirates in August to interview members of the large expatriate Soqotri community living there, I found that my image had traveled before me. "We saw you on television," many Soqotrans told me, referring to a brief interview in a Yemen TV documentary on Soqotra. "When you came to my door, I knew you already," said one man, "and I had seen you wearing a hijab which made me happy then and it makes me happy now."

Yet, the downside of this mutual embrace—I dress according to Soqotri norms and Soqotrans respect me for it—is that I am still only participating halfway. I speak Arabic and I wear the hijab, but I have not converted to Islam. "You are so close!" many people remark. And because I am "so close," they think I ought to be more serious. "That's a beautiful outfit," a SCDP employee commented when he saw me one day wearing a *niqab*, a black veil covering my face. (I don't usually wear the niqab except on special occasions when other village women wear it as well.) "But there is something more beautiful," he said. "What?" I asked. "The *jilbab*," he said, referring to a black cloak worn over the 'abaya that is usually a sign of increased modesty and devotion. In other words, I can "dress the part" but this will not ensure my entrance here, or in Heaven. Most of the frequent encouragements I receive to convert are out of genuine concern for my well-being and my soul. Some exhortations are even humorous. "You think *this* is hot?" one of the tourist-police asked me on a sweltering June day before pointing expressively to the ground. "Wait until you experience Hell" is what he meant. Does he ask the bikini-clad tourists this, I wonder? Or does he take license with me because I do dress "like a Soqotran"?

It is now Ramadan and I am fasting. This makes sense when I live in a small village where I take all my meals in other people's homes. Besides, I had wanted to fast, even while in Hadiboh (where I rent a house), so that I could participate in the rhythms of this vital month. As always, my Soqotran friends are generous hosts and I receive more invitations to *iftar*, the breaking of the fast, than I can schedule. However, some friends remind me lightly that fasting without praying (as a Muslim) achieves nothing but hunger and thirst.

I am struck by how Zeno's paradox of motion—that a body can reach a given point only after having reached half the distance, before which it must reach half of this half, and so forth, and thus never reaching the ultimate goal—might be applied to anthropological fieldwork. The closer I get to becoming a member of the community of my field site (and regardless of whether, given this example, I convert or not), the clearer it is that I will never truly reach a "fitting in" point.

Being a Daughter

In writing about these early experiences and dilemmas concerning my desire to "give back" to the community and my attempts to "fit in," I make it sound as if my strategies were calculated or as if my responses to certain situations were based on premeditated reflections. In reality, many of my decisions were made on the spot and as often as not were made for me—by other actors with other interests or by realities I had not foreseen. I had not foreseen, for example, the huge impact of my emotional unpreparedness on my research. I have spent years living in different cultures—as part of a high school exchange program, as a college student, as a traveler, as an employee—and I figured, quite presumptuously, that I had I mastered obstacles such as "culture shock" and the emotional strain of being away from family, friends, and comforts. But this fieldwork has required so much more of me, affectively, than these earlier experiences. Primarily, this is because I have now taken on the responsibility and the anxiety of rendering these erstwhile strangers' words and lives accurately and meaningfully to a critical academic audience. I feel responsible to these Soqotrans. In addition, my personal life has not proceeded according to research schedule. Instead, my emotional states have determined my work and relationships in the field and have also prevented me, at times, from being fully "here."

I started my fieldwork only two months after the unexpected death of my father. In fact, I was in San'a, Yemen, when I received the 3:00 AM phone call summoning me home. After scrambling with my family to arrange the funeral, I then spent the busiest month of my life packing up my father's apartment and his architectural office, what seemed like grappling with half-completed drawings and impatient clients, paying bills and searching for clues by which I might extricate "him" from the entanglements of a life suddenly departed. By the time I arrived in Soqotra, still in shock, I had nearly forgotten the purpose of my research here. "Culture shock" was probably my awakening. Imagine the bewilderment of any Soqotran to notice my teary response when first asking my name. "Nathalie, daughter of whom?" Everyone would ask. "Peter, son of whom?" They continued. And for at least the first three months here, I would weep—hearing in my genealogical name, Nathalie Peter Fritz, a roll call of fathers deceased.

I write of this here because I cannot deny the centrality of this event to my fieldwork experience. For example: it was mid-December, I had been living in Qayher for six weeks, and I was about to spend a week in San'a with my husband. A teenage mother in Qayher—I'll call her Aisha—had been reluctant to show me her swaddled baby; when I eventually caught a glimpse of the infant, I think I may have recoiled. The baby's large head did not befit her withered and bony limbs. Suffering from a stomach obstruction causing continual vomiting, the baby had been starving slowly for four months and now had acute pneumonia as well. I asked whether she had been taken to the island's one hospital in Hadiboh and was told, "Yes, but there is nothing they can do." Further questions were discouraged. What could I do but accept their resignation? But when a visiting British doctor diagnosed this as a case of pyloric stenosis—not uncommon in infants but requiring a minor operation—I learned that the family had been advised in fact to take the baby to San'a or Aden for treatment. There was something they "could do"; they just could not afford the airfare and hospital charges.

It was two days before my own San'a departure and I was in a quandary. Do I fly the baby to San'a with me? Do I take on the responsibility—not just financial, but also ethical—of this critical operation? What if the child, weakened by the pneumonia, dies during the procedure? What if the child dies anyway, in a few days, in the house right next to mine? Do I intervene? How will this affect my research? This strikes me as a strange question, now, for it implies that the successful completion of my research is more important than the child's life. Yet, after the years of graduate preparation required just to begin my fieldwork, I hesitated to do something that might jeopardize my presence here. At the same time, I felt confronted by the limits of cultural relativism. As an affluent and rather secular American with some faith in medical science, am I not treading upon what many believe to be God's will? I discussed this dilemma with a Jordanian SCDP consultant, who immediately quelled my fears. A baby was clearly starving to death; we could get her on the next outward flight; what else was there to do? This devout Muslim kindly donated a substantial amount of his personal money and said he would have the tickets ready for our departure. It was now just up to me to convince the family and fetch the child.

I returned immediately to Qayher, sickened with anxiety. I thought I knew well enough to approach Aisha's father since her husband had migrated to the Yemeni mainland for work and had no idea that his daughter was ill. But Aisha's father seemed nervous. "You will have to ask the owner (*sahib*) of the child," he replied, meaning her paternal grandfather whose decision would stand in the place of his absent son. Since the baby's parents are first cousins and the maternal and paternal grandfathers are brothers, I was a little stunned by the formality of his response and this delineation of responsibility. The paternal grandfather, "Othman," was also nervous and perhaps embarrassed. He would have liked to take her to the mainland earlier, he explained, but he didn't have the money. With the Jordanian's support, I was able to promise Othman that we would cover every cost, including unexpected ones. Eventually, Othman agreed to let Aisha and the baby travel with us, but he would have to come as well. Both Aisha and Othman packed some personal items into a plastic bag and an hour later we were heading to Hadiboh.

Traveling for medical purposes—from Soqotra to San'a or from San'a to Europe—is not unusual in Yemen, where the regional public hospitals are crowded and expensive medical equipment often remains unused due to the lack of technicians. Aisha had never left Soqotra, but Othman, her uncle and father-in-law, had been to San'a ten years earlier seeking medical treatment for his wife before she passed away. For many Soqotrans, travel is associated with hardship and crisis.

The children's ward in the public hospital in San'a was packed with sick children and entire families who seemed to be camping out beside them. My husband and I could not imagine receiving treatment there and paid an extra fee so that Aisha, her child, and Othman could be moved into a private room. The doctor in the private ward asked us if we were "those people who travel around the world and help poor people so that you can then convert them to your religion." "No, we are not missionaries," we answered. It happened to be Christmas Eve.

For a week, the baby underwent treatment for her pneumonia. There was nothing to do but wait. Othman and Aisha passed the hours watching the Asian Tsunami coverage on television. By the day of the operation, each one of us felt quite tense. Aisha was afraid for her child and wanted to return to Soqotra immediately. Othman tried to reassure her. "Look how many people are dying each day," he said, pointing to the television. "If she dies, we will just make a little grave for her here in San'a, and then we will go home." I wondered if this is exactly what happened when he was here previously, with his wife. He then took me aside and asked, "After the operation, will she [the baby] still be able to have children?" "Yes, of course," I said, understanding then the stakes involved in "letting" the child live. I, too, had a worry that I did not share with him: what if these four months of near starvation had irrevocably damaged her physical or mental development?

Fortunately, the operation was successful and Aisha and Othman returned to Qayher with a healthier child. The girl—Bilquis is her name—is now a chubby toddler adored by everyone in the village. One unintended effect of this intervention is that the people of Qayher, who were already quite gracious before, have treated me with even greater kindness ever since. Some of the people in the Protected Area remain dubious, however. Why provide medical intervention for a weak infant when so many adults urgently need treatment? When I left the hospital, sobbing after hearing that the operation had gone well, I realized what I had been trying unconsciously to achieve. I had managed to get this child to a distant hospital, whereas I had failed to do the same for my father.

Eight months later, I am driving with Aisha's brother from Qayher to Hadiboh. The steep descent from the plateau is harrowing and the dirt track itself is precarious. Aisha's brother, twenty-something and without driving experience, berates me for being too cautious. "You are scared! You need a strong heart," he says, "you have to have courage." "I used to be courageous when I was your age," I say. "I used to be strong, but then that changed when my father died. When death entered my family."

I notice that I have adopted the metaphor of entry, of being vulnerable, of having a permeable self.

A Comeback

Some months ago, before the monsoon season started, I was sitting in a neighboring village with a group of women, waiting for our training to begin. A European nongovernmental organization (NGO) had decided (with Soqotran input) to implement a community gardening project in a few select areas around Soqotra, including in this Protected Area. The idea was simple and sound: establish a community garden and support it with fencing, irrigation pipes, seeds, and training so that it can serve as a nursery for the families' home-gardens and a center for education regarding agricultural techniques. The women were annoyed, however. They had no interest in agricultural training in a community garden if they weren't going to be remunerated for their attendance, whether through salaries, food, or fencing (for their own gardens). To make matters worse, the NGO vehicle was already two hours late and the sun was intense. I, too, started thinking that I had better things to do than to wait for this training to begin, even though I didn't have children to feed or dinner to prepare. When finally the NGO staff arrived, the women were ready with their demands. "We will not come to any of your trainings if you don't pay us or give us fences," they declared. A tired foreign agriculturalist tried to explain that the trainings were meant for their benefit. "Aren't you going to give us anything?" The women insisted. "Or have you come all the way to Soqotra to give us nothing?" "We're giving you the training," the agriculturalist said. "But we're not goats!" one of the women replied. "We know how to garden! You've come all the way here to tell us how to plant some tomatoes?!"

From early on, I was warned by foreign expatriates and even Soqotrans that the people living in this Protected Area were "difficult," "severe," "fundamentalists," "traditional," and "opportunistic." Indeed, they only have to point to examples such as this—when people demand payment for training, or for responding to surveys, or for pulling foreign weed species in their own backyards—to confirm their view. However, as an anthropologist writing about the Soqotran attitude toward foreign development workers, researchers, and myself, I must be careful about the images that I present. I certainly do not think of my neighbors as being greedy and this is not how I wish to portray them. Yet unfortunately, the mere snapshots of daily life conceal as much as they may illustrate. For instance, these women desired fences over training because they saw no point in cultivating gardens that their goats would instantly devour. Additionally, the women preferred immediate material aid because they had learned not to rely on long-term promises made by outside donors. Furthermore, at the time of this incident, Hadiboh-based conflicts between development organizations were being played out in the Protected Area such that villages meant to benefit jointly from home gardening projects and tourism were pitted increasingly against each other. All these background factors point to a more sympathetic interpretation of these "demanding" women who were in fact being quite "reasonable," given the history of foreign intervention in Soqotra. To avoid inadvertently depicting my neighbors in this negative fashion, however, it might be easier for me just to omit these examples from my writing. But this may be worse. It is during these tense and embattled situations that the Soqotrans living in the Protected Area reject the inferiority that they see reflected on to them by the outsider's gaze. "We're not goats!" they affirm.

This reputation of being "difficult" and also insular does not square, moreover, with the inhabitants' own perception of their area as a wellspring that had "spread knowledge" to the rest of the island at a time when Islam elsewhere was "weak." Men are proud of the religious erudition of their forefathers. A few months ago, Othman showed me a "Soqotri" manuscript (written in Arabic, but by a Soqotran) that had belonged to his father. The *sira* (accounts of the prophet's life) was written as a palimpsest on the pages of a German shipping-log, its original entries still legible. I could read that on December 12, 1886, the ship's crew had been given 6 *Stangenspargel,* 2 *Himbeer, Saft,* and 1 *Fass Sauerkohl* (asparagus, raspberries, juice, and sauerkraut). Had this log traveled to Soqotra with the Vienna Academy of Sciences expedition in 1896? Can it be read as a reminder of how foreigners and locals have used each others' material culture to produce and document the knowledge that is relevant to them—even in such an "isolated" place?

My very first encounter with Soqotrans was during a two-week visit in 2003 that coincided with the bombing of Baghdad, a Pentagon tactic referred to as "Shock and Awe." It was not really a coincidence that I was visiting Soqotra; it was because of this war that my preliminary research plans in Yemen had been impeded and Soqotra Island was the only "safe" place (outside of San'a) where foreigners were permitted to travel. Meanwhile, the

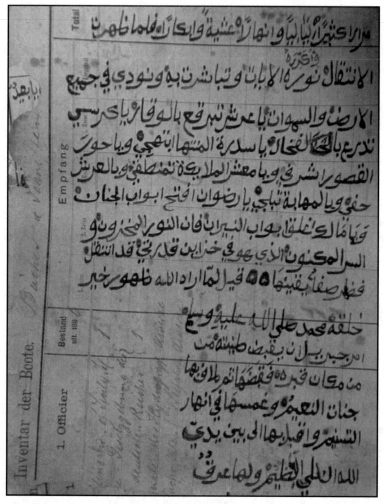

A Soqotri manuscript and a German book list.

very idea of conducting research in the Middle East during the height of my government's involvement there seemed reckless. Eager for an escape, I traveled to Soqotra thinking that I would learn something from watching the war unfold from this "periphery" of the Arab world. Yet, even given my graduate training, I had erred in thinking that this island (and the Protected Area within it) was "peripheral." This is perhaps how mainlanders view it, or tourists—but not the inhabitants, for they consider themselves quite central to this world. In fact, it is because of its "isolation" that Soqotra attracts an unusual set of international visitors: government dignitaries, film stars with TV crews, and investors. Most of these visitors spend an evening in the campsite and it is not unusual for an ambassador to enter Qayher. The director of the Protected Area thinks that Soqotra should be given a seat at the United Nations. (I should note that he is *not* advocating for independence from Yemen, but simply expressing his understanding of Soqotra's significance to the international community.) Two days ago, Othman told me that he had given Soqotra a new name. "Everyone comes here," he explained, "and so you will come back, as well. I call Soqotra 'The Planet of the World [*kaukab al-'alam*]' because of its exalted position and because it's more beautiful than all of the world together."

So how do I reconcile this sense of global significance with the simultaneous self-disparagement that pervades? Again, this is a research question that has turned into an actual and daily challenge. While I have been trying to understand and describe the Soqotrans' relationship to their environment and the outside world, Soqotrans have been defining me and evaluating my place in their lives. While I reflect on my mobility and training and yet, at the same time, am aware of my failures to even partially "fit in," Soqotrans reflect on what they consider to be their own ignorance and yet, at the same time, are proud of their stewardship of this unique and globally significant biosphere. While I may only ever reach "halfway" in my comprehension here, Soqotrans are reaching out halfway, too.

Research Lessons

Last week, I visited a Soqotran poet, "Koikihen," who is collaborating with a British linguist in collecting, recording, and translating Soqotri poetry. Koikihen had just returned from a research trip to Scotland and was busy setting up a Soqotri herbal pharmacy with paraphernalia he had brought from abroad. While we talked, he was filling little plastic bags with the pulverized leaves of the *sibra* tree. He is "a real plant doctor," Koikihen tells me. "There is another one in Hadiboh, but he dabbles in magic. He's more like a soothsayer. I am different, though, because I am straight with people and I give people the proper plants in a scientific manner. I have these books, see?" Koikihen has plants that are effective for skin diseases, post-partum hemorrhaging, fertility treatments for barren women (he glances at me, promising to give me these herbs before I return to my husband in the States), stomach problems, headaches, and joint pain. He suggests that we, too, collaborate in our research as he must collect more poems and I am looking for "facts." He then launches into a lecture on research—how to do proper research, who has done false research, how one needs to search for truth. It's a speech I've heard before. The following comments, however, were new:

> The truth comes from research that is done on foot. You need to walk into the country [*badiya*] and talk to people there. You can't go to the market [*suq*] where people will tell you anything. Seventy percent of what they tell you will be wrong. The strong informa-

tion comes from the badiya, not from the coast. Truth comes from old poetry, from tiredness, from sun, and from walking. This is true research.

Respectfully, I take notes but I am also intrigued. Just how often do I receive teachings on *how* to do research and *how* to be a researcher, rather than "the facts" themselves? Even these lessons came early. During my very first week in Qayher, while waiting for my house to dry, I took refuge from the heavy rains by rereading the one major anthropological work on Soqotra: an English translation of the results of a Soviet team that conducted a four-field anthropological study here in the eighties. The sheikh from a nearby village was quick to tell me that the Russian ethnographer, Vitaly Naumkin, had not been thorough enough. "Fitaly," as he is affectionately known here, had merely recorded the words of one informant, the sheikh said; I must always get my information from more than one place or person, he warned. Many people counsel me like this on how I should conduct research. I have been told that I must triangulate data, trust no one, and dig deep. "Imagine a plate of rice," my friend, Salim, told me. "On the surface it is cold while it is the food underneath that stays warm."

I have also been told that to do good research, I need to have a wide heart [*qalb wasi'*]. In fact, there is a need to have two hearts, Salim says: one for outside the house and one for inside. If one's inside heart is upset or angry, then it is important to have another heart reserved for use outside of the house, for other people, so that one's own frustrations will not be taken out on them.

When Salim first told me this, I jotted it down even though at the time it had seemed trite. Yet in the past 11 months, I have been experimenting, really, with the ways in which to "do" research and to "be" a researcher. These "Soqotri" lessons, if taken seriously in the beginning, may have helped. In a sense, I have been grappling with this very issue of "two hearts." On the one hand, I have been trying to resolve my outward stance toward the community in which I live and the informants I depend upon. How much should I do or give in return? Or am I not like a missionary who tries to "help poor people so that [I] can then convert them to [my] religion"—convert them into becoming willing interlocutors with a belief in my anthropological project? On the other hand, I am wrestling with my inner stance while conducting research. Do I remain the detached observer who can make sense of conflicts and contradictions by not becoming too emotionally involved? Or do I adopt the "widened heart," allowing myself to be frustrated and to be judged, to grieve and to delight in all of these unexpected encounters?

Notes

[1] *Qat*, or *catha edulis*, is a mildly narcotic leaf that is grown in mainland Yemen and chewed frequently, if not daily, by a large percentage of the male population. It does not grow on Soqotra and its use on the island is restricted to Hadiboh, to which it is flown in weekly.

[2] The Soqotri language is an oral language that has no written alphabet. Soqotrans learn Arabic in school and use Arabic for all written and official communications. When Soqotrans do "write" Soqotri, they use the Arabic alphabet, which cannot in its current form convey all Soqotri sounds. Most of my communications are in Arabic.

[3] Michael Herzfeld, *The body impolitic: Artisans and artifice in the global hierarchy of value.* (Chicago: University of Chicago Press, 2004), 21.

[4] In brief, Soqotran society was traditionally composed of the Arab ruling, religious, and merchant classes (immigrants and sailors from Mahra, Hadramawt, and the Gulf) who lived in Hadiboh or along the coast; the Bedouin pastoralists living in the hinterland; and the coastal population of African descent. While the socialist government sought to erase class and racial distinctions, today one hears references to a *moral* hierarchy based on who shows more shame (*'aib*) and who has been here the longest.

Acknowledgements

My research in Soqotra was generously funded by the Fulbright-Hays Dissertation Fellowship, with additional support from the American Institute for Yemeni Studies and the Socotra Archipelago Conservation and Development Programme. I remain especially grateful to my many Soqotran hosts. Here, I would like to thank Andrew Gardner, Sherine Hamdy, David Hoffman, Miranda Morris, and Justin Stearns for their insightful responses to this essay.

Anger Management:
Working Through Identity
and Objectification in Indonesia

Greg Simon
University of California–San Diego

Anger

When I picture myself moving through the streets of Bukittinggi, Indonesia, during my first months of fieldwork here, I picture myself angry.

After living several months in this small, mountain city of markets and mosques, traders and tourists, I have found myself thinking: I am being abused. I am like an animal at the local zoo (where I was once transformed into a roaming exhibit); people stare at me, point, make jokes about the *bulé* (literally, an albino person). They comment—to each other, as if I were not present—on my skin, my nose, my height, my movements. I tense whenever I go to use the local dialect, Minang, knowing that every time I do, they will be sure to laugh and parrot me for others and remark at how very clever I am. Not clever enough to be taken seriously: when they turn back to speak to me, they continue to use Indonesian, the national language, or simply use broad hand gestures. Sometimes they greet me, in barely audible tones, only after we have passed each other moving in opposite directions. They do not so much as pause in their steps, but they quickly, and this time at full volume, remark to their companions that I am arrogant for having not responded. Or they zoom by in pairs on motorcycles, screaming at me and then laughing as they speed away.

When I remember myself during those first months here, I remember myself bracing for an attack.

Encounters

The ethnographic "encounter" enjoyed a blitz of attention in anthropology in the years before I began my own graduate work. This was part of the self-reflexive move in the discipline that sought to address directly, and critique, the basis of what we do as anthropologists, and particularly as ethnographers: go places, interact with people there, and then write about it. Along with the emphasis on writing, this movement focused on the process of ethnographic research as an "encounter" between an anthropologist and all those people—known as "the other"—that the anthropologist interacted with during the course of fieldwork. With this in mind, we were forced to acknowledge explicitly the fact that an anthropologist's knowledge does not descend from the sky, but is born of a human process in which a person interacts with other people. This led to the insistence that we should not falsely veil our work with the shade of objective truth. Instead, we need to face fully our distortions and biases, our relative positions of power and privilege in comparison to the people we study (including our power to define them for the elite audience that reads our work), and the limits of our methodologies. Anthropologists were no longer to present themselves as if they were authorities sitting above the fray of social life, but as actors situated within the world of social interaction.

I arrived in Bukittinggi about a year and a half ago, early in 2002, ready for my own encounter. I came here with an intellectual appreciation that much ethnographic knowledge is subjective, or situated knowledge, and should be treated as such. At the same time, I had always dismissed these concerns as secondary to the *real* work that I intended to do. It had always been clear to me that the focus of the ethnographic work I wanted to carry out must remain squarely on the people I encountered and the undeniable fact of their lives as something meaningful and independent of my practice of anthropology. Avoiding the arrogance inherent in writing about others' lives with a voice of ultimate, detached authority was something that I thought (and still think) could be managed without resorting to an equally arrogant stance in which the anthropologist and the process of doing fieldwork are assumed to be as, or more, interesting than the lives of the people being studied. I did not want to do fieldwork in order to go back home and write primarily about doing fieldwork. I wanted to do research to try to understand a little piece of what goes on in the lives of some human beings, and a little piece of what it means to be human.

In the field, I have discovered the tenacious power of the encounter. Its heart lies not in the academic concerns, however legitimate, in which scholars have wrapped it, but in the immediate, emotional impact of using one's own self and one's own life as a tool through which to learn about others. What is at stake is not merely the integrity of the anthropologist's work but also the integrity of the anthropologist. The anthropologist's own self becomes a tool for research, and this does have implications for the assessment of that research. More palpably, sometimes painfully for those of us doing fieldwork, it has powerful implications for our own experiences of who we are.

Assigning Guilt

While discussions of the ethnographic encounter have paid great attention to the biases and distortions caused by our cultural assumptions and our relative positions within relations of power, there has been less attention paid to the distortions that may result from the psychological strains of doing fieldwork. It is easier and less risky to acknowledge that we are biased by something as abstracted and inescapable as "relations of power" than it is to acknowledge that some of the very tools we use for our research—our empathy, our ability to think and feel through what we see going on around us—are flawed as a result of our own emotional lives. Pointing a finger at power does not truly call into question our own individual competencies; it can remain academic. Admitting something like anger towards the people we study may pose the danger (I hope not realized here) that we expose ourselves as, to put it bluntly, not good enough people to do this job well. Further, if we are relatively more powerful than those we study, it seems even more perverse and arrogant to judge them in anger. Who do I think I am to come here and feel angry? Aren't anthropologists supposed to be humble before the people they study, to help others in the world see what they have to teach us, to champion their underdog causes and undermine the easy assumption that "they" just do things the wrong way? But the fact is we have mental as well as political situations, and the emotional strains of fieldwork are not something we are necessarily trained to handle.

Day after day, I saw red when faced with an enthusiastically smiling visage; I was prone to feel my blood pressure rise when greeted with a hearty, "Hello, Mister!" and I was vulnerable to feeling a prick of irritation at the curious probe of a stranger's questions. I found myself primed for fight or flight. With increasing frequency, I would notice myself trying to avoid interaction with people whom I did not already know and feel comfortable with. Seeing a stranger looking towards me, perhaps about to speak to me, I might find myself turning away as if frightened, or directing a steely stare in their direction as if hardening myself for their approach. It was all done in an effort to protect myself. But it also made what I needed to do—meet people, interact, have conversations—that much more difficult. So I would despair at my prospects for carrying out successful research, and I would lay blame: Minang people are hostile, unwelcoming, mean-spirited, and indifferent to making any genuine connection with me.

I felt horribly guilty at this thought. Wasn't this, after all, exactly the kind of bigotry that anthropology is supposed to confront and defuse? I also knew, rationally, that this character-ization of Minang people was not true. Not only did it brush broadly over the behavior of the thousands of people around me, each with a different personality and attitude, but so often this characterization of Minang people as hostile also seemed to be exactly the opposite of what I have experienced here from the very beginning. In between these failed encounters, I was also spending hours enjoying people's hospitality and conversation and developing genuine friendships. Both then and now, in people's homes or in other relatively intimate settings, the level of kindness and hospitality that is directed towards me continually sur-passes my expectations. I receive frequent invitations to visit people in their homes (and sometimes, perhaps even sincerely, to move in) or to attend weddings and parties, and at gatherings I am always an extra-special guest, given the most careful attention and defer-ence. People I have met only briefly before have told me that I am like their very own child, that they miss me when I am not around. Some, though materially poor, give me gifts. Oth-ers talk about how wonderful it is that I have come from so far away to be in their corner of the world, and how brainy I must be to be a graduate student. Even those comments people make about me as I walk by are, as often as not, compliments of a sort. People remark on how white I am, how tall, and how pointy my nose is: all attributes widely considered by people here to be desirable. Sometimes they simply say, "Look, a beautiful person." It is not possible for me to pass off all of this as simply a matter of niceties. When I discuss with local friends the attention I receive in public, they tell me how excited everyone is to see foreigners (even though this city hosts a constant trickle of them) and even how Westerners are regu-larly considered smarter, sexier, harder working, and worldlier than people here.

When I would think of this treatment, I could not possibly believe that people here were somehow innately characterized by hostility towards me. Yet neither this knowledge nor the guilt I felt kept me from feeling—not always, yet certainly too often—that I was under siege, surrounded by hostile forces. The warm glow of my friendly interactions would quickly turn into an inner boil out on the street, and against my own better judgment, I would find myself quickly assuming a fiercely defensive posture once again.

Being George Bush

I remember: After more than half a year here, I find myself sitting in a public car on my way into town. More than a dozen people—men and women together, small children on their laps—can cram into the back of these small vans, sitting along the sides, facing each other. The car is not quite full today. A man has just boarded, and is now asking me all the usual questions, and I am giving all the usual answers, as I do several times a day: *I'm from America; I've been here for eight months; I'm thirty years old; I'm doing research here; yes,*

A quiet day in Bukittinggi's "Chinatown," at the center of the city.

I'm married; no, I don't have any children yet (yes, I use birth control); yes, I think people here are very nice . . . . Everyone else in the half-full car is listening. No matter what I actually say, he laughs at me every time I answer a question because I am speaking the local language, Minang. I don't even smile: the laughter grates on me. I am giving short, grudging answers, almost as if resentful at having to speak at all. The course of these question-and-answer sessions has become so predictable that it quickly catches my attention when he breaks the standard routine with a novel query: "Do you act like George Bush?" With the previous year's invasion of Afghanistan, and with a U.S. invasion of Iraq seeming more likely every day, it is not unusual for Bush to be discussed. Still, Bush is universally loathed here, so a question connecting me to him is a loaded one, reasonably comparable—if not completely equivalent—to a Muslim man in the United States being asked if he shares attributes with Osama bin Laden.

I grunt, "George Bush," a little dismissively, but inside I have tensed. I ask him what he means. He looks at me steadily. "Do you often go attacking other countries?" I surprise myself by responding with the question, "What do you mean '*often*'?" In the back of my mind, I am already wondering why I am being so oddly defensive of George Bush, rather than simply distancing myself from him. People in the car assume that I do not know what the word for "often" means, so now others jump in to the conversation: "'Often,' it means 'frequently.'" "'All the time,'" someone else offers. "Yes," I reply, now also feeling tweaked by the assumption that I would not know a simple word, "but what countries are you talking about?" "Iraq!" the

Women and men buy and sell along a narrow lane in one of Bukittinggi's marketplaces.

man declares. "But he hasn't attacked Iraq yet," I hear myself counter, even though this isn't the point, this isn't what I really want to say. "Oh, but he's attacked them psychologically!" the man announces with a smile and an air of finality, as if putting me in my place. I am flustered, and I feel everyone's eyes on me. The man now turns his attention towards others in the car and suggests, "Ah, maybe he's a spy! Are you a spy?" This is now the cause for general, if nervous, amusement in the car, except I am not laughing, nor is my wife, sitting in the car with me. His tone changes to a softer one of admonishment: "You're not angry, right? It's okay, right? You know it's just a joke. You know people in Bukittinggi are friendly and good," he enthuses. I nod unconvincingly in agreement. An older woman, trying to help repair the situation, adds sincerely, if a bit more sheepishly, "We like Americans."

I ask the driver to pull over, and brusquely exit the car before my destination, angry with the man and angry with myself.

Marginalized Identities and the Cycle of Objectification

The hostility surrounding some of my interactions was something that concerned me in my early months here. It was also something I wanted to avoid thinking about and would rather have had it magically resolve itself so that I could get on with my work. This was not going to happen—not only because incidents such as the one described above kept occurring, but also because such events are not simply unpleasant experiences to endure while trying to do my job. Understanding them is part of my job.

I need to face the nature of my interactions with people not only to make my life here less distressing but also to get a feel for the social world I am investigating. I have come here with an academic background rich in studies of psychological anthropology and a plan to study the ways that Minangkabau men experience themselves as moral actors within their families and in the context of Indonesia's current political and economic turmoil. This involves extended interview series with individuals during which I spend hours discussing each person's life and experiences, trying to make sense of the ways they fashion their own sense of morality and self. These issues require me to carefully gauge the emotional tenor of the conversations in order to understand what concerns are drawn deeply into individuals' moral outlooks, and how those concerns affect their own lives. As an anthropologist, I also know that to make sense of what they tell me, I have to be able to frame it within its social environment, as it acquires meaning in the context of the world they live in. I have to develop not only an intellectual understanding of the organization of this society but also an empathetic sense of what the city and social interaction in the city are like. How and why do people react to each other in certain ways? What does it tell me about the way they structure their lives and about their conceptions of themselves and what is important to them? The emotional tenor of interactions on the street—even interactions with a foreigner—offers insight into such matters. Getting a feel for what is going on around me is crucial, both for my sanity as well as for my work.

In order to do this, it was much more useful to objectify the anger than it was to objectify the people with whom I was angry. Blaming them and defending myself with the idea that they were simply hostile, malicious people obviously did nothing to bolster my empathy and insight. Similarly, it was facile to declare myself inherently and unreasonably hostile, and leave it at that. I strongly suspected that my sense of being *surrounded* by hostility resulted from the fact that I was always carrying it around with me and often projecting it onto others. However, to look no further than this would not only prevent me from understanding the roots of that hostility but would also constitute a failure to fully examine the nature and causes of the treatment I received. Yes, I had clearly and senselessly been cold in that car, as if the man were doing something wrong by asking me questions in the first place. Yet there was no doubt that the man had attacked me with a line of questioning that, while couched in a composed smile, contained an underlying hostility. There was clearly something moving both directions in these interactions. Approaching this anger as a part of my work, as something to be held up for examination and analysis, allowed me the distance necessary to face it more directly.

First, I accepted that the most obvious dimension of my troubles stemmed simply from the fact that shifting into a fieldwork setting can be the cause for an enormous adjustment. To take the prototypical ethnographic fieldwork experience as the example (fieldwork outside the ethnographer's native society), there are of course the mundane adjustments to different food, weather, diseases, ways of using bathrooms, and so on. There may also be more radical adjustments: using a foreign language or several foreign languages, interpreting different styles of communication and body language, adapting to different assumptions about privacy, and so on. The list is long and familiar to anyone who has knowledge of the concept of culture shock and its causes. I had even experienced it all myself a decade before as an exchange student living in a different part of Indonesia (although I recall the struggle then, while certainly difficult, as less intense and certainly less characterized by hostility).

Graduate students conducting dissertation research, however, face an added dimension to their adjustment. While for many anthropologists, dissertation fieldwork may very well be the most intense and sustained research experience of a career, it is ostensibly part of the process of professional training and preparation. This is the time to nourish a new identity as a professional researcher. It is an identity that may start out fragile for many of us, insecure in what we are doing, anxious with the dread of failure. When I arrived in the field, my identity as a professional researcher was little more than a skeleton, waiting to be given weight and flesh. This takes time to develop.

In the meantime, when I feel the need to fall back on parts of myself that seem more secure, I often find these elusive as well. There are moments here, especially when I am alone with my wife, when my self is transparent, so comfortable that it feels authentic. Slowly, I have developed friends here who seem to see in me some things that I myself recognize. But when I am out in the streets, I am a "tourist," a "Westerner," a "foreigner," a "bulé," and a "mister" to those who have never met me, and I may be called any number of things by those who have: George, Georges, Georgie, Krem, Kran, Geg, Eric, Frank, Greek, Jon, Rudi, and various indistinct grunting sounds. The visions people have of me—I am a beautiful (white!) sex symbol, fabulously wealthy, worldly, poised on the brink of an academic title that will place me in the highest reaches of social prestige, wealth, and power—are so far from my own vision of myself. I also come from a place where there are no sexual morals ("You two aren't *actually*, officially married, right?"), where members of a family are bound by no ties ("If you ran into your brother's wife on the street, you wouldn't acknowledge each other, right?"), where there is no sense of community ("You'd never do this in your country, right?" "Do what?" "Chat with someone."), and where the presence of criminals, the unemployed, fish, rice, and trees are all debatable. When I see myself through the eyes of people here, I am unrecognizable—and those eyes are always on me, wherever I go, watching whatever I do. I am objectified, a thing both marvelous and despicable, but never quite fully human.

In the early days of my fieldwork, it was hard to find something to fall back on when I was out in the streets of the city and I wanted desperately to assert myself as a real person. This is why it was so important for me to turn to analyzing the disconcerting ways that people conceived of me and make it part of my work. That not only gave me something significant to hold on to, but I also found that it told me a lot about the way many people here think about their society's place in the world. These reactions to me served as a starting place to begin exploring not only people's vision of the world and their place in it, but also the emotional tenor and depth of that vision. Examining the marginalization of my own personal identity led me to appreciate the greater marginalization of their society as a whole.

The narrative of modernity may be passé in some academic circles, but it is strong in the minds of many here. When I listen to people here talk, I envision a world that is on a relentless, global march forward, always progressing (for better or worse) in knowledge, technology, culture, and wealth. Bukittinggi is a city, not an isolated, insular village. Through tourism and travel, television and telephones, and the flow of consumer goods, it keeps up a steady interchange with the rest of the world. People imagine themselves as part of global society; yet they do not generally imagine themselves to be living in anything but a backwater of that society. It is a society that appears dominated by Westerners, with their wealth, scientific achievements, military power, stable governments offering high-quality education, and pop-culture cachet. It is also a society that, people often believe, sees them as little more than poor, corrupt, and prone to terrorism. Nationalism in Indonesia is no longer a reliable refuge for pride. When I ask people here what they think is the best thing about Indonesia, what Indonesians have most to be most proud of as a nation, by far the most common response is a long pause followed by, "nothing."

"What are you looking at?" Bob Marley and Osama bin Laden, painted on a wall in the city, make an intriguing pair of international celebrity portraits.

In this imagined master narrative, people here are likely to see themselves as watching the action from the sidelines or perpetually trying to catch up. They are likely to see the their own society's accomplishments—the beauty and wisdom contained in Minangkabau traditions and their emphasis on equality, cooperation, and empathy—as dismissed or threatened with extinction in the face of modernization or as turned into an exotic object for the tourist trade. Even in the moral universe, where Minang people often see their adherence to Islam as making them relatively central, there is a widespread belief that the Islamic community is marginalized and even under assault on a global scale. There is also a sense that their own position is often undermined by the fact that many of their fellow "Muslims" are hypocrites, not practicing the superior morals that they preach. (Compounding matters, West Sumatra seems to be far from Islam's Arabic, Middle-Eastern heart.) Overall, it is a vision of the world in which their own society is devalued and relatively powerless to make its case for its rightful status as, at the very least, an equal.

Let me be clear: this global arc is by no means the only, nor is it the primary lens through which individual people here view their lives. To judge their interests and identities solely or principally through it would be little better than to judge them as mindless hostiles and would simply continue the cycle of objectification. Yet this *is* a real part of the way people here understand their place in the world, and it is a lens that my presence invites people to adopt. My body acts as a living symbol of the West and modernity, global society, wealth, power, and culture—in all of their glory, temptations, awesome accomplishments, and arrogant, destructive power. It is MTV, the Internet, and George W. Bush rolled into one. Looked at this way, it no longer seems paradoxical at all that I can be both put on such a pedestal, treated with the greatest respect and admiration and yet also subjected to an underlying hostility. My presence may offer the people here an exciting link to the action—but also a reminder that they may be judged or treated as insignificant, unable to measure up, or not fit to be taken as seriously as some others in the world. "Many people here," a friend recently told me, "don't know how to act around a Westerner because they feel you are somehow greater or more important than they are."

Desire, envy, resentment, fear, possibility: this is the emotional load set off not by me as an individual but by me as a symbol of something so much larger. If people react to this with an underlying hostility, I can all too easily become hostile in return; if people are especially excited at my presence, especially demonstrative of my special status as an exotic, I feel objectified just the same. Both of these reactions to me threaten to undermine a sense of security in my very self. Being treated as less than completely human made me want to either avoid interaction with people or battle them. When I was finally able to put enough energy into analyzing my own situation, I found in myself a reflection of the people around me. They, too, often feel that they live in a world that is liable to dismiss them as less than fully human.

Resettled—and Unsettled

The conclusions I reached about the source of my anger, and particularly about my symbolic meaning for people here, may not seem surprising. I admit, none of it came as a revelation to me, but more like the gradual discovery that a theory I had already assumed to be true was also *real.* Understanding one's need to adjust to a new identity, and understanding that one has meaning for others as a symbol, not just as an individual, is an intellectual exercise. Actually adjusting to the new role, and actually accepting that these emotionally charged and uncomfortable symbolic meanings are being applied to oneself, takes something more: it takes a conscious effort to resettle the self, to move it from an old home to a new one.

It was, in part, analyzing my anger that allowed me to settle into a new home. After all, amid all of this tearing down of the structures of identity in which I normally take refuge, there has also been a building up. I have gone about doing my research and become increasingly comfortable with this identity. For me, this new identity was reinforced as I came to understand my anger as part of my fieldwork, as something to observe, record, and analyze. Incorporating my anger and its sources into my work literally gave me a way to work through it.

Looking out from my new home, through the window of the researcher, I have developed some distance from that person under attack. The emotional strains of fieldwork have by no means disappeared completely, nor do I expect them to. Yet I have settled, even if ten-

The author, second from left, and friends in their neighborhood coffee house.

tatively, into this new identity, and as a result, I do not walk around primed for anger anymore. Letting go of the need to constantly defend "myself" has not only allayed my anger, but also increased my ability to feel empathy for people here, to understand intellectually and emotionally what they were telling me about themselves and their place in the world.

I have no doubt that my experiences have been both unique in detail and commonplace in their greater outlines. I suspect that all of us who do fieldwork face variations on these themes as part of the endeavor. We all must work through the temptation to objectify as well as the indignity and pain of being objectified ourselves. We all must work through the untidy construction of a new identity, gathering and buttressing new pieces, holding tight to what we can. It is a difficult process, but I do believe I have become better at it as time has passed. It has been beneficial to my work, and often personally rewarding. Still, as I complete my fieldwork, there is one question about this resettling that continues to puzzle me: when we shift to a new identity, what can we allow to get left behind and what must we absolutely retain?

A Final Encounter

My mind returns to the scene: I have been in Bukittinggi for over a year, and my new identity has begun to develop some tender roots. I am sitting next to my friend Din in the marketplace when the man arrives. Din knows him, and they chat. Soon the man's attention turns to me, and he begins to ask who I am, what I am doing in Bukittinggi, and so on. It does not take long, however, until he is done questioning and has launched into a long, winding monologue, clearly enjoying the fact that he has an unusual and attentive audience to lecture. I am juggling a bunch of mental notes, trying not to drop any of the things he is telling me so that I can set them down in writing later, when he moves to a topic that grabs my complete attention.

He explains: *Jews, or "Zionis"* (as he used the two to mean the same thing), *have their own indelible character based on their heritage and genes. This character is bad. It is hard and crafty and hateful. And their plans are different from the Catholics. See he connects my secrecy about what I'm researching* (what secrecy?) *with researchers who have been kicked out of the country, like that one who was supposedly researching something near the coast, but was really working for the Christians in order to convert people.*

See, what they do is they give people humanitarian aid, food and medicine, and then try to get them interested in their religion. That's their plan. But the Jews/Zionists are different: they want to destroy Islam. They want to make sure that Islam is divided into factions fighting against each other, so that Islam will be ruined. This is made clear in the Koran. And wherever you seen Muslims quarreling with Muslims, it is really the Jews that are behind it. And the Jews control the economy of the United States and of the world. And it has been revealed that the money behind the purchase of that recently privatized telecommunications company here, it was from a Jew. A Jew! It's been revealed that this is so. The Jews are the worst.

And do I know whom he likes the most? He likes the Germans. I might want to know why he likes the Germans. Because he and the Germans have the same idea: get rid of all the Jews. He likes that. That's his thinking, too. He likes the way the Germans think. And see how the Germans and French and Russians opposed the U.S. over the war in Iraq?

He's enthused, grinning, eager to teach me and to prove his intelligence to this exotic foreigner. And what am I doing? How do I take this? How do I react to this? I've certainly heard anti-Semitism before—it's in the newspapers almost every day—and I am familiar with many of these conspiracy theories. I know people, friends even, who believe them, or at least believe that they are, well, true *enough* in essence—and it is hard. But never have I before been so directly faced with a smiling man, doing everything he can to gain my approval, to prove to me his intelligence and talents, to be my friend, who is at the same time praising the idea of murdering me, my family, and committing genocide against the community to which I belong. He has no idea. He has no idea that he is grinning at me, and trying to win me over, all while saying horrible things about *me*, telling me what *I'm* like, how horrible and evil *I* am, and advocating my death. He has no clue.

(But does Din know? Din sits there and listens. Din stares into the distance. Din's face shows no hint of emotion or concern. He is my friend, and he knows I am Jewish—I know he knows, I know he must remember. Or has he, like some others, found the idea so unreal that it is hard for him to keep it in his memory?)

What does my face look like? I know I am nodding a neutral "I'm listening" nod ("that's very interesting"), I know I am trying very hard to be a researching scientist. A professional anthropologist: this is who I am, right? I know that my jaw muscles are clenching, that my heart is starting to pound. I know that I am terrified that he will ask me my religion. Not terrified of what he'll do: I know he's not about to heed his genocidal predilections right there in the market—or anywhere, for that matter. He's all talk. I know he can't even conceive of the fact that I could be a flesh and blood Jewish person. I know that if he found out, he would be—what? embarrassed? flustered? Or would he simply keep talking, talking, talking, and have it not matter a bit to him, not enter any sort of reality that he's just said these things about *me*, the person sitting there in front of him? I know that whatever he knows, he will continue to be nice to me, to try to befriend me, to try to maintain the proper respect of the face-to-face interaction. Jews aren't real to him, only theoretical. I am not real to him.

Yet I am still terrified. He's still talking, and I'm still nodding. I don't want to deal with it. How do I deal with it? Shouldn't I confront such hate, such challenge to my identity, such horror, with vehemence? I will be embarrassed to reveal that I took those words and just sat there. I want to believe that it makes me more powerful, wiser—that my outward calm and dispassion shows my maturity and professionalism. But I also know that inside I'm actually frozen, without a clue about what to do or what to feel. My humanity is being attacked, and here I am, pathetically, doing nothing about it. Pathetic. I don't want to be there. To be here. I suddenly feel more foreign than any stare or incomprehensible sentence has ever made me feel. I don't belong. Leave me alone. . . .

Before I leave the market, he asks me for about the fourth time whether I want to talk to him again. Do I want to talk to him again? I ask myself. Yes. He's interesting, and he's not a dull person in any sense of the word. He talks. He wants to talk to me. He would want to be part of my project. No. He's too hard to handle. I couldn't get him to focus on anything; he wouldn't take any of it seriously. He just likes to hear himself talk. And then there is the matter of the fear and hatred. (Whose fear? Whose hatred? Take your pick.) No small thing. But he wants to talk. How can I reject that? Isn't that what I'm looking for, isn't that what I'm supposed to be doing here?

Do I want to talk to him again? "Okay," I say before I leave. He wants to touch thumbs, a kind of ad hoc salute of friendship, before I walk away. I smile and touch thumbs. I turn around and walk away. He has no idea. I head out of the marketplace to go home, and everything seems normal outside. I do not feel angry, but I am lost.

Acknowledgments

I wish to express my thanks to everyone whose insights helped me to improve this essay, especially Andrew Gardner, David Hoffman, Akihiro Ogawa, Steven Parish, and Jenny Simon. The material in this essay grew out of a research project supported by the National Science Foundation under Grant No. 0130317; the Anthropology Department at the University of California, San Diego; and the United States–Indonesia Society. Any opinions, findings, and conclusions or recommendations expressed in this essay are those of the author and do not necessarily reflect the views of the National Science Foundation or any other person or institution that provided support or advice to the author.

Fieldwork in Coca Country: Investigating Democracy and Development in the Bolivian Andes

Caroline S. Conzelman
University of Colorado–Boulder

La Coca No Es Droga

A light wind cools the back of my neck, alleviating the heat of the afternoon sun that has dispersed the morning's rain clouds. Still bent in half toward the ground, legs and back straight with arms outstretched toward the low plants, I glance up to marvel at the long row of steep forested valleys with a patchwork of terraced fields hugging their flanks. A dozen pairs of hands move rapidly around and within the stocky bushes along the narrow terraces where we are, deftly plucking the small emerald-green leaves from their stems and filling the cloth pouches tied around ample waists. The steady battery of snaps amidst the silence is hypnotic. My inexperienced hands endeavor to keep up, but I haven't yet mastered the precise thumbnail grip, quick flick of the wrist, and ability to cup several sets of leaves in my palms without some fluttering to the red earth. Each time the owner of the field comes around to collect our leaves, she acts impressed with the amount I have accumulated, and tells me that I am learning quickly and will soon be an expert *cocalera*.

We are harvesting coca, a leaf whose cultural and economic importance in the Yungas valleys of the Bolivian Andes permeates rural life here. The ways that different groups of

119

actors—rural indigenous agriculturalists, town merchants, government functionaries, and international development workers—in this region honor, promote, or try to control the use of this controversial leaf serve to illuminate the complex relationships between varied political structures and continuous processes of change. My study of democracy and development in the Coroico municipality,[1] now three months along, has at its core the investigation of the beauty and vulnerability of lives rooted in coca.

Morning mist in a Yungas cocal. (Photo by author.)

Coca production is legal in the Yungas—though limited by law to 12,000 hectares (30,000 acres)—and has been going on here for at least 1,000 years.[2] Coca plants are well-suited to the acidic, rocky soil and irregular climate of this subtropical region on the eastern slope of the Andes mountains just over the pass from the highland capital city of La Paz. Most Yungas inhabitants are bilingual Aymara[3] and Spanish speakers and sustain diversified rural livelihoods with small-scale exports of coffee, citrus, and coca. A family's coca field yields three to four crops a year and depends on the reciprocal labor of extended families and communities. Its cultivation is labor-intensive in such precipitous terrain—traditionally providing near full employment in rural areas—and the leaf is simple and cheap to process and transport to markets. Its price is relatively stable and earns a profit many times that of other crops, so no matter what other economic activities a family may engage in, they likely maintain a piece of land for growing coca to weather the slow times of the year.

The leaves are sold nationally for *mate* (herbal tea, either as the raw leaf or in tea bags), medicines (tonics, salves, and supplements), and mastication (the most common use, done the same way you would "chew" tobacco). They are shared at social events and meetings to represent the bonds of reciprocity that exist within and between Yungas communities. But coca's importance runs even deeper than all of this: it is considered the sacred or divine leaf, a gift from the Creator, and thus the intermediary between the human world and the supernatural. When people cultivate or chew coca, they are linking themselves to an ancient identity and way of life.

Alison Spedding (1994), a British anthropologist who has lived in the Yungas for 20 years, maintains that coca is an immutable element of the social and spiritual order in this region. Infuriating to people here, coca is frequently conflated with the drug cocaine (and it is not cacao—you couldn't make chocolate from coca if your life depended on it), but as the ubiquitous t-shirt slogan declares, "*La coca no es droga*!" (Coca is not a drug!). Coca leaves need only to be dried in the sun, swept up with a broom, pressed into huge bags, and trucked out of town to the legal market in La Paz; they require no chemical inputs[4] and provide a host of nutritional and medicinal benefits to the indigenous workers who use them.[5] Cocaine,[6] on the other hand, is made by clandestinely processing vast amounts of coca leaf with a series of noxious chemicals[7] that eventually isolate the scant cocaine alkaloid and concentrate it into a powder, which is then illegally trafficked across distant borders and finally snorted up the nostrils of elite users and addicts for an expensive and dangerous high.

"Alternative development"—a euphemism for coca substitution projects promoted by USAID (the United States Agency for International Development) in its wildly futile effort to halt the demand for cocaine in the U.S. by eliminating the supply of the leaf in the Andes—provides funding and training to help people adopt other crops or a different vocation, even in the legal areas. In the Yungas this translates primarily into projects to promote tourism and specialty coffee exports. Yet, to date, no other good can imitate the financial security and cultural legitimacy of coca.

Democracy and Local Politics

With so many competing forces and such high stakes within the charged atmosphere of the U.S. "War on Drugs," Yungas politics is nothing if not impassioned. I needed the first few months of my fieldwork to parse out the different elements that are at play and how they interrelate here in the Coroico municipality, like a biologist studying an ecosystem. Bolivian political parties and USAID are central players, but there are four localized systems at work. At base are the rural indigenous areas and their system of relationships, reciprocity and spirituality, derived from Aymara tradition and Catholic ritual; then there are the agricultural trade unions, or *sindicatos*, that link together each of the municipality's 99 rural communities and the central town of Coroico to form political advocacy blocks in ever-expanding hierarchies up to the national level; then there is the municipal government with its elected mayor, city council, and many committees; and finally there is the departmental government with its appointed officials.

Each one of these political structures evolved in a different historical era for distinct reasons, and each exemplifies a particular form of democracy. This confluence of paradigms I find fascinating and is where my ethnographic gaze can play its most critical role. While political scientific analyses of democracy are essential to explicate broad trends and systems, anthropologists are better able to witness dialogue around the idea of democracy and to discover how it is understood, utilized, or abused by individuals in varied contexts. I am searching for answers to such questions as: What is the meaning and function of democracy in each system? How do different groups of actors make use of each system to articulate their agenda around development and coca production? Is there a flow of ideas between systems, and are practices affected? If so, are there new forms of "hybrid" democracies[8] emerging?

In the world right now, the word "democracy" is tossed about as carelessly as a child's toy. I cringe as I read news reports documenting the debacle of U.S. intervention in Iraq; the tired language of "the U.S. bringing democracy to other countries" harkens back to insidious Cold War politics in Latin America. What is missing from most discussions of the topic is the recognition that democracy matures gradually and fitfully out of a particular context to eventually serve the needs of the majority and functions according to a shared understanding of life's priorities and responsibilities. Such a governing system cannot be imposed from the outside without violence and the pointed denial of the right to self-determination. I am curious about the unique set of circumstances and reasons behind the different extant forms of democracy in the Yungas, and how the Western model of representative democracy—as embodied in the municipal system—interfaces with other designs. The extremely delicate context of coca just throws all of this into sharp relief.

People here often ask why I chose to study in Coroico, an area famous for its stunning vistas and tranquil rural character. Seven years ago I came to a town near Coroico with a group of advisors to the Unidad Académica Campesina, the only college in the Yungas. We were here for one short week, but I was captivated by the conversations I had with local people and the potentials I saw for research projects I could create. In my graduate work that followed, I focused on the political economic history and culture of Bolivia and the Yungas for all of my major papers, and slowly carved out an intellectual space for myself.

The demographics, geography, and history of the area also make it advantageous for my research objectives: Coroico's proximity to La Paz allows local leaders to negotiate regularly with national government officials; its multiethnic populace with an Aymara majority links it to a rich cultural history; its agricultural base has a strong tradition of activism; several international NGOs with permanent projects are established here; the ascendant industry of tourism diversifies (and complicates) the economic opportunities available; and the legal standing of coca production and its interest to the U.S. government intensify the significance of every other topic. And, I am still dedicated to supporting the extraordinary college here. I give lectures, advise on ethnographic methods and grant writing, and have hired four thesis students as research assistants.

It is funny how simplistic and naïve those tight, logical grant proposals appear amidst daily life in the field. Everything seems pertinent and important to investigate now because everyone else here is intertwined with all aspects of their society, religion, economy, environment, and more. It is easy to lose track of one's ultimate goals or get bogged down with information, and this requires a constant reorientation toward the final product. Advisors who well understand the local or national situation are a crucial component of a successful project. Contemplating the complexity that is revealed by spending a long stretch of time in a foreign setting is like watching the stars gradually appear in the growing night until you stand unbelieving under the vast canopy.

Reciprocity in Fieldwork and Development

I am finding it difficult to balance my tendency to act like the biologist I once was—assembling a systemic view of things and getting the "facts" right—with my responsibility to perform as the anthropologist I am now—analyzing relationships between different segments of society and processing the meaning of complex ideas, like democracy. This is why my relationships with friends, research assistants, and local leaders are invaluable, for they help me sort out the interactions I witness during meetings and interviews and interpret the concepts I wrestle with. Even market women, truck drivers, and old men resting in the plaza talk with me about their lives and perspectives on things. I am paying four research assistants to help me conduct interviews in rural communities, translate Aymara into Spanish, and transcribe my recordings, but how can I compensate all the other people who give so generously of their time and ideas? This is where my motivations for pursuing a Ph.D. overlap with a principle of enormous local importance; it is also a central anthropological concept: *reciprocity.*

The ancient Aymara practice of reciprocity, called *ayni,* connotes the reciprocal relationships and mutual aid that are fundamental to healthy sustainable communal life in the Andes. I am not yet sure to what extent its original structure remains, nor how increasing participation in the international economy, migration, and tourism is affecting community-level organization, but ayni persists as the give and take of labor and responsibility in some

The author interviewing one of the first Yungas sindicato leaders. (Photo by Freddy Mamani Castro.)

Yungas communities where I spend time and also as a potent ideological concept deployed in many social situations.

I use it myself to explain to people that I am not here to extract information as if it were a colonial-era resource, take it back to my country, and manufacture it for my personal profit. I am here to generate a study that will be of use to communities and organizations in Coroico—as well as help me obtain the Ph.D. I will have my dissertation translated into Spanish to put in Coroico's municipal files and the college library, and I hope to use my degree for the benefit of Bolivians through a job that allows me to work toward a more informed and less manipulative U.S. foreign policy agenda. This is indeed what people here would like me to do. They ask me, "You are going to explain to people in your country what coca is, and what is really going on here, aren't you? You understand more than many people here since you talk to people on all different sides."

In addition to these long-term strategies, my practice of ayni also has immediate impacts during my year here. By hiring college students as research assistants with some of my grant funds, they are able to earn money toward their thesis expenses (a hurdle that prevents many students from completing their degrees), and gain practical research experience for their thesis projects. They are also able to complete their annual community service requirement by offering their skills to the communities where we conduct interviews. For example, one of my assistants is studying veterinary medicine: I paid for a set of supplies so that in appreciation for people's help with my study, he can provide vaccinations, surgeries, and other medical care to the animals in that community. I also often make copies of articles and books from La Paz for my assistants and the college library.

The hottest commodities I have are my digital camera and voice recorder. I am regularly asked to photograph and record meeting procedures, and then I burn a CD for the participants with the documentation. I also print out piles of photos that I distribute to the people I know and work with, something that brings them and me great pleasure. I am teaching two weekly English classes to groups of adults who have asked me for assistance, sporadic anthropology classes at the local university, and computer skills to individuals in town. I have been asked to be the godmother (*madrina*) to several of my friends' children, which requires occasional gifts of clothes and school supplies and initiates a more abiding connection to these families. Through all of these efforts, I am attempting to show my gratitude to those who are helping me, and to become a part of this broad community of integrated relations—and, yes, to justify in a way my intrusion into people's lives.

Development policies as implemented by some organizations in the Yungas run blatantly counter to the ayni concept. As sociologist Marcel Mauss (1990/1950) pointed out about the dynamics of gift exchange, bestowing a gift on someone is rarely an act of altruism, in which nothing is expected in return. Instead, it is a deliberate act in the negotiation of relationships, in which reciprocation is expected and even required if the initial receiver intends to maintain his or her dignity and social standing in society. Over time this back and forth builds long-term relationships of mutual aid and trust. Compared to this, then, the standard development practice of a wealthy entity donating "aid" money or technical assistance puts unfair pressure on the poorer receiver to reciprocate and is a bastardization of appropriate social conduct.

Knowing that they can never repay the funds that flood in for "alternative development" projects in the Yungas, coca growers, or cocaleros, are duly suspicious of the true purpose of this money. What will they have to give back to the U.S. if not money? When a top U.S. Embassy official made a point of saying in a speech here last month that USAID donations are not contingent on people in Coroico doing anything in return—trying to quell the suspicion that their funding is tied to coca eradication conditionalities—he further complicated matters by creating a dangerous imbalance of power. As one indignant sindicato leader said on the radio the following day, "Could it be that we have held out our hand for this money? No! We didn't ask for this, so that the U.S. could come here and tell us what to do!" In such a situation, the giver—thinking himself magnanimous or imagining the receiver as incapable of reciprocating—holds tightly the reigns of power by keeping the receiver in a lower social position. Such manipulative behavior can also create dependency and loss of sovereignty, and this is exactly the relationship between the United States and Bolivia.

In reality, aid money is almost never given with altruism in mind,[9] even though the popular sentiment among people in the U.S. is that our government is just lending poor people a caring hand. Aid money can be used to bend people to the will of the giver (at home or abroad—consider welfare in the U.S.), whether or not the intentions are noble. Governments always (some say must) hold their national interests as the highest priority, and they distribute or withhold aid money in order to secure the behavior they desire. The following story illustrates a classic use of this tactic.

In May 2004, the Bolivian Senate passed a highly controversial resolution that would grant U.S. citizens, U.S. or U.S.-trained military personnel, and foreign contract workers employed by the U.S. immunity from being tried for human rights violations or genocide by any foreign judicial system. The agreement would proscribe their prosecution in Bolivia or their extradition to the International Criminal Court, requiring instead that the alleged offenders be returned to the U.S. for trial.[10] Why would Bolivia's representatives agree to such a deal, given the history of human rights abuses during militarized coca eradication exercises, and right when revelations of U.S. soldiers torturing prisoners in Iraq are all over the newspapers? Because the Bolivian government has become dependent on U.S. aid money to remain fiscally solvent, it is forced to choose between its dignity and the continuation of the considerable funding it receives.[11] Particularly in light of such blatant attempts by the U.S. administration to manipulate the Bolivian people, I think it is extremely important to practice ayni with the people I live and work with. It has become a cliché for anthropologists to promise to "give something back" during fieldwork, and it is only a rare topic of discussion in my department. But I don't think it can be emphasized strenuously enough how vital reciprocity is during fieldwork.

I Am Not My Government

Tory[12] and I wandered the streets of Santana[13] before the regional Agrarian Sindicato Federation meeting, chatting with people along the way as usual. This town is deeper inside the coca producing region than is Coroico, hours away from trunk roads and rarely visited by foreign tourists. We happened upon an old *hacienda* compound—a vestige of the feudal system that controlled agricultural production in the Yungas before towns were built by freed indigenous peasants, or *campesinos*, after the 1952 Revolution—and as we strained to get a glimpse over the wall, a couple came along with their big red plastic bags of freshly picked coca leaf and went inside through the gate. Just before they closed it I caught their attention and asked if we might have a look around inside. They nodded and continued with their loads around the corner. We stepped slowly into the compound. The crumbling low adobe dwellings lining the path might have looked just the same a hundred years ago, with rusting tools stacked outside and a puppy picking at the leftovers from breakfast. We moved on to admire the vines laden with bright flowers overhanging the large blue house, when a small door off to the side caught my eye. It was open a crack, and I went to confirm my suspicion: there was the hacienda's original *cachi,* the large slate patio used to dry coca. The couple that had let us in were scattering handfuls of the leaves onto the flat stones to soak up the morning sun, and we stood to watch their practiced motions and listen to the sound of the leaves rustling against each other.

Now that campesinos have reclaimed the hacienda and its grounds for their own use, sections of the huge old cachi are rented out on rotation. Many families have their own modest cachis, or build one to share between neighbors. Even so, the scale of this one reveals the large volume of coca that was produced when the majority of land and people were controlled to produce for the profit of the elite few. Coca production in the Yungas has shown a dramatic increase over the past few years, and newly cleared patches in the forest are visible from any road.[14] However, several coca growers have told me that less coca is grown now than during the feudal era. This perception only deepens their anger toward those who would tell them to reduce cultivation. Because there appears to be a large potential demand for the legal use of coca leaf in neighboring countries, cocaleros would like to be able to more extensively commercialize and export the leaf. It is a cruel irony that poor Bolivians have a crop that provides wide employment at the local level, requires no chemical applications, gives three to four harvests a year, brings a better price than any other agricultural good, is widely used for quotidian and medicinal needs, and connects people to their cultural heritage but is outlawed by the international community, even for its non-narcotic uses.

Standing in the back of the truck that morning for the hour-long ride to Santana with 30 campesinos from Coroico, all of us jostling with the rough road and lively conversations, I felt happy about the solidarity I am building with this community. We all crowded into local cafés for a typical lunch of vegetable soup and plates of chicken, rice, and potatoes, sharing coconut soda at tiny linoleum tables. The Coroico group then went to meet up with members of other sindicatos while Tory and I explored the town. When we headed up the hill to the schoolyard, the meeting was getting underway. At one end of the concrete soccer field, one of the leaders was reading aloud the afternoon's agenda off a chalkboard. Some people had secured spaces in the shade of the field house near the head table, while the rest of us lined up on the step bleachers in the baking sun. After a few minutes, I was asked to come to the microphone and explain our presence—two red-haired freckle-faced girls writing in notebooks and taking photos in the middle of a cocalero meeting. My introduction was met with smiles and nods, and though my heart was pounding, I was glad to clarify what we were doing there. They have every right to ask and no real reason to believe what I say, since we represent the forces they are struggling against. As I scribbled notes and looked out toward the mountainsides replete with coca terracing, the meeting proceeded through the first few items.

Sindicato meetings such as this are run in an open fashion and led by the input of those in attendance; people just have to take the initiative to stand up and speak. At times they have to work to get the attention of the leaders to be called on, something the women have trouble with, I've noticed. People have no qualms about interrupting each other, but generally a speaker is allowed to carry on for as long as it takes to get through his litany of observations and opinions. This method is not deliberative, as comments are not necessarily followed by discussion of that point. Remarks just pile one on top of the other, and there is no one who keeps notes on what is said. Decisions are made when people have no more to say, and one of the leaders announces what he perceives to be the general consensus. He asks whether there is agreement, some in the crowd mumble or call out yes, a resolution is created, and the next topic on the agenda is introduced.

In the middle of one man's commentary two hours later, I noticed him gesturing specifically toward Tory and me. He was talking about the attention being paid to the Yungas by the American Embassy in light of U.S. satellite data publicized a few months ago showing a sharp increase in coca production in this sprawling region. A large structure is being built along the highway between La Paz and the Yungas, and people worry that it is to be a military installation, which could signal the start of overt and possibly violent pressure to eradicate coca here.[15] The speaker expressed his discomfort with the fact that two people from the United States were listening to all their remarks, and since they were about to broach the subject of how to respond to this unwelcome situation, he suggested that we be asked to leave. This volleyed the responsibility to the three men running the meeting. The leader of the Federation noted that, hypothetically, anyone here could be a spy, but he agreed that they should not risk allowing us to stay in case we were in fact agents of the CIA or DEA.[16] Everyone turned their heads in unison as he shifted his gaze to us and said, "So we must ask that you vacate this meeting." I nodded with what I hoped came across as respectful deference. I put away my notebook, pen, newspaper, camera, and banana peel, and with a wave and a thank you, we walked into town and caught a ride back to Coroico.

I had to ward off feeling rejected, or embarrassed, even though this was not the first time I had been barred from a sindicato meeting on account of my nationality. In this instance, since I had only been in the area for a month, the young leader from Coroico whom I had only just met could not risk standing up for me in a crowd of more radicalized cocaleros from a different municipality. I respect their choices in how and when to accept me; the responsibility is mine to develop relationships with them, and to prove that I am seeking a balanced understanding of the situation. Even at the meetings I do attend, I have to weather cold looks of suspicion from people I don't know. I just smile warmly and try to look relaxed, and I keep my notebook and camera in my bag. If I can strike up a conversation with whoever is looking at me askance, this defuses the tension. After I explain what I am doing here, a discussion of U.S. foreign policy usually ensues, followed by questions about how much it costs to live in the U.S. and what kinds of jobs are available for Bolivian immigrants. Now, after three months, more people are used to seeing me poking around. I am often invited to sindicato meetings and am able to participate in their camaraderie. I am frequently asked with genuine concern how my work is going, with tidbits of advice or insight thrown my way.

The reality is that coca growers simply must take precautions in this very real and very deadly war that is being waged on poor agriculturalists in Bolivia by foreign military and economic coercion. If ever I receive apprehensive looks, or when someone only half-jokingly suggests that I am a spy, I make it clear that I do not represent my government. I openly disagree with foreign policy that subjects people in other countries to intimidation, suffering, and upheaval for a grave social problem that actually exists in my country. This political hypocrisy is not lost on people here either, since they directly experience its impact. When I explain that most people in the U.S. simply do not understand what coca leaf is, what or even where Bolivia is, or how U.S. policy affects innocent families here, they look surprised. Then I say that I hope my work will help ameliorate this deficiency.

Coca and Community Organization

My experiences harvesting coca have helped me think differently about the kinds of politics this daily agricultural work inspires in Aymara communities. I usually pick coca with a group of women from Maracata,[17] a small town perched on a curve of the mountainside with broad low hills scored by coca terraces filling the huge valley below. Walking through these fields, or *cocales*, along meandering paths, one can see small bands of workers who spend the day together: the men clear the trees and brush, make the earthen terraces, and plant the seedlings in new fields, while women and children do most of the harvesting in the mature cocales. No weeding is required, and the red or yellow seeds are collected once a year. Though land parcels are individually held, extended family members and neighbors work together, rotating from one field to the next throughout the year. It would be impossible for one person or nuclear family to manage a single plot's three to four harvests a year; keeping apace with the agricultural cycle requires the collective, focused efforts of the group.

When my women friends arrive in the field to pick coca, they begin by chewing the leaf together, catching up on town gossip, and tying cloth pouches around their waists. Then, beginning at the top of a steep, narrow section of terraces,[18] each woman steps to the end of one row, bends down and begins with the first bush. Lined up vertically, they move slowly across the column of terraces at roughly the same pace, alternately chatting, listening to a transistor radio, or caught in meditative silence. When a woman has collected all the leaves from one row, she moves down to the next one available and continues filling her pouch. The owner of the field collects the leaves throughout the day in large red sacks. Once in the morning and once in the afternoon, the group takes refuge under a shade tree and again chews coca together. For lunch everyone convenes inside the thatched-roof shelter situated in each field. Spooned from large pots, heaping bowls of rice, spiced meat, vegetables, cooked green bananas, boiled potatoes, and hot sauce are passed around to each person. I like to bring disks of dark chocolate for our dessert.

It appears to me that the relaxed efficiency of this daily work pattern and the egalitarian structure of the work groups[19] inspire similar attitudes in other community settings. Imagine people working like this according to a steady rotation of labor day after day, year after year, alongside multiple generations of extended families and community members, with no status or power hierarchy other than the person coordinating the plan for the day. Now imagine these same people coming together for a meeting: the community would consist of one big network of interlocking relationships between people who literally could not survive without the ever-shifting balance of reciprocity. There seem to be few permanent positions of dominance or servitude in the fields, and few in the political structure of Aymara communities. Just as the field owners in charge of the day's work rotate, so do the positions of community leadership alternate from family to family for one-year posts. Differentials in wealth and power do exist, however, and women do not share equal social status with men, so certainly there are exceptions to my hypothesis. But this general dynamic illustrates a fundamental characteristic of community democracy that I will be able to compare with the other political systems at the municipal and national levels.

Being Systematic: You Need a Schedule, Not a Recipe

Now I am six months into my fieldwork in Bolivia, and I continue to be amazed by the steady barrage of opportunities that present themselves. I don't have time to do all the things or meet with all the people I would like, and this is frustrating. It is difficult just making time to write about the myriad experiences and conversations I have each day; I find it takes me anywhere between two and seven hours a night. And it is true what the prophet Russell Bernard (1995) admonishes about spending a year in the field: If you do not write it down, it is gone. Just poof, disappeared from your memory, as if you never had the experience. During certain spells I operate on a level of perpetual exhaustion from writing so late, but every day is another adventure and I want to capture it all. When possible, I get in bed with some time to read one of the many books I have with me, and I write regularly in my personal journal as well. I try to give myself one day a week to sleep in and take care of things around the house and maybe go for a swim at one of the nearby hostels. But regardless of the madness quotient of any given day, I love the 15-minute walk along the dirt road between my house and town where I can gaze out over the wide green valley, breathe deeply, and let my thoughts sort themselves out.

One thing I do consistently even in my normal life is keep track of my daily activities in a desk calendar. I have an almost uninterrupted record of my life that dates back to high school in the 1980s and consists of events such as "Nationalism class 6-9," or, "lunch with Jack at Chautauqua," or, "The Dead at Cal Expo with Shari." Looking back through my time so far in Bolivia, each week has been jammed with random happenings and interactions, punctuated by scheduled interviews, meetings, visits to rural villages, and work in the fields. The one week or so a month I spend in La Paz I have to race around interviewing people in universities, organizations, and the government, and taking care of the bureaucracy of my life here—though I usually manage a visit to my favorite Latin jazz bar, Thelonius. Spending time in the city is like going through a checklist, where I only have so many days to accomplish certain objectives. Resourcefulness and unflappability are required no matter where I am in Bolivia, but in La Paz I am autonomous and anonymous, so it is a very different experience from being in the Yungas.

In Coroico, each day is completely different, guided by particular events and my energy level, though there are certain trends that my days have been following. One kind of day goes like this: Wake up at six, take photos of the snowy peaks across the valley illuminated by the sunrise, go back to sleep; get up at eight, pick oranges from the tree by the door for juice, make coffee and pancakes, write until ten; listen to the local radio news and record key segments and interviews until noon; walk into town with my dog Eva[20] and find people to have lunch with at Apimania or the Cocalero; visit Don Pepe or Doña Fidela or others I need to talk with; stop by a development NGO to sign up for a site visit later in the week; make the rounds to buy groceries and chat with each shop owner; walk home at six to make dinner for Eva and me; then write and read all evening.

Another kind of day goes like this: Drag myself out of bed at six-thirty, make tea and oatmeal, give a chicken head to Eva; walk into town for an eight o'clock interview with the mayor or other local leader; visit town hall employees to observe their office routines and learn how the municipal government works; take lunch by myself on the Back Stube's patio so I can write about the morning and read the newspaper; sit in on a town council meeting and then maybe record the life history of one of the town's elders; walk home for dinner; hitch a ride back to town to teach an English class or to attend another meeting; maybe have a beer with friends afterwards on the plaza; home again to write for several hours with coca tea, a disk of Doña Celestina's homemade chocolate, and the Allman Brothers live on CD.

Still another kind of day works out like this: Spring out of bed at seven, pluck two bananas from the bunch outside to make a smoothie with milk and honey; pack my hipsack with a windbreaker, sunscreen, camera, and water; rub bug lotion on my ankles, wrists, and neck; set out on the hour walk with Eva to a village in the countryside, with one stop to buy a dozen meat *empanadas* from Doña Amanda; by nine meet the group of women in their *cocal* to spend the long glorious day picking coca, immersed in rousing conversation; leave at four to follow the winding paths back to the main road and catch a ride in the back of a pickup truck to Coroico; buy cheese, beets, potatoes, and chicken innards; walk home to make food for Eva and write for a while; then head up through the forest to my landlord's house for a dinner shared with neighbors, followed by drumming around a bonfire, the smoke trailing out over the vast valley below.

Three typical days that are anything but similar or predictable. I have never been the nine-to-five type of girl anyway, but after following this irregular pattern for six months, I am beginning to get a queasy feeling in my gut; I can always tell when something is out of kilter in my life when I get that almost nauseous feeling that comes and goes at first and then becomes more persistent. Then I know I have to identify what is bothering me and decide what to do about it. I have been thinking about the kind of data I will come home with at the end of the year, and all I can envision is a gigantic heap of information lacking structure or coherence. I love the chaotic happenstance of how things come together, and I enjoy the ebb and flow of my daily activities. But interpreting the current of life here is difficult, I am realizing, because there is little consistency to how I spend my time, week in and week out.

To what depth of local experience am I reaching? What do I truly understand about life here, when my agenda is so completely different from that of local people? Maybe I should recalibrate my weeks more to the rhythm of local life, especially since my research relies on qualitative methods. Participant observation does not imply an unstructured amalgamation of information based on random experiences; I think it should be deployed as a grounded method. For example, I could structure my days like this: every Saturday morning go to the plaza to witness the market scene when campesinos come from all around; every Sunday observe who is coming to meet with the mayor or the town council and why; I could do one development site visit a week, one day picking coca, and take Mondays off along with the rest of the population. With such a system I could generate quantifiable data from the variations, and at the end of the year be able to identify patterns through the seasons and shifts according to the influence of local and national events. This, I am coming to believe, is what being systematic really means. Such conscientious research requires a schedule of activities that creates regularity of experience and observation, not just the collection of data that you assemble at the end in the required proportions like a recipe. Such a simple perspective, yet why was this not clear to me at the start? Can I make up for the considerable time I have lost?

What Does It All Mean?

Ultimately, my presence in Coroico community affairs is not nearly as significant to people here as it is to me. I will probably never be a permanent component of the Yungas ayni structure. If people gather in the mayor's office and I am not there to hear them, did a meeting actually take place? Of course. People's struggles and achievements persist whether I am here to document them or not. There are plenty of officials, organizers, academics, and journalists who make the issues of democracy, development, and coca production in Bolivia their daily bread. There is a constant stream of articles and newspaper reports written by people with a much more profound grasp of the historical and social context here than I will ever achieve. What will I be able to contribute, besides a headache to those subjected to my interloping attendance at their meetings? How valuable will my presence and work really be to the people here? And how will I relate all my data back to what now seem to be remote anthropological theories? Well, all that remains to be seen. For now, my desire is to use this rare opportunity to learn as many interesting things as possible and to serve the people with whom I live and work to the extent that I am able. As any spiritual guide would say, a positive mental approach to life can produce favorable outcomes. So, by cultivating my sense of adventure, open-mindedness, and trust in the people around me, I am sure to reap fascinating experiences, new information, and valuable relationships. The rest depends on this.

Notes

[1] Municipalities are like counties in the U.S., of which Bolivia has 327. Coroico pertains to the Nor (northern) Yungas province in the department of La Paz. Bolivia's nine departments are analogous to U.S. states. Coroico is also the name of the municipal capital, population ~3500.

[2] It is thought that coca was cultivated in the Bolivian Yungas for use in highland communities for centuries before the Spanish arrived in the early 1500s, though the little archaeological evidence that exists in the Yungas has yet to be adequately explored. Botanical and archaeological data show that coca leaf cultivation, use, and trade in the Andes region in general dates back at least 4,000 years (see Mayer 1978). The other well-known coca producing region in Bolivia, the Chapare, was colonized only 25 years ago and is an illegal zone. Its coca leaves are not of sufficient quality for most traditional uses.

[3] Aymara speakers are thought to be descended from the pre-Incan Tiahuanaco Empire near Lake Titicaca. Aymara is one of Bolivia's four national languages.

[4] This is the common discourse, but more and more cultivators—perhaps as many as 90%—are using chemical fertilizers and pesticides on their coca fields, with no regulations or understood usage guidelines (according to an agricultural researcher in Coroico I spoke with). This alarming practice has the potential to severely damage this ecologically sensitive region's water and soil, not to mention the health of those who use the unprocessed leaf.

[5] Compared with other foods from Latin America, coca has been shown to rank higher than average in calories, protein, carbohydrate, fiber, calcium, phosphorus, iron, vitamin A, riboflavin, and vitamin E (Plowman 1979, cited in Davis 1996 and in Museo de la Coca 2000). In other words, the normal amount (about 100g) of coca chewed by someone in the Andes in one day more than satisfies the Recommended Dietary Allowance for all of these nutrients. It is thought that coca evolved together with potatoes—another native Andean plant—because it helps regulate blood sugar produced by potato starch. Coca's high calcium content also indicates an evolutionary advantage because dairy products did not exist before the Spanish arrived (Davis 1996:419); fresh milk is also too expensive now for many to consume regularly.

[6] Cocaine is only one of 14 alkaloids that coca contains, all of which provide particular medicinal benefits.

[7] Precursor chemicals include sulfuric acid, ether, diesel, caustic soda, potassium permanganate, sodium bicarbonate, kerosene, gasoline, hydrochloric acid, acetone, ammonia, rubbing alcohol, and paint thinner (listed in Bolivia's antinarcotics law). It takes 355kg of coca leaf to make one kilogram of cocaine (Riley 1993: 78).

[8] Geographer David Slater (2003) suggests that interaction between indigenous politics and Western-style democracy in Bolivia could produce a unique hybrid form; I see potential hybrids between more than just these two options.

[9] I am avoiding a discussion of whether it is even possible to be genuinely altruistic, a subject of significant debate.

[10] The Bush administration is pushing for this agreement in countries around the world, not just Bolivia.

[11] Ironically, the U.S. was threatening to withhold millions of dollars destined for the armed forces—funds needed to fight the U.S. "War on Drugs," and thus to be certified to receive the next year's funds. Many Bolivians are furious and are incorporating this issue into their protest marches against an already contentious national political agenda. The resolution now goes to the House of Representatives to be considered.

[12] Tory is an undergraduate anthropology major from the University of Colorado at Boulder, a former student of mine, here for three months to do a study for her honor's thesis and be my research assistant.

[13] Place name has been changed.

[14] This recent expansion of coca production in the Yungas seems to be a result, at least in part, of the "successful" eradication of coca in Bolivia's Chapare region, where coca feeds the cocaine trade. This is a textbook case of the principle called "the balloon effect": when a commodity that is in high demand is forcibly destroyed in one place, its production will merely shift elsewhere. It is unclear where all this new coca grown in the Yungas is going, but as several cocaine processing labs have recently turned up in the Yungas, the U.S. is beginning to pay even more attention to this region. *Cocalero* leaders in Coroico strenuously condemn narcotrafficking and argue that the legal coca market is larger than Bolivia's laws recognize.

[15] Both the Bolivian and U.S. governments have announced that they do not intend to forcibly eradicate coca in the Yungas, acknowledging coca's legal status and cultural significance in this region. However, people are wary of such government promises. In 2001, the military was sent in to destroy coca fields in the southern Yungas that lay outside the legal boundary and were deemed to be in excess of the total acreage allowed by law. Forced coca eradication continues with U.S. backing in the Chapare region.

[16] These acronyms—which stand for the United States Central Intelligence Agency and the Drug Enforcement Administration—are universally known by people here, said with Spanish pronunciation.

[17] Place name has been changed.

[18] Each terrace is about 25 feet wide: they lay end to end across the width of the field, and cascade downhill in long columns.

[19] Work groups of men follow a similar egalitarian pattern in the new *cocales*.

[20] I was blessed to be adopted by a remarkable dog from the streets of Coroico in the first month of my fieldwork. She accompanies me everywhere, but sometimes makes her own rounds about town and meets me back home in the evening. We walk for hours together to and from rural communities, I can throw her into the back of a truck and she deftly balances along the bumpy roads, and she sleeps quietly under my chair during meetings. I feed her a thick soup of rice with chicken heads, feet, and innards, which I cook each day since I don't have a refrigerator.

References

Bernard, H. Russell. 1995. *Research Methods in Anthropology: Qualitative and Quantitative Approaches* (2nd ed.). Walnut Creek, CA: Altamira Press.

Davis, Wade. 1996. *One River: Explorations and Discoveries in the Amazon Rainforest.* New York: Simon and Schuster.

Mauss, Marcel. 1990/1950. *The Gift: The Form and Reason for Exchange in Archaic Societies.* New York: W.W. Norton.

Mayer, Enrique. 1978. El uso social de la coca en el mundo andino: Contribución a un debate y toma de posición. *América Indígena* 38(4): 849–65.

Museo de la Coca. 2000. *El Museo de la Coca: Guía.* La Paz: ICORI.

Plowman, Timothy. 1979. Botanical perspectives on coca. *Journal of Psychedelic Drugs* 11(1–2): 103–17.

Riley, Kevin Jack. 1993. Snow Job? The Efficacy of Source Country Cocaine Policies. Ph.D. Diss., Rand Graduate School. RGSD-102.

Slater, David. 2003. On the spatial dynamics of democratic politics: Analysing the Bolivian Case. *Development and Change* 34(4): 607–32.

Spedding, Alison. 1994. *Wachu Wachu: Cultivo de coca e identidad en los Yunkas de La Paz.* La Paz: HISBOL—CIPCA/COCAYAPU.

Acknowledgements

I would like to thank the U.S. Fulbright Program and the NSEP David L. Boren Graduate Program, as well as the University of Colorado Department of Anthropology, for their generous support of a total of 18 months of dissertation research in Bolivia. I am grateful to Andrew Gardner and David Hoffman for their patient and detailed reviews of this essay. Thanks also go to Jack Powelson, Tom Perreault, Ann May, and Jim Schechter for their helpful comments on the original version e-mailed from the field, to an anonymous group of CU undergraduate reviewers, and to Alicia Davis for a critique of the final draft. My most profound appreciation, of course, goes to all the people in Coroico and La Paz with whom I worked and played.

Dispatch from the Sahelian Range: Renegotiating Expectations and Relationships among the Wodaabe of Niger

Karen Marie Greenough
University of Kentucky

Before I returned to Niger at the end of July 2003, a colleague and I discussed dissertation fieldwork. "I'm not sure where I'll be researching," she said. How strange that seemed to me. The very reason I'd decided to get an anthropology degree was so that I could return to live and work in Niger. Nomadic pastoral life—caring for cattle, sheep, and goats and the challenges of living in the forbidding semidesert of sandy steppe and broken red-black rock—had all captivated me. Friends' kindness kept tugging me back to the town of Tanout where I'd been posted as a Peace Corps volunteer in the 1980s. I returned in 1991, and in 1994 began to live in the Damergou rangeland with Wodaabe Fulbe[1] friends. I went there not as an anthropologist but to simply experience nomadic life among people who generously accepted me. For over four years, I spent more and more time traveling with different families on the range. After near-death by malaria, a metaphorical wake-up call, I have since capitalized upon this experience to enter graduate school. Now I've become, though sometimes ambivalently, an anthropologist.

While finishing my master's degree in spring 2003, I told my advisor I would spend fall semester in Niger. Late summer and autumn in the States coincide with the good seasons in Niger—the rainy season (*ndungu*) and the short hot season afterward. Among the

Wodaabe these are seasons of plenty, of gatherings and dancing. I'd not been to the lineage gathering, called *worso*, in five years. Our director of graduate studies kindly obtained a tuition grant for me from the University of Kentucky's Graduate School. My advisor worked out my schedule of independent study. To begin earning credits toward my doctoral degree I would read ethnographies and carry out research among my Wodaabe friends. Once in Niger I frequently questioned the wisdom of undertaking all this work.

Ever since my Peace Corps days, my brain has compartmentalized my Nigerien life from my American life. Even now, when I am in one place, thoughts of the other become misty and dreamlike. Now that my Wodaabe friends and family have become my "research community" I must construct a strong bridge to carry the heavy, analytical thinking I use in school across the Atlantic and Sahara and into the Damergou. This time when I traveled to Niger my burden seemed to disintegrate on the way like dust in the Sahelian wind. In the anthropology department I speak of the constraints that development discourse places on nomadic agency. I discuss how I am interpellated[2] by various Nigeriens. I consider hegemony and the muted voices of subaltern women. In Niger, I strategize how I will find my "brother" Daneri's camp.[3] On the range, Daneri and I decide which of my old sheep or buck goats to sell, when to buy heifers, how best to care for our horses, and what to do with my camel. I accompany my "mother" Tsibi and my friend Halima to birth celebrations and grief-filled funerals. I commiserate with Mariama over her rocky marriage and try to keep on Togindo's good side. Yet anthropological thoughts and questions do make their way, italicized, into my Nigerien mental compartment.

Interest in gender studies has grown within pastoral research and I felt I should be well placed to approach this topic. I decided to collect women's life stories for my fall semester project. Perhaps this project could evolve into my dissertation topic. But the presumably straightforward request, "tell me your life history," turned out to be much more complicated than I'd anticipated. When my Social Theory and Method crumbled, I felt lost without structure to guide my research.

On the Range Just After Ndungu

While October begins in the States, here on the Sahelian range the few months of ndungu, the only time it will rain during the year, end. It is hot today as I set pen to paper to write this essay. I sit on my woven palm-frond mat, in the shade of a spreading, thorny acacia tree, trying to collect my thoughts, scattered in several directions. This acacia stands in a glen of bushes and trees, at the bottom of a broad valley. A prehistoric watercourse once ran through this valley, gathering ancient streams from the Aïr Mountains to flow south into tributaries of the Niger River. Now only football-field-sized depressions are left. They collect rainwater from flash floods that occasionally rage down the grassy hills through sandy arroyos. Wodaabe and other pastoralists camp along this valley so that they can water their livestock at these short-lived ponds.

The open range is bounded only by the Sahara desert in the north, where grasses, bushes, and small trees give way to sand dunes, and by millet fields about 40 kilometers to the south of where we are now camped. A small town, Tanout, lies more than a hundred kilometers to the southeast with only a few small villages and hamlets between here and there. Our camps have been methodically arranged just behind me along the edge of the glen. Before me cattle paths weave through the thick grass, between the trees and bushes, toward a long pond a half-kilometer south.

How to describe and explain everything here—the land, my relationships with the people among whom I live, my struggles with fieldwork? I review my journal.[4]

> *11 Aug Mon:* What theories? The idea does not make much sense here and I decide to abandon most of the methodology that I'd planned. I'll just ask for life history and proceed from there. I suppose the idea is to discover **their** epistemologies and so does it make sense to begin with Western epistemologies?

> *23 Aug Sat:* Read some in a major comparative ethnology of the Fulbe. Then I got depressed. The whole purpose of my research seems rather inane. Anthropology in general seems inane. I just want to live here.

> *24 Aug Sun:* I feel like giving up on this research until I get with women I feel much more comfortable with: Tsibi and Halima.

> *25 Aug Mon:* Got Hadija on tape about her *te'egal* marriage. She described how women can own their own personal livestock. They can even have their own calf rope separate from their husbands'. I forgot to ask about women's work and returning home for first birth.

> Read the ethnology the rest of the day. It's striking how ideal and generalized such an ethnology can be as compared to real life and real individuals. Talking to Hadija, I get back the theoretical **sense** of women's agency. Perhaps I will be able to do this.

The very idea of fieldwork has become problematic while living again with my Wodaabe family of several years. Simply remembering esoteric words like *problematic* and *agency* feels peculiar here. This is home, and while a place of work—fetching water; milking cows, goats and sheep; preparing food; herding, watering and caring for livestock; caring for children—it is a place to *live* life and carry out the necessary tasks to sustain it, not to analyze the practices that organize it.

This summer I found that during the five years in which I'd had only sporadic contact with my family and friends on the range, the Gojen-ko'en lineage in the Damergou had divided into two factions. The southeast faction lives just north of Tanout, and the northwest

faction spends ndungu and the season after in this valley far up along the highway to Agadez. In August I spent three weeks in camps with the southeast faction. Then, after a week in
Tanout and Zinder, I traveled up to my "family's" camps, part of the northwest faction. I have
spent most of my years among the Wodaabe with Daneri, my Gojen-ko'en brother, and his
mother Tsibi, who is like my own mother.

> *8 Sept Mon:* Left Zinder before sunrise and took a market van north. The driver said he
> was going to Tanout, but he left me in Bakin Birji [a market town 100 km south of
> Tanout]. It was noon before I got to Tanout. There was a van waiting to go Takoukout [a
> market town on the way to the camps]. I rushed around gathering stuff for camp and
> forgot (I realized later) the ropes and my plastic tarp. I'd not had breakfast or tea. I was
> told by different people in Takoukout that I should go north to Ankafar. I traveled in a
> market truck with Bamo. He was on his way home and said he'd take news that I had
> arrived. I spent the night in the hamlet of Ankafar hoping Daneri would come in the
> morning with my donkey.

> *9 Sept Tues:* Iggoi came from the south with a donkey and his young son who seems to
> have epilepsy. He'd been to a traditional healer to get medicine. Daneri did not come to
> Ankafar, but friends came with camels and took my heavy stuff. I rode on Iggoi's donkey
> with his son—Iggoi walked. Their camp was not close—the journey took us three or
> four hours.

> *10 Sept Wed:* We encountered Tsibi and Daneri's brothers mid-move, coming south. It
> was a long move, and it turns out they left Daneri and others north of where we met up
> with them. Very nice to see Tsibi and the others.

> *11 Sept Thurs:* Talked to Tsibi about getting her *tarihi* [Hausa for history]. She didn't
> understand at first, but once she did understand ("You know," I reminded her, "you've
> told me before how the tent was different.") she was all for it. Daneri came with my don-
> key around noon. I accompanied him back to his camp quite a bit north. This is home
> and I just want to stay here.

I am most at home with Tsibi, Daneri, his brothers and cousins and their families. And
here I sit now, just south of their camps.

I Remember Worso, Drought and Plenty

Today, thankfully, the hot, dust-driving wind that tormented us over the past week, coming from the east like a furnace blast, has abated. When the wind turned away from the
west a few weeks ago, ndungu ended. Now days will shorten into the cold season. Though
the humid western breezes are gone, yesterday we trekked under low gray clouds that spo-
radically spit tiny drops of rain of stinging coolness. Yesterday we left worso. Over a hundred

A woman travels through the rangeland with her child and donkeys.

households came together in this annual extended family reunion. This year, because the rains had been so good, not only did the Gojen-ko'en hold their worso, they also hosted a *dado*, a huge, weeklong party bringing together men and women of various lineages for nights of dancing and singing, including the men's competitive *gerewol* dance. Following an extremely difficult dry season, a magical atmosphere excited the end of this bountiful ndungu and the preparations for worso. At worso, Gojen-ko'en would celebrate births and marriage contracts with roasted sheep and visit with relatives and friends they had not seen for months or even years.

I'd arrived in Niger in the middle of ndungu, which had started much earlier than usual—a blessed reprieve after the tough drought year. Stories of hardship surrounded me: lack of grass; long treks far south in search of pasture; selling some animals to buy straw, millet stalks, and grain to feed the rest. Then debilitating diseases accompanied the herds returning north. "But," people said, "we thank God because we came out of this with calves, lambs, and kids." No one old enough could help but make comparisons with the devastation of the 1984 drought. The subsequent famine through 1985 killed children, parents, and grandparents as well as whole herds, an impoverishment with which most pastoralists still struggle.

While discussing plans for the upcoming dado, the men complained that they had no elders to manage the dances. I suddenly realized how true this was. Among Daneri and his cousins, only one cousin's father, very old now, is still alive. Daneri's father, three of his father's brothers, and his oldest cousin all passed away, most of them during the 1984–5 famine. "It was having to eat strange food that killed them," my friend Halima told me. Both her parents had died. She explained that the Wodaabe used to drink just milk with a little millet. When there was no milk, they had to eat bran and other foods they couldn't digest. She told me this during worso, while we sat with the wind at our backs. I embroidered a dance shirt for a friend, and she carved moons on her calabashes.

The hot east wind unfortunately blunted the festive spirit as did the location chosen for the worso, an uncomfortable compromise between the southeast and northwest factions of the lineage. We camped among a few hills, barren but for already grazed stubble. Over the season many other people's camps had left shreds of debris littering trampled clearings: burnt wood, discarded tent posts, scraps of cloth. Daneri and his brothers found campsites on a hill with good-sized acacias for shade and some thick bushes for wind breaks. Other families camped in the valley near the dancing ground amid small, thin milk-sap trees that provided little shade or shelter. Good pasture and ponds with decent drinking water were not close. The well water was brackish, and after people fell ill, most girls fetched decent water from distant ponds. Several men missed much of the dancing searching for their livestock that wandered off during the night to find better grazing.

The visiting, feasting and dancing helped to bring back the magic, though. Every evening we watched men and boys dance in firelight far into the night. I slept after midnight and awoke at sunrise to the distant echoes of a round of singing and dancing. Gojen-ko'en women and girls worked hard every day to provide large calabashes and bowls of milk, porridges, and meat for the many guests. Southern villagers set up a small market near the dusty dancing ground. They cooked rice and beans, macaroni, and fried cakes and sold all this food plus everything from batteries to aspirin. After dancing all night, Gojen-ko'en men gathered their livestock in the morning and then turned the pasturing and watering over to their sons, while they visited and rested up for more dancing. Overall, the Gojen-ko'en, men and women, deemed the worso and dado a success.

I Consider the Seasons, the Division of Labor, and the Environment (Soft and Prickly)

Yesterday, we returned to our rainy-season valley, a few kilometers south of the worso site. A gust of wind bursts through the glen. I hear girls laughing and donkeys snuffling. Daneri's stepdaughter Mbodi returns from the cement well a few kilometers south with the family's two plastic 25-liter jugs loaded on one donkey and my goatskin waterbag tied under another. I help her uncinch the bag and fill my large calabash, lifting it carefully into a nest I've woven from the top branches of a stiff bush, out of reach of goats and calves. Mbodi's cousin returns from the pond with my washing calabash and his clean clothes, and wonders over my pens and notebooks. (A satisfactory solution to school for nomadic children has yet to be found.) Later, Mbodi's older brother passes by, collecting firewood to make charcoal for tea. Half lost in my writing, I feel him watching me. He suggests I move. "The sun has reached you," he says, and I suddenly feel its heat on my back. I realize that noon has passed. "Mbodi is pounding millet for cold porridge," he adds. A few trees behind me I can hear the steady thumping of mortar in pestle. I stand to drag my mat and books to the thickest shade east of the acacia. Late in the day, Mbodi's uncle exclaims in wonder that I have been writing all day long.

My ability to read and write creates an unbalanced relationship here, which I try hard, unsuccessfully it seems, to redress. That ability, my whiteness/Americaness, and my some-what more ready cash, tips a perceived balance of power uncomfortably on my side. What to do with this power, less real than imagined? (*No, I can't get you a visa to America. I can't get you a rich project from a powerful development agency. I can't give you a ride anywhere because I don't own a vehicle. And I can't loan you money because I've run out of cash.*) I am feeble, though, because I am not Bodaado and must depend on the skilled Wodaabe who sustain me, physically and socially, in this pastoral life.

Now that the rains have ended, we camp again in valley bottoms without fear of flash floods, in lees of glens that provide shade and windbreaks. During ndungu storms trouble us. Violent winds threaten tents and tear at the plastic tarps with which we rush to cover household gear. The humidity draws out swarms of stinging and biting mosquitoes, flies, and lice. We move every few days—the cattle will not stay in a place soiled with wet manure—from the top of one hill to the slope of another. We women only hope that the men find campsites with shade. In the morning the women and girls take apart their tents and the poles of their beds and tables. They pack these, their calabashes, mats and other gear onto the donkeys. They follow the men and herds, set up camp—put together the beds, their tents, and the tables for their calabashes—under the hot noon sun, and then prepare afternoon and evening meals. Now that ndungu is past, we stay in one place for a few weeks. With no rain, the women don't put up their tents. We all sleep in the open.

Our new campsite is located in the valley bottom—a pleasant and shady site. The nights are cool and the wind seems to have driven away the worst of the grasshoppers, which landed in our water and food, leapt down our shirts, and got tangled in my hair. In the half-light of dawn I wake to the fragrance of tiny, green flowers of a bush that hedges my small camp. Fragrance is a seasonal extravagance in this dry air normally scented only faintly by dust and straw. From the ponds, the black acacias' little, yellow, pompom blos-soms emit a heady sweetness that surrounding breezes carry up the hills. Birds call, sing, and chirp in the glens. Yesterday as I set up my camp a myriad of pale butterflies flitted around the green-flowered bush.

The grass in the valley bottom is soft. On the hill slopes, burr grass grows ubiquitously. We constantly pull its little stickers from our clothing, our toes, our blankets, and from the ropes that tie baggage and hobble donkeys. Then we dig tiny broken thorns from our fingers. The herdboys run through the grass with pants hitched far up their thighs; small children wear no clothes at all. We women hold our wraparound cloths higher than mini-skirts when necessary; my white thighs gleam over crisply baked shins.

The boys take the livestock to the pond every morning before they lead them to pasture. Watering at ponds is a luxury of ndungu and the short season after. The pond water, though muddy, is drinkable, but many girls make the four-hour trip to the well to draw water for their households because their mothers refuse to drink pond water. Once the ponds have dried, the young men will spend the rest of the year pulling water for the livestock from wells 70 to 100 meters deep. A man lets a 35-gallon bucket-bag plunge into the darkness of the well, its heavy rope whistling through his open hands and over the pulley. Then he pulls and releases, pulls and releases over distant splashing echoes from the well bottom, until the bag is full. "Go!" he shouts at the child who has attached the other end of the rope to the donkey harness. She drives the team of three donkeys down the path from the well. The donkeys strain against the weight. When the bucket-bag arrives at the well mouth, two men lift and carry the heavy, slopping bag to the watering troughs where cattle crowd and shove each other. Boys control the thirsty cattle by hitting their long horns with staves.

Now, in this season when ponds still lie in the valley bottoms, the young men, reprieved of the heavy well work, care for their riding camels, lie in the shade, work on their boom box cassette players, drink tea, and eat whatever food the women prepare for them. Mbodi has finished pounding the millet. She brings me a small calabash full of the coarse flour mixed with buttermilk.

I help Daneri's daughter carry water from the well.

I miss cooking my own food. "Where are all your things—calabashes, bowls, and pots?" the women ask me. In the 1990s I cared for a small boy and learned to milk my cow and churn butter. I pounded grain, fetched water, and cooked porridge. Although I miss maintaining my own household on the range—miss some (imagined?) control over my life—when I remember all the truly hard work, I am very grateful to Mbodi and other women who bring me food and water. I still pound millet occasionally to help the girls of my family. I also do it for the exercise, to surprise people who don't know that I've learned to pound millet, and to "participate-observe"—or so I tell myself. Participant-observation supplies me with an expedient excuse for not conducting interviews, for avoiding my journal and field-notes, for not thinking about anthropology. Often participant-observation falls conveniently under the category of "just living life" on the range.

I Contemplate Wodaabe Marriages and Other Aspects of Our Social Organization

I have been reading a book on kinship and apply the concepts to Wodaabe social organization, which I find fascinating. The Gojen-ko'en are dispersed in different regions of Niger, as are most Wodaabe lineages. Most Gojen-ko'en still live in the Ader region located a couple hundred kilometers to the west of where we are now. Some families live near Agadez. People from here make trips to visit relatives in both places. Women who have been married into families living in a different region find themselves sometimes painfully separated from close kin.

The Wodaabe practice two types of marriage. Parents, particularly mothers, arrange endogamous[5] *kovgal* marriages for their young children. Kovgal contracts take years to conclude. Sheep or oxen given by the boy's family to the girl's family secure first an engagement and then, a few years later, the marriage. The girl will usually not live with her husband, though, until she has borne one or two children with him.

A separate marriage practice called te'egal encourages exogamous marriages. Men seduce and steal the young wives from other lineages. "That's the whole point of the gerewol," Daneri's brother tells me when I remark on the warlike dance of an unwarlike people.[6] "We want to show that we are better than the men of the other lineages so we can steal their women." Men are often ready to live with a wife some years before their kovgal wives are ready for husbands, and young kovgal wives usually live with their mothers until after their second child is a year old. These factors incite many men toward te'egal, and polygyny if they're successful. Many such marriages are short-lived. While in a kovgal marriage a woman receives a dowry of household goods from her parents and kin, in a te'egal marriage she must rely on her husband for everything. A te'egal wife may also find herself a lonely outcast.

19 Aug Tues: The men brought back a woman from a dado and the women here are wondering what's going on. Pamaril, Riskuwa's wife, is somewhat upset that she's been asked to provide food for the guest.

20 Aug Wed: It turns out that Riskuwa stole the woman and killed a sheep for the te'egal marriage yesterday. Pamaril is upset that she was never told.

22 Aug Fri: I hoped to interview Pamaril but she is much too disturbed by the new wife. No one knows the name of the woman's kid and the other women make up nicknames for him. She, they call Bodaado. She has nothing except a plastic sack of clothes and things.

My "brother" Daneri takes care of my livestock and I usually camp with his immediate family. They camp together off and on seasonally with the families of his brothers and cousins. When I move to Tsibi's camp, Daneri scolds me for camping with her, though she is his mother and my "fictive" mother. He says *he* should take care of me, since my livestock are under his care. He's right, but I love spending time with Tsibi, who is an excellent teacher. This was not a problem in the past when Tsibi camped near him with her youngest daughter, his sister. Now Daneri's sister lives with her husband and Tsibi camps with Daneri's younger brothers, often with some distance between the camps. When I return, Daneri's daughter upsets me and he insists I've been unreasonably angry with her. He hints that I've insulted his wife. (*How do I deal with such emotional situations and remain an objective observer, an anthropologist?*) Scolding me seems to re-establish his status over me as household head, and to put him on better footing with his wife.

Daneri inherited two children, Mbodi and her older brother, when he married their mother, Togindo, by levirate.[7] She first married Daneri's oldest cousin by te'egal. The levirate marriage was necessary, Togindo felt, so she could stay with her children, who were kept by their deceased father's cousins. Daneri and Togindo's young sons now herd the livestock, and Mbodi's brother, in his early twenties, helps with well watering. Daneri's second wife, his cousin married by kovgal, has just had her second child and still lives with her mother.

Daneri's three younger brothers join him during these two seasons. His second brother is already talking about heading south, though, moving his family and livestock closer to their eventual dry season camp. His youngest two brothers are discussing their return to city jobs in Nigeria. Neither of these men have enough livestock to support their families on the range. The minimal wages from their work as security guards provide a small supplement to their pastoral livelihood.

Mbodi, born nineteen years ago after the last drought, has just given birth to her first child and has entered a special stage in her life. To indicate this, she wears a long string of amulets instead of a shirt. She must not speak to men outside her immediate family. She goes nowhere except to the well and back. After a year or so, when her mother grants her permission, she will put on a shirt again, and she and her husband will begin to sleep together again in the bush behind her mother's camp. After Mbodi's second child, Togindo will buy the bed and calabashes that will finally establish Mbodi's own camp. Among the Wodaabe all of the camp furniture and utensils belong to the women. Mbodi's younger sister is married but hasn't been given to her husband yet. When Togindo feels she is old enough, she will give the couple permission to spend nights in the bush until Mbodi's sister becomes pregnant. Until then she sleeps with whomever she pleases (except her husband whom she avoids). Before a girl is given to her husband secretive sex is encouraged, even by her parents. Mbodi's sister talks about eloping with her husband, though, whenever she fights with her mother.

I help Mbodi pound grain. As she is confined to the camp, most of the chores fall on her shoulders. We have a much more congenial relationship now than we had five years ago, when she was a guy-crazy teenager. We continually joke together, and I promise to buy her a shirt when she complains of flies biting her exposed back.

Tsibi told me that a woman has asked Togindo for her and Daneri's youngest daughter, about eight years old, to marry her son. Such a marriage contract would take a few years to complete and conclude during worso. During worso the boy's family will show their cattle wealth to the girl's family, designate a cow or ox for the girl's bridewealth, and give two sheep to the girl's family. During this worso I joined the women who followed the men who drove the groom's family's cattle to the bride's uncle's camp. (*Why the bride's uncle and not her father? I must ask Tsibi.*) The women, carrying calabashes on their heads, sang, "Welcome us, welcome us!" Once at the camp they danced, tipping the calabashes to scatter millet onto the ground. (*And the symbolism of all this?*) The men drove the cattle in a circle and one man pointed to the bridewealth cow with his long staff. "That's her!" he shouted. They tied up a couple of sheep for the bride's uncle to slaughter. "Marriages were much more expensive in the past when we slaughtered cattle," Hadija had told me earlier during her interview. "Now they are nothing."

A Night in Tanout

Tonight, in the town of Tanout, I work at a friend's house because she has electricity. I type this essay on my laptop in the quiet coolness of late night, sitting on a small stool, at a low table, under a dim light bulb. Now I try to reach the root of my research problems. Worries over language prevent me from asking questions: I don't have all of the vocabulary I need to ask the questions I have. Yet too many questions, scattered unmethodically all over the ethnographic spectrum, crowd in my brain and get jammed together. When I do ask, my questions intrude on the work of family and friends and break up the flow of everyday life. "Tell me your life history" makes no sense to the women. I have not yet found a word in our

Fulfulde dialect for *story.* The word that I thought meant *folktale* actually means riddle. I use *tarihi* for "history," but the women do not understand because this Hausa word does not match their concept of life story. Finally, I say, "How does life when you were young differ from life now?" I stumble over the Fulfulde words for "differ" and "different," and fall back again on more familiar Hausa.

For all my years with the Wodaabe, I seem to have mastered only the tip of the iceberg of complex Fulfulde vocabulary and grammar. I know enough to hold a conversation of my own, but I cannot completely understand conversations between others. Fulfulde pronouns do not differentiate gender, and names create confusion—most people have at least a couple, as well as a nickname or two. Speakers cannot name certain people: first child, spouse, and other affines.[8] They call them "this one." I go astray within a maze of individuals with unfamiliar or unmentioned names and unspecified genders. I trip over complicated verb tenses with their various prefixes, infixes, and suffixes. My mind drifts and soon I lose the story's thread.

I also fail at recording notes. I hate writing in my journal, facing that blank page where I must capture dynamic life and freeze it. I catch up guiltily on a week's worth of journal notes in one morning, desperately trying to remember the fading impressions of profound thoughts. My biggest problem is that I cannot see a purpose to my fieldwork. What possible benefit can this research bring to my women friends? "Making known their lives" seems a weak excuse for academic exploitation, but is it?

Ostensibly I study applied anthropology with an emphasis on "development." "What projects have you brought us?" I am asked on the range and in town alike. "I *hate* projects," I reply. Most projects I've seen turn so-called "beneficiaries" into beggars and rarely conclude satisfactorily. Wodaabe family and friends wonder when I will get *real* work—work that will bring material benefit. They tentatively ask, "Don't you have enough schooling?" I tell them I will get more respect from city folk and Westerners if I get more education.

I have a vague idea of initiating of collaborative *research* with pastoralist *women*, yet I have no idea how to approach this. I have more experience working with *men* on *projects.* Then again, what exactly would we research?

November, Back on the Range

I spend a day under the scant shade of an acacia sapling with my good friend Halima. I lie on a mat with my tape recorder on and ask her questions about the changes that she's seen over her lifetime. These interviews are difficult to arrange. For example, I have yet to catch Tsibi alone sitting for long in one place. When we do sit together and I take out my notebook, she hesitates. "I don't know anything about writing!" she exclaims.

2 Oct Thurs: Tea in the evening with Tsibi. I asked her about some Fulfulde words. I can't tell if she's just agreeing with me to make me feel good, or because she thinks I'm testing her. The young men kept teasing her: "She doesn't know anything. She's old and crazy."

One of the women weaves a bed mat.

I worry about my theoretical deficiencies, especially when it comes to feminist theory. I want a Fulfulde word meaning power, as in: *Do women have power in their relationships?* But then, what good does *theory* do when a husband is beating his wife?

> *15 Sept Mon:* In the morning Zare complained about her husband to Mariama for a long time. Later Mariama's husband, Dego, fought with Mariama. He had taken her sheep, which he sold, and now he tried to take a small amount of cash that she wore in a pouch around her neck. I watched from our camp as he beat her with his heavy staff. I kind of ran over and called for him to stop. (What keeps me from wanting to get involved?) His friend was telling him to stop. When I got there he was picking up things to take to market and he left.

> *16 Sept Tues:* Mariama's hand and ribs hurt her but it doesn't seem as if anything is broken. In Zare's camp Mariama's daughter described how she and her sisters were all crying when Dego hit Mariama. "You don't think Mariama's used to beating?" Zare said. "That's what husbands do."

Several times Mariama indicated she wanted to leave Dego. Now she told me outright that she wants to return to Ader where her siblings live. She is ready to leave all her children. "Even though you are a kovgal wife," I said, "with no family nearby, you must feel like a te'egal wife." "Yes," she replied. "It's difficult to live where you have no relatives to help you." I told her I've always thought of Dego as an intelligent, calm, kind man. I suggested that his deep depression over their first son's death still affects him. She agreed he's completely changed.

I remark to Halima on Zare's marriage and her constant jealousy of her husband's second wife. "Their life together has just become a necessity," I say, meaning they get no enjoyment from it. Halima asks rhetorically, "Aren't all our lives together just necessities?" I become depressed again. But I can't help feeling, for some reason, that somehow these stories must be told. If I dig deep enough, I must be able to find some happiness in the strength of these women who raise their children and arrange their marriages, and then help to care for their grandchildren. I want to learn, I remember, their epistemologies, but even the word overwhelms me.

Epilogue: February at the University of Kentucky

Just before I left Niger, I realized that during most of my stay, I simply needed to decompress after two stressful years of concentrated study. I finally did tape some interesting stories with my best friends, women and men, and began to write more thorough and timely journal notes.

I entered graduate school with the idea that while I had much experience, I needed a foundation in social theory to understand and explain this experience. In the field, I found this is still true, yet the theories I learn in school seem to stay there, incapable of transfer to range life. Perhaps the theories will become clearer as I transcribe the recordings I brought back from Niger.

I've just spoken with Daneri, who traveled to Zinder for my phone call. I've already sent money for his care of my livestock and I ask him to buy me a heifer. We talk briefly about ideas for future projects. I tell him I'm not sure I can make it to Niger this summer. Perhaps, I say, if I find a cheap ticket. The next day I finally mail the box I've promised full of gifts for the women who helped me, including a blouse for Mbodi.

Though the researcher leaves the field, does the field ever leave the researcher? In my case, the field is one of my homes. It never leaves me, even if its reality wavers and fades once I am back in the States. In the classroom, everything I read and write connects with the Wodaabe, and perhaps in this way I build the bridge I need in order to take Theory and Method back into the field. I've decided to focus on a different neighboring group of pastoralists for my dissertation fieldwork. I promise myself, however, to continue to collect Wodaabe women's stories and work on careful translation. Perhaps in this way the women will speak for themselves to the world.

Notes

[1] All foreign words, unless otherwise indicated, are Fulfulde, Wodaabe dialect. The singular of Wodaabe is Bodaado.

[2] *Interpellated:* to have one's identity (one's subject position) created by the people with whom one is interacting,

[3] In the text and my edited journal notes I have changed all names.

[4] Journal entries have been edited and all names have been changed.

[5] *Endogamous:* marriage "within," in this case within the family lineage. An *exogamous* marriage occurs between lineages.

[6] Though individual Wodaabe fight with swords over wells or women, and engage, sometimes fatally, in bow and arrow skirmishes with farmers over pasture, they do not raid as do eastern African pastoralists.

[7] *Levirate:* when the younger brother of a man who dies marries the man's widow. In this case Daneri married his older cousin's widow.

[8] *Affines:* persons one is related to by marriage; in-laws.

Belief in "Cancer Alley": Church, Chemicals, and Community in New Sarpy, Louisiana

Gwen Ottinger
Chemical Heritage Foundation

By eight-thirty every Sunday morning I am in church. This baffles my family and old friends. I explain that my newfound religion is in the interest of fieldwork. To the members of St. Matthew Baptist Church, however, I say no such thing. I say very little, in fact. At first, I participated in church activities fearing all the while that I might be asked for an expression of my faith. But several months later, I've grown comfortable with my brothers' and sisters' assumption that I believe as they do. I still avoid speaking roles—which I now understand are offered as gestures of inclusion—mostly because I do not feel proficient in the language of praise. But I am anticipating my last Sunday in church, just a few weeks hence, when I will want to thank these generous Christians for their hospitality. I have been practicing: "God has been good to me," I will say, "in so many, many ways. I have been truly blessed to have been able to make St. Matthew my church home. . . ."

A Leap of Faith

St. Matthew only became my "church home" when my research took a radical turn halfway into my fieldwork. I originally went to New Sarpy, Louisiana, where St. Matthew is located, because of the oil refinery next to the town. New Sarpy and Orion, as the refinery was then known, are located on the Mississippi River between New Orleans and Baton

153

Rouge, in the heart of a heavily industrialized region known to many as "Cancer Alley." A year ago, residents of New Sarpy were actively campaigning for Orion to buy their homes at a price that would allow them to relocate to comparable homes elsewhere in the parish. The residents' group, known as Concerned Citizens of New Sarpy (CCNS), was supported by the Tulane Environmental Law Clinic (TELC), which had filed a Clean Air Act lawsuit against the refinery on their behalf, and the Louisiana Bucket Brigade (LABB), which helped residents conduct a community health survey and, using low-cost, easy-to-operate air samplers, demonstrate high levels of toxic chemicals in the air they were breathing. Orion, of course, denied that it had broken the law or that its operations posed any threat to residents' health.

I saw this confrontation between New Sarpy residents and Orion as a perfect fit for my interest in the intersection of science and public discourse: there was an active argument in which technical information, some of it even *produced* by nonscientist community members (using the aforementioned air samplers), played a key part. Yet even when locally produced information was combined with more official scientific studies, available information was arguably insufficient to demonstrate a conclusive link between petrochemical plant emissions and human health effects; moreover, it was questionable whether any scientific evidence would have the power to prove that the refinery had a legal or moral obligation to relocate the community. The mixing of science and politics was thus inevitable. Making the technical information generated and used by residents a central feature of my proposal, I secured funding for my fieldwork from the University of California's Center for Information Technology Research in the Interests of Society (CITRIS). I got to know New Sarpy residents through LABB, where I volunteered my technical skills—acquired during my undergraduate engineering training—to help them increase their ability to monitor refinery emissions and interpret monitoring results.

From the time I arrived in New Sarpy in July 2002, I devoted myself to following CCNS's campaign against Orion. In that first month, Orion offered community members cash payments or grants for home improvements *if* they would drop their lawsuit against the company. CCNS leaders angrily denounced the offer at first, insisting that their lawsuit was for clean air and that they would *not* drop it for some meager sums of money. By November, however, many residents' homes had been damaged by flooding from a hurricane; top refinery officials had convinced key community leaders that they were genuinely interested working with residents to "build up" the community, and—most importantly according to CCNS leaders—Orion announced a settlement with the state Department of Environmental Quality that seemed to simultaneously address residents' air quality complaints and severely undermine their lawsuit. A week before Christmas, CCNS members decided to drop their lawsuit and accept Orion's money. With that decision, the campaign ended, and the focus of my fieldwork evaporated.

St. Matthew (front right) and its industrial neighbor (back left).

So I started going to church, as part of an effort to understand New Sarpy as a community separate from their campaign. It was not an obvious move: scholars who study science
and politics, including many anthropologists, understand communities of experts and processes of knowledge production to be global, and consequently many develop "multisited
ethnographies" to study the dynamics that interest them. Following their example, I might
have chosen another campaign to study so that I could follow the networks of activists, scientists, and lawyers that had supported CCNS. Instead, I followed a hunch that the geo-
graphically bounded communities were also still important. The idea of "community"—
especially who belonged to it and who had power to represent it—had been central to the
campaign and its outcome. Residents described New Sarpy as a "tight knit community"; they
also told me that in New Sarpy, people left each other alone. That such a complex, fluid
notion was so important to participants in a science-heavy conflict suggested to me that
studying this community and how it was constituted would *somehow* provide insight into
the politics of science and technology. But as I focused my attention on New Sarpy, I had no
idea what I might find, no idea how learning about everyday life in a town where no one
cared any longer about monitoring data or health studies could possibly speak to my
research questions about the use of science in political controversy. For that matter, I did not
even know exactly how I would study "community" without knowing what that idea meant. I
hoped for the best.

Encountering Belief

Although it took me six months to become a regular churchgoer, religion had figured prominently in my fieldwork experience from the first. In Louisiana, where counties are called "parishes" and one can ask "are you Catholic or Baptist?" without irony, public expressions of faith are everywhere. Some are ritualistic: community meetings in New Sarpy and surrounding towns are opened with a prayer and closed with a benediction—when they can be properly dismissed before descending into chaos. Industry-sponsored meetings don't open with prayer, but a blessing is always said before a meal, which these meetings frequently include. The person in charge of a meeting may honor other attendees by asking them to pray. Alternatively, he or she may pray him or herself in order to retain control of the meeting and instruct others on desirable behavior through the prayer. For example, CCNS's president once opened a meeting on a contentious topic with a prayer that asked God to help participants stay focused on the group's goals, be respectful of each other, and not "get ugly" with anyone.

Public statements of belief are not limited to these rituals, however. Christian individuals will talk about the role of God in their lives to encourage, instruct, or inform their listener. Stories of the sick being healed, money appearing when it was most needed, or God guiding someone's actions figure prominently in narratives of daily events or personal histories. Expressions of trust in Jesus and His ability to provide come up as people talk about the problems they face or the worries they have for their families or their neighborhoods. "Witnessing"—serving God by bearing witness to His power and goodness—is so much a part of ordinary conversation for some people that I have at times felt bombarded by these expressions of faith. Even when offered casually, they require the polite listener to accept God in order not to challenge the storyteller's version of events.

Community

When I began to focus my attention on "community" in January, I chose to attend St. Matthew because the congregation had made me feel welcome during an exploratory visit last summer. My first visits were nonetheless awkward. I was conspicuous as the only white person in the church, and I seemed in need of constant instruction: I came in the wrong door of the church, didn't know where to sit (or that I should hail an usher to help me!), and couldn't navigate my brand-new Bible. The familiar songs sung by the congregation were unfamiliar to me, and I had to learn the words—and how to clap on the right beats of the music.

I met a few people during my first weeks at St. Matthew, but my participation in Sunday services seemed insufficient to really involve me in the church. I approached a woman who had been kind and welcoming and told her that I wanted to get involved. She asked if I wanted to join the church. I explained that I did not, because I was only in the area temporarily, but I wanted to help out. The church's sign advertised after-school tutoring two days a week, so I mentioned the tutoring program as something I might assist with. She invited me to attend meetings of the Women's Ministry, of which she was in charge, and introduced me to the woman who ran the tutoring program. "Praise be!" said the second woman, raising her face and hands heavenward, and the next day I began tutoring two eight-year-old boys. I soon learned of the church's Mission Outreach program, which delivers hot meals to sick and elderly members of the community two Saturdays a month, and began volunteering for that as well.

My participation in St. Matthew's activities constituted part of my effort to figure out how, and whether, New Sarpy's collection of households constituted a "community." Puzzled by residents' conflicting descriptions of their town as "tight-knit" and hands-off, I sought evidence of community in New Sarpy. The unincorporated town has no unified civic association, no regular public meetings, and no central gathering place within its borders. The town is split in two by a railroad track running parallel to the Mississippi, with blacks concentrated "back of" the tracks in the lower-lying areas further from the river, and whites "in front," or closer to the river. Moreover, the campaign against the refinery involved only a portion of New Sarpy as a whole: four streets, each running two blocks from the river to the tracks, known as the St. Charles Terrace Subdivision. Overall, the subdivision has equal numbers of white and black residents, but the "front" block is predominantly white, while the "back" block is overwhelmingly black.

While I came to understand St. Matthew as a key New Sarpy establishment, at first I was doubtful that participation there would help me gain insight into the community. Few of the people I met at church lived in the St. Charles Terrace subdivision, where I intended to focus my attention, and many of them didn't even live in New Sarpy at all. I realized over time that, in most contexts, New Sarpy's black residents didn't think of the subdivision as separate from the rest of New Sarpy. They recognized the geographical boundaries, but their social and family ties extended across the entire town. It took even longer for me to catch on that almost everyone at St. Matthew, regardless of their current place of residence, had ties to New Sarpy, and, furthermore, that most of the black residents of New Sarpy have ties to St. Matthew. Church members who live in neighboring towns may have parents or in-laws who still live in the neighborhood, for example, and residents who now attend other churches may have been baptized or married at St. Matthew. In fact, church members say that one of New Sarpy's other churches was formed by people who split off from St. Matthew 20 years ago.

Participation at St. Matthew did not, however, help me to learn about the white section of New Sarpy. Nor were white residents similarly connected to one another through a single place of worship: they belonged to churches of various Christian denominations, all in other towns. In the absence of any central institutions in the white community, I resorted to visiting individual households, starting with people whom I had gotten to know through the campaign. I eventually learned that in the white part of the community, as in the black part, family members live in clusters, with maybe 15 or 20 families (black and white) accounting for most of the subdivision. One generation, now in their 70s and 80s, mostly settled in New Sarpy as young adults in the 1950s and 1960s and raised their children in the neighborhood. Those children, now grown and raising children of their own, make up another portion of the residents.

Understanding how people in New Sarpy are connected to each other and to their town took a great deal of work. Having uncovered these networks of relations, I take them as part of the substance of community in New Sarpy and as evidence that such a thing does exist. But I have also been preoccupied with what I imagine to be another aspect of community: how people stay informed or create shared understandings of local issues. Because I feel as though I haven't made progress on this question, I despair of my understanding of the community in general. Nevertheless, I do have evidence that information does travel, despite the fact that residents report that they don't socialize much. For example, during the campaign residents knew rapidly what CCNS and the refinery were up to. A shared rationale for what CCNS should do was somehow developed. And news of who's sick or who died traveled more quickly than the local newspaper or church bulletin could carry it.

When I ask residents how they learn what's going on in the community, they say they hear it around, or they just like to talk to people. More revealing are my casual conversations with people about what has been going on in their lives recently. My friend might say, for example, that she made gumbo yesterday and took some across the street to share with a neighbor; that her friend across the street took her to the hospital over the weekend; that people have been calling to find out what's going on; that the neighborhood children think her kitchen is Grand Central Station. Of course, recent events are just as likely to have taken residents away from the neighborhood—to shop, to go to the doctor, or to visit children or parents in other towns.

From residents' offhanded remarks, I am left with the impression that information is shared through a thousand tiny interactions that occur as residents run across the street or ride (in the car) out to the main road, but I bear witness to few of these. I am a frequent visitor to New Sarpy, but live three miles away, in the closest apartment I could rent. I wonder how much of a difference living there would make in my exposure to these fleeting interactions. Would I be automatically included in them by virtue of proximity, or does their substance lie in duration, kinship, and some perceived commonality? Would I notice that I had (have?) become part of the information-sharing network, or take it for granted as residents do?

When I got my very first reminder call on the eve of my last Women's Ministry meeting, I thought triumphantly that I was finally in the loop. When the meeting included a going-away party for me, I began to wonder if I had indeed joined the ranks of regulars, or if they were just ensuring that the guest of honor showed up. Watching each lady come into the church with a dish for the meal, I thought of the larger-than-usual gathering and the well-coordinated potluck supper as more evidence of the networks operating in the community. Then it hit me that I was not looking at evidence, but participating in community life itself. In looking for the big picture, perhaps I have been missing the extent to which I have been sharing in the small, fragmented, fleeting interactions that comprise community.

I still think of my questions about community—how people are related to each other and how information is passed around—as very grounded, humble questions. Yet they seem not to resonate with the residents of New Sarpy. When I ask people specifically about community, they do not tell me about their relatives living on the adjoining lot or about their chats with other residents. I'm sure that part of the explanation is that they are taking these things for granted, as I suspect I have been. What they do say, though, has surprised me: they tell me that New Sarpy is a nice, quiet community. They don't have any problems here, they say, mentioning New Orleans' high crime rate by way of comparison. Some even say that it's a close-knit community, but more often (and sometimes in the same breath) they say that neighbors live and let live. Complaints about the community are along the same lines: about the young people hanging out on street corners, the growing drug problem in some parts of the community, or the neighbors who fail to keep their places up. While comments like these initially led me to believe that perhaps there was no real sense of community in New Sarpy, I now wonder how residents come to understand their community in this way despite their relatively dense, long-standing relationships.

Quietly Not Believing

One evening in early May, I attended a meeting of Concerned Citizens of Norco (CCN), a group of black residents of an adjacent town who, after a protracted struggle, had won their demands for relocation from their industrial neighbor, Shell Chemical. A noted environmental justice activist who had been working with the group spoke at the meeting. She began by saying that she wouldn't talk long because her sinuses hurt as they always do when she visits Norco. She then remembered the first time she had visited the town. She was on a bus with other activists, and the bus broke down. They sat on the bus in the bad air of Norco for three hours waiting for another bus to come for them, she said, and it took her a week to recover from the effects of breathing all those industrial fumes.

Having by then spent many Sundays in church, I recognized her comments as following a familiar form—that used by Christians when they "testify" to knowing the goodness of the Lord. In religious testimony, a speaker will usually offer an overarching statement of faith to confirm his or her belief in God; for example, someone might say, "God woke me up this morning and started me on my way." The speaker will then tell of a moment where his or her belief was solidified. In one testimony I heard, a woman told how a relative's illness, which doctors had pronounced incurable, was cured through prayer. The personal account is, of course, offered as evidence of the value of faith and prayer, and the speaker frequently ends by saying so explicitly and admonishing listeners to stay strong in their faith.

The activist, in comparison, testified to knowing the ills caused by the petrochemical industry by first expressing her personal belief: by saying that her sinuses hurt when, and only when, she was in Norco, she identified Norco's looming chemical plant as the cause of her sinus trouble. The pivotal moment in her belief—as she told it in her testimony—came when she was stuck on the bus in Norco. Having experienced the effects on her health that came from breathing Norco's polluted air, she became convinced of the harms of the industry. She ended by encouraging her listeners to be strong in their fight against Shell: she said that CCN had won relocation because their cause was just, but that they shouldn't rest until Shell made its Norco facility a "green" plant.

When I recognized the parallels between this activist's speech and religious testimony, I also began to understand the fervent opinions about the chemical industry—locally as pervasive as religious testimony—as a matter of belief. One kind of believer *knows* that the plants adversely affect people's health. Asked how they know, they will tell you that it's because they have experienced the effects firsthand: the bad smells, the days when it's harder to breathe, the relatives with cancer. Asked what could convince them to the contrary, they deny the possibility. If an appropriate study were done, they insist, it *would* show the effects. To believers, belief comes prior to evidence. The truth of the matter is so obvious that one can't sincerely disbelieve: Ida, a lifelong New Sarpy resident, told me how she had confronted an acquaintance who was trying to defend the chemical industry. Ida reported that she had asked her friend if she could honestly say that she did not think the chemicals from the plants harmed one's health. She told me triumphantly that the woman had had to change the subject, because she knew that the chemicals were harmful, but did not want to admit it.

On the other hand, many residents of New Sarpy and neighboring communities believe just as sincerely in the goodness of the industry. Their evidence is different—long-lived neighbors and relatives, prosperous lives built on industrial incomes, diligent, trustworthy acquaintances who are plant workers—but, just like those who believe the opposite, they are quick to declare their position publicly and to bear witness to things that support it.

Before I understood these opinions about the effects of the petrochemical industry as expressions of belief, though, I had concluded that most people were, in fact, agnostics, lacking belief in health effects due to industrial emissions. In January, a member of St. Matthew was driving me around New Sarpy, showing me where she'd grown up. I asked her what her parents did for a living. She told me that her father had worked for a predecessor of Orion Refining. In the same breath, she told me that he'd died of cancer. So I asked: did she think the two were related? She didn't know, she said quickly. Similarly, a man who lives on the street closest to Orion told me that he didn't care to live there any more. At 75, he was sick like he had never been before in his life. I asked if he thought he was sick from the plant. "Well, it could be," he said. "It could not be. I don't know for sure." A third resident told me she didn't know what to think about the plants' effects on health, though she thought there was cause for concern. But she told me that you couldn't be worrying about it all the time; the sixth chapter of Matthew says not to worry. She said that you had to do the best you could, but all the rest you should leave in the hands of God.

Only once during my stay have I witnessed comparable doubt about religion. I was invited to the home of a former New Sarpy resident, Martha (not her real name), for dinner with a few of her female friends and family members, two of them natives of New Sarpy. As we sat around the dining room table after dinner, Martha joked that she was the "atheist" of the group. Her friends responded with absolute seriousness. One told her that she could tell as she was watching Martha in church on Sunday that Martha was only holding back because she was afraid of where her belief might take her. Another told us of the emotional moment when God had called her to be baptized. She declared that Martha would be all right, for God was always on time. He maybe wouldn't call her when she thought she was ready, but he would be on time. Martha didn't argue with her friends, nor did she appear to be comforted. She continued to look doubtful and concerned.

In this intimate exchange, I began to understand why public discussions of the chemical industry's effects on health are dominated by believers on the two sides of the issue, even though I have found agnosticism on the subject to be more common than belief. Believers have a lot to say: arguments can be made, examples cited, personal testimony given, and reassurances offered to skeptics. Agnostics can only shrug. Such consuming doubt can only be expressed as "I just don't know." Once one has admitted to not knowing, there is little else to say. As a result, while agnosticism may be expressed privately—with the potential consequence of having some listening believer try to fill the vacuum of not-knowing—it seldom makes itself known in public.

I believe that petrochemical company emissions have health effects untold by current scientific studies. I don't know if I believe in God or in Jesus Christ Our Savior. But at St. Matthew I have been circumspect about my agnosticism, thinking that I would only be accepted if I passed as a believer. Listening to Martha's friends, believers themselves, react—with acceptance, compassion, and hope—to her agnosticism, it dawned on me that perhaps the community of the church was not based *solely* on shared belief and that perhaps my belief had not been assumed and acknowledging my doubt would not have made a difference to my acceptance at the church.

Belonging

On the Sunday after Mother's Day, St. Matthew held their annual Women's Day celebration. As a member of the Women's Ministry, which sponsors the event, I had participated in its planning and even devilled four dozen eggs for the occasion. Nonetheless, as with most other events during my fieldwork, I had no idea what to expect until I walked in to the church.

The morning program was much the same as any other Sunday morning worship service, with a few added features (a special welcome to guests, for example, and a liturgical dance). In addition, instead of deacons leading the prayers and the pastor preaching the Word, girls and young women had all of the speaking roles, and only the girls from the youth choir were on the choir stand. I finally caught on that the whole purpose of Women's Day was to honor the women of the church when, at the very end, the organizer of the program made presentations to a number of the younger women (childless, and under 40) who had served the church over the past year.

In the midst of my revelation, I realized they were calling on me to come and receive one of the small trophies they were handing out. It was in recognition, the organizer explained, of my faithful work with the tutoring program and with the mission program. In the afternoon program, where the older women were featured and acknowledged, I sang with an expanded version of the women's choir. As the organizer acknowledged each of the guest choir members, she called my name and admitted, "of course, we really consider Gwen one of our own. . . ."

I was deeply touched by these gestures, and I treasure my little trophy, with its depiction of a cross and praying hands, and the inscription "Women's Day 2003." Yet I am also profoundly baffled. I had never anticipated that by showing up and lending a hand—with the selfish hope of making connections that would allow me to get on with my fieldwork—I might become an integral part of the church. I certainly had no idea that this had actually come to pass. While I had slowly been developing relationships with various church members, none of those relationships have even yet grown beyond the context of the church. I thus imagined myself to be peripheral to their worlds. Understanding that I *do* belong, in their minds, has added weight to my growing suspicion that St. Matthew is a community in itself for church members, overlapping but not coextensive with other ways in which they may be connected to New Sarpy.

While St. Matthew's members indicate that I have become one of them, my presence has not yet become taken-for-granted. The extent to which I am still remarkable makes me an outsider yet. During one recent week, Reverend Douglas was visiting New Sarpy from Texas, where he has lived for many years. Rev. Douglas is a native of New Sarpy, and still has a home in the St. Charles Terrace neighborhood, plus relatives who are active members of the church. He visits New Sarpy every few months, and when he does he participates in the activities of the church. As during his last visit, we were both among the workers in the mission program on Saturday morning and had the chance to talk some. The next morning, Rev. Douglas preached as a guest minister. Before he got to his sermon, though, he acknowledged me: he told how he had gotten to know me a little through the mission, and that he doubted that he would have another chance to meet me before I went back home. "Keep me in your prayers," he asked from the pulpit, "and I will keep you in mine." Then he spoke to the congregation. They deserved credit for their hospitality, he told them; it was because they were open and welcoming that I was there.

Perhaps I read too much in to his words, but I found in them confirmation of long-standing suspicions. I was surprised to be so welcomed into this all-black church. I explained it to myself as being no more than Christian to welcome all comers to church. As I've had more opportunities to understand the racism of the South through the eyes of my black friends, though, I have come to think that the arrival of an unknown white person must have aroused some suspicion, and that it took real generosity for the members of St. Matthew to welcome me as they did. I don't know if this is true. We are certainly not on such familiar terms that anyone has said to me, "We didn't know what to think of this white girl waltzing in here." But Rev. Douglas' words suggested to me that, in order to welcome me, the congregation perhaps did need to suspend their doubts and draw on their best Christian spirit.

If church members seem now to delight in my company, as I do in theirs, I wonder if it isn't the more so because they measure our interactions against whatever expectations they initially had. One church member commented that I had "mixed well"—surely, I thought, a comment on my ability to fit in despite my race. Another church member later made the same comment, but supported it by saying that I had contributed more and generally behaved better than some long-standing members of the church community, forcing me to reevaluate my assumptions about the range of relevant expectations.

As I have become more a part of life at St. Matthew, I have been surprised to find that who I am as a person has started to matter. The leader of the mission program tells me that I have helped her learn humility and that I have provided her with an example of serving God peacefully, without complaint. This touches my heart, and I try to find truth in it. I do not think of myself as humble nor as possessing any great ability to keep my mouth shut. I conclude that what she sees must be an artifact of my deciding that part of my job as a field-worker is to be agreeable. But as others comment on my ready smile and my desire to be helpful, I realize that cheerfully pitching in *is* typical of me in many settings. It has caught me off guard that people seem to know me personally, even though I thought that I had left my personal life in Berkeley.

In April, I was married by a Justice of the Peace in St. Charles Parish, the timing of the marriage dictated by legal and financial concerns. While I told a few of my friends in New Sarpy that I was engaged to my long-standing boyfriend, whom they had met during his brief visits to Louisiana, I did not tell any of them that we married. At the time, I thought little of it: it seemed easy enough to separate the two parts of my life. I have since come to regret the way I have handled the situation. Understanding better the extent to which I have become part of the community, I now wish that I had told them about our marriage, even with its associated ambiguity (namely its hastiness and the fact that we are still living apart). In fact, given that the Justice of the Peace preached a sermon during our purportedly civil ceremony—which should not have been unexpected to a professional observer of South Louisiana culture but yet was—I wish that we had asked one of St. Matthew's ministers to marry us. Whether or not I entirely share in their belief, I understand their belief, I share their community, and I trust in their caring for me.

Transporting Belief

One of the leaders of Concerned Citizens of Norco's successful campaign against Shell Chemical told me in an interview how she relied on God's guidance during the campaign. She complained that this is the part of her story that the many people who have interviewed her inevitably leave out. But it was important that she tell me anyway, she said.

That part of her story deserves to be told. Yet I'm not surprised that it hasn't been. I was jolted by a Berkeley friend's reaction when I told her about the importance and ubiquity of religion here, expressed in part by people saying that they will pray for you. "No, thank you!" she exclaimed, horrified. Although I tried to explain, she failed to understand how offering to pray for someone is a kind, caring gesture.

As I bid St. Matthew good-bye, I *will* ask that they pray for me. I hope that their prayers may guide me in portraying belief diligently and earnestly to the decidedly secular academic world.

Epilogue: Being Faithful

Belief is nowhere to be found in my dissertation, completed nearly two years after I left Louisiana. I discussed neither the relationship between conviction and evidence nor the role that New Sarpy residents' deep faith played in sustaining their opposition to their giant industrial neighbor. On one hand, it seems a surprise that these issues, which loomed so large for me as I left the field, would not have played a larger role in my analysis. But on the other hand, it is unsurprising in the same way that my ending up in church and being married by a preaching civil servant are unsurprising. In reclaiming my own, theoretically motivated interests as I wrote my dissertation, I moved further and further away from the things that mattered most to the people from whom I learned so much. The same process occurred in reverse when I entered the field: the two-sentence explanation I originally gave to account for why I was there, focused on abstract issues of science and politics, was quickly replaced by the statement that I was interested in how communities and industry get along—something that is of great concern to just about everyone that lives or works in southeastern Louisiana. These changes in the way I think and write about my fieldwork mark honest efforts to translate ideas and commitments from one world into terms that make sense in another, and I do believe I did the best I could. Yet what was lost in the translation *was* important, and its absence saddens me.

Although belief dropped out of my scholarly writing, it sticks with me in my personal life. In the very difficult year that followed my fieldwork, I prayed, remembering the spirit that filled St. Matthew during Sunday morning services. Whether that spirit was God or the enthusiasm of a hundred believers, I could not say. I remain agnostic. But my previous disregard of spirituality has been transformed by my experience at St. Matthew into a reflective not-knowing. I now have a basis for pondering religion, for attempting even to be thoughtful (rather than simply irate) about its role in contemporary politics. If the people of St. Matthew would be dismayed by my agnosticism—and I am not convinced, in fact, that they would—I hope that they would consider themselves to have done a service in bringing about this transformation. In any case, I am grateful.

Laboring under Illusionism:
Notes from the Study of French Magic

Graham M. Jones
New York University

Making Yourself Useful

The elegant French stranger tugged at the lapels of his trench coat, shielding his cheeks from the biting December wind as we strode briskly through New York's Greenwich Village. Under my arm, I clutched the reason for our meeting—an unwieldy package inconspicuously wrapped in brown paper.

We stepped into the warmth of a dimly lit dive bar, deserted in the mid-afternoon, and chose a booth far from the door. A haze of smoke still seemed to linger despite the city's recent smoking ban. Eyeing each other intently through two pairs of fogging glasses, we ordered a round of colas.

A devilish smile flickered across the stranger's lips as I slid the package towards him. He held it slightly aloft, gauging its weight. "Oh man, 15 pounds!" he breathed in heavily accented amazement. "I won't be able to get all this back to Paris."

"It might be too much," I conjectured.

"Yes, but these are very precious." Opening the wrapping with expectant fingers, he plucked forth a handful of wriggling little rubber bands and spread them triumphantly on the table. For a moment, we simply marveled.

These were not ordinary rubber bands, but Alliance brand Pale Crepe Gold 16s and 19s. Made of pure rubber and sold primarily for commercial uses, they have a quasi-mythical status among magicians around the world. While synthetic or composite rubber bands quickly fray and snap, the more elastic, more durable Pale Crepe Golds are ideal for mind-boggling manipulations with tell-tale names like "Jumping Rubber Bands" and "Linking Rubber Bands" that commonly figure into close-up magic routines.

Almost a year ago, while conducting six months of pre-field research for a dissertation on entertainment magic in France, I met a talented young Parisian conjuror particularly interested in rubber band tricks (and other forms of magic involving digital gymnastics). In August, he placed a three-dollar order for two pounds of Pale Crepe Golds, unavailable in France, from a major American office supply chain. After six or seven weeks passed without word, he began to send increasingly bitter and generally unrequited e-mail messages (which I quote verbatim) to a company sales representative as the affair lurched towards a farcical conclusion:

> *October 12:* I'm still waiting. And I'm upset now. I paid for something I never receive and you never answer my mails. Be conscious that it's not a correct way to treat people.

> *October 19:* Enough is enough, I let you one week to contact me about this order. If I had no answer be sure I will do my possible to have justice, don't think I cannot do anything because I am far away, you could be surprised. . . .

> *October 24:* After my many, many emails that you left unanswered about my package that never arrived, I decided to take action to the relevant authorities. I think you asked for it. I have filed a complaint to the relevant FBI service, for Internet trouble. Lieutenant E . . . advised me that foreign matters of this sort take no time to be solved, he will get in touch with you during this week. Best regards

> *October 28:* Are you kidding me? I'm afraid there is a big misunderstanding . . . or this is all a big joke. I received the merchandise this morning, two months after I placed my order. . . . And this is NOT what I've ordered. Instead . . . you sent me [another brand] of rubber bands. Do you really think I would make an order all the way from France if I didn't want a really specific brand of rubber bands?

Desperate, he turned to me, hoping I could track down Pale Crepe Golds *somewhere* in New York.

I had returned from my first visit to France in June, and was working on completing the steps requisite for my return the following year—grant writing, comprehensive exams, and human subjects review. Schematically speaking, the pre-field research I had just completed was a stepping-stone towards actual fieldwork—a time to develop questions rather than answer them, mull over methodologies rather than employ them. In essence, in the early days I was essentially creating a field site—a social arena for living and researching—through the relationships I was building with French magicians.[1]

This process did not stop when I returned to the U.S., and I was trying to remain in active contact with the magicians I met during my first trip, mostly via the Internet. A learning experience in its own right, sending materials available only in the U.S. became important as a way for me both to thank people for helping with my research and to further cultivate bonds of reciprocity and trust. I began strolling regularly along Canal Street, weaving in and out of its vaguely anachronistic industrial outlets and Chinese or Indian haberdasheries on the lookout for everyday objects that my informants could transform into the stuff of dreams.

Many magicians are themselves inveterate browsers. In his autobiography, David Bamberg (a.k.a. Fu Manchu) defines magicians' practice of "exploring shop windows on the chance that they [might hold] something that could be used for a magic effect" as *snuffling around* (Bamberg 1991: 88).

Pierre Brahma, one of France's most renowned illusionists, writes eloquently about an epiphanic snuffle that changed the course of his career:

> I liked to drift along [department store] counters, picking through the myriad things offered up to shoppers' cupidity. Often an idea for a new trick would spring into my head upon seeing an object with no seeming connection to the world of illusion. On this particular day, I was passing through the jewelry isle when I stopped short before a display of thousands of cascading necklaces—fine pearls, Czech glass, gold and silver. A kaleidoscope of colors played before me for 50 feet, a veritable Cavern of Ali Baba, a sea of jewels. It struck me like a bolt. I was going to make illusions with jewels. (Brahma 1998: 80)

In the coming years, Brahma developed a groundbreaking routine with jewelry and precious stones that would take him around the world.

For me, snuffling was full of revelations too. I learned to see the material excesses of consumer society as I thought a magician might: an inexhaustible and scarcely tapped source of artistic raw material. So far, I have conveyed goods ranging from hundreds of paper lunch bags, jumbo ziplock baggies, Listerine breath strips, yards of reflective contact paper, Sharpie markers, "Iraq's Most Wanted" playing cards, and three collapsible laundry hampers to my informants for use in their acts. I anticipate returning to the field like an old-time peddler, suitcases brimming with an orgy of gewgaws and household products.

Needless to say, I was primed to spring into action when my friend contacted me about the Pale Crepe Golds in November and quickly sent him several pounds. Weeks later, he asked me to transmit, via a magician acquaintance of his vacationing in New York, another shipment of rubber bands—by all appearances, a lifetime supply (it wasn't). "What an incredible addiction!" I thought.

But as I waited to make the drop-off in the chilly winter air, worrying whether the middleman and I would pick each other out of the heavily bundled throng, I realized that I too had fallen under the sway of an odd and contagious passion. For I found myself immersed in a world where even buying routine office supplies could become an enthralling game of cloak and dagger.

My fieldwork was taking shape, unassumingly, out of small, unexpected, and often funny adventures like these. Through a series of five loosely-related vignettes, I want to illustrate this process, exploring how, in the earliest phases of graduate-level field research, the process of learning to inhabit—if only peripherally—an alien social world is itself productive of ethnographic insights that may later be subsumed by more "sophisticated" ways of knowing.

Along with the excitement of discovery, these stories also reflect the inevitable frustration, confusion, and embarrassment that beginning ethnographers must endure and that are doubtless intrinsic to all ethnographic inquiry. Indeed, to the extent that the ethnographic method is a scientific one, I should hope that there is nothing at all uncommon about my solutions to methodological problems raised by this somewhat peculiar subject.

Taking Part

My journey to Paris earlier this year represented a pilgrimage of sorts. It was there, in the mid-nineteenth century, that Jean-Eugène Robert-Houdin (whose name Houdini adopted as a kind of homage) staged his seminal *Soirées fantastiques*, establishing many of the conventions of magic as we know it today and earning the moniker "Father of Modern Magic." I was looking forward to studying the way that entertainment magic is produced as an art form and reproduced as a social activity in contemporary France, with an eye on the factors that have reshaped it since Robert-Houdin's time—among them the rise of mass media, the astronomical growth in the practice of magic by amateurs, and the expanding (but increasingly fraught) intervention of the French state in funding for popular performing arts.

Still I fretted that imperatives of secrecy would lead French magicians to reject an ethnographic observer out of hand. Before I left New York, an American magician ominously warned that I was "delving into the most secret society in the world," further intimating that French magicians are notoriously protective of their secrets. My fears of categorical rejection, however, proved unfounded, as Parisian magicians warmly invited me into their clubs. But their openness was beguiling.

My first direct contact with the Paris magic community was at an informal monthly dinner in a pizzeria, recommended to me by a young French magician who I met backstage after a small-time performance at a New York elementary school. I arrived early to introduce myself, describing my project and nonchalantly mentioning my contact's name. I was surprised to learn that he was among the young lions of French magic ("you can even buy his videos in Las Vegas!" one magician gushed). Indeed, when he showed up late that evening, he was no longer an awkward foreigner struggling to connect with a group of restless children, but a dashing, larger-than-life celebrity.

Because of my singular letter of introduction, rumor unfortunately spread that I was a mysterious New York magician with stellar credentials. Before long, I was surrounded by people beseeching me to perform. "Where are your cards?" someone asked suspiciously. "Show us some real New York City magic!" another implored, perhaps thinking of "street magician" David Blaine, a young biracial Brooklynite (like me) who recently leapt into the international spotlight with edgy, urban stylings (totally unlike mine).

The admission that I was *just* trying to write my doctoral dissertation on magic only seemed to serve as a mark of further distinction, stoking expectations even higher. I demurred until I was alone at a table with several particularly friendly young magicians and performed a few simple card tricks that I had learned for just such occasions. It was a relief to thoroughly disabuse them of any illusions about my skill.

Eventually, I clarified my "purely academic" intentions and became a regular at several monthly magic club meetings. I imagined that I would ultimately conduct the majority of my research in these contexts, observing magicians' interactions with each other and participating in their shoptalk. Although it seems foolish now, I didn't anticipate that actually doing magic, in earnest, would be necessary to learn about the culture, structure, and group dynamics of the Paris magic scene—my ethnographic bread and butter.

I was therefore surprised that as I became a more familiar presence at magic events, participants' requests to see "what [tricks] I was working on" only increased. At first I assumed this was a way of policing access to what is an undeniably secret world and of asserting hierarchies of expertise within it. It must be said that the world of magic in France as elsewhere is overwhelmingly male and there is much showboating and jockeying for prominence within it (some might even say that the magic itself is a way of expressing—and creating—social dominance, since it hinges on tricking people using knowledge they do not possess).

At the very least, by putting me on the spot to display skills I had little mastered, the "old-timers" were sending me the message that "newcomers" were welcome to participate in club activities provided they manifest serious devotion to magic, which they sometimes lovingly referred to as the "Queen of the Arts." But I also think they were tacitly *telling* me something essential about the nature of the social relationships between magicians.

A secret art, magic can also be a solitary one, requiring long hours of monkish study and practice. Magic clubs are one of the few contexts in which magicians can delight in a mutual appreciation for skills necessarily hidden from outsiders. It is safe to say that sharing an impassioned interest in illusionary techniques and the rich human stories in which they are embedded draws magicians together for purely social reasons. In the context of these meetings, being recognized as an engaged, engaging person hinges on participating in interactions that quickly shuttle between talk and performance. Because magicians discuss magic while and by doing it, practicing along with them soon struck me as essential for entering into their ongoing dialog.

Far from seeking to exclude me, then, by pressuring me to perform even as (or especially because) they recognized my limited ability, members were making an inclusionary gesture. Placing me in the position of a novice, they constituted me as a potential beneficiary of the expert instruction that only they could offer. Perhaps most importantly, they were thereby giving me an opportunity to study magic by taking part in one of the forms of social activity—apprenticeship—that keeps it a flourishing popular tradition in France and around the world.

In addition to learning informally in clubs and from friends, I purchased a number of magic books and videos, and enrolled in a weekly class on card and coin magic. Although practicing magic was often the last thing I wanted to do during my time off from attending magic events (and thinking obsessively about magic, more generally), I eventually built up a small repertoire of tricks, and even began to perform selectively for nonmagicians.

My informants were pleased with my investment in learning magic, but disappointed with my slow progress. By the time I left in June, they were advising me to prepare for my return with diligent training. "When you come back, you're going to know lots of tricks. You're going to amaze us," one stated unequivocally. Another, who had been my instructor in two magic workshops, advised, "You need to start performing more, and making use of what you learn. We're not sharing all this with you just for fun."

These weighty expectations, coupled with my own growing enthusiasm for magic, gave rise to a heady delusion. I confessed to my closest informant that I wanted to become a *full-fledged* magician. In an ironic reversal, he cautioned, "don't let yourself be distracted. Doing magic can take over your life, and you'll never finish your dissertation!"

With more realistic goals, I have continued to do magic while preparing my return to the field, though more often than not, I feel guilty for not practicing enough. Given the portability of playing cards and people's seemingly universal interest in magic, it is easy to conduct highly instructive para-ethnography (i.e., fieldwork outside one's field site) by performing card tricks for friends and relatives. For example, at a recent family gathering, my sister's boyfriend asked if I had learned any tricks in the field. When I "demonstrated" a method for identifying a chosen card apparently by observing the dilation of a volunteer's pupils, he talked about the feat for days. Though he may have been humoring a prospective brother-in-law, this experience suggested that, under the right circumstances, even an elementary trick can leave a long-lasting impression, one that only grows with continued retellings.

All this made me wonder if, perhaps in some cases and for some types of projects, "being in the field" is as much a state of mind as it is a physical condition. Certainly, for me, the practice of magic (which would go on to take forms that I could not have foreseen at the time) became not only a pretext for interacting with informants, but also a way of exploring the inner workings of their art—even when far from my actual field site.

Toeing the Common Line

During the period of my pilot study, I met a distinguished American sociologist whose pioneering research on artists and musicians was a major inspiration for my project, and who had himself practiced magic as an adolescent. I invited him and his wife, a photographer and scholar, to a magic show hosted by Paris's largest magic club.

The day of the show, I attended a magic bazaar and series of workshops sponsored by the club. My American friends arrived early for the performance that evening. Sitting in the lounge outside the theatre, we chatted about my research. Eager to show off my "insider" status, I introduced them to several magicians, and recounted the day's events. They asked if I had purchased anything at the bazaar, and I promptly produced a stack of instructional books from my knapsack. As they flipped through a brand-new treatise on tricks with rings and cords published by one of the club's members, I described the buzz the innovative techniques it contained had generated that afternoon. I hoped to learn some of the routines myself, in fact.

Suddenly, a voice bellowed over my shoulder. "You're not sharing secrets with laymen, are you?" I immediately recognized the Parisian cockney of a stout journeyman magician and fixture of the local magic scene. Turning to meet his withering gaze, I flushed with shame and snatched the book back from my friends. The veteran sociologist intervened to defuse the tense situation, explaining in impeccable French that he had been a magician as a boy, and posing some well-informed questions about the upcoming show. Still, I had been caught *in flagrante delicto*, flouting the cardinal rule of the magician's code: *Protect secrets*.

In my defense, I had no reason to think that my friends would make an effort to penetrate either the book's jargony French or recondite illustrations. They were not considering it as a source of secret information but, with professional detachment, as an example of the kind of artifacts I was encountering in the field, something generically reflective of my ethnographic experience. Speaking in English further distanced me from the activity going on in French all around us. Nevertheless, in my interest to receive potentially valuable insights from sophisticated outside observers (and perhaps to impress them with insights of my own), I let my anthropologist self—a creature of university classrooms and professional conferences—eclipse what might be called my ethnographic *fieldself*—the persona I had assumed as a necessary means of adapting to the social conditions of my field site.

In expressing solidarity with academic colleagues, I simultaneously disaffiliated myself from club magicians, committing a gaffe that threatened to undermine their hard-won trust. Thankfully, I had done no irreparable harm, but I learned a valuable lesson about the danger of role-dissonance in the course of research and the importance of abiding local behavioral norms.

Getting Your Questions Straight

Midway through my pre-field visit, I stayed after a club meeting to talk with three friends. They were concerned that, although I had become an almost ubiquitous presence in the Paris magic scene, I wasn't doing any work (recognizable as such) on my dissertation, nor could I even clearly explain what it was about. As they pressed me to articulate my hypotheses and methods, one asked if I was planning to do any interviews.

"Definitely, but I'm not sure if I'm quite ready yet."

"Why don't you interview them?" she sniggered, gesturing derisively at her friends.

Frankly, I was grateful for the entrée. "I'd love to, if they'd be willing. . . ."

"I'd do it," one volunteered, "but not if you're going to ask dumb-ass questions (*questions à la con*)."

"What's a dumb-ass question?"

"Like, 'How'd you get into magic?' or 'Which magicians do you admire?'"

"Those aren't dumb-ass questions; we talk about that stuff all the time!" the third retorted.

"Sure, but that's why they're uninteresting."

"So what would you like me to ask?"

"I don't know. . . . Like, 'What do you want to *say* through magic?'" While I haven't yet gotten around to interviewing this young man, I have a good sense of the issue he wanted me to address—the meaning of magic. I often heard French magicians debate it among themselves, arguing about how to "get a message across" (*faire passer un message*) or "express oneself through magic" (*s'exprimer dans la magie*), and about whether a magician needed to "have something to say" (*avoir quelque chose à dire*) to be a successful performer. Along with them, I struggled to understand what it might mean to *make a statement* in the idiom of magic. To me, magic tricks initially seemed to have little discursive content beyond the sense of surprise they produced, and I wondered why the problem of meaning should command so much of my informants' attention.

For reasons intrinsic to the art of conjuring, lay audiences generally lack magicians' appreciation for technical virtuosity. Not surprisingly, when magicians were asked to rank their least-favorite audience remark on a popular French magic Web site, "You make a living doing *that?*" was at the top of the list. What's more, the problem of underappreciation may be especially acute in France, where magicians often complain (only half-jokingly) that deep-rooted Cartesian rationalism makes their audience "the worst in the world," unable to appreciate magic effects because of a hyper-rational mania for demystifying illusion. Even if this "folk theory" is only a shorthand way of accounting for the rigid hierarchies separating high and low culture in France (something that has much more to do with institutional legacies rather than worldviews), it has a strong hold over the imaginations of French magicians themselves.

In order to make magic meaningful for a wide public, many magicians therefore feel they must overcome or at least redirect their own fascination with illusionary techniques, concentrating instead on spectators' sensory and psychological experience. It is a telling paradox that some of the oldest, simplest magic effects are more likely to dazzle lay audiences than the most technically sophisticated, cutting-edge tricks. Thus, Henning Nelms, in his landmark treatise *Magic and Showmanship*, warns magicians,

> Everything you do, literally everything, has a different value for conjurors than it has for laymen. Conjurors are fascinated by subtle devices and difficult sleight of hand. Laymen are incapable of appreciating either the subtlety or the difficulty. In fact, if the performance succeeds, the layman cannot even guess what methods have been used. On the other hand, laymen are easily impressed by illusions, whereas conjurors are immune except in rare cases. (Nelms 1969: 17)

Faced with this predicament, some magicians choose to remain steadfastly amateur or to go "underground," indulging their infatuation with technique. Free from the exigencies of entertaining lay audiences, a few ultimately become major technical innovators; many are relegated to the status my informants defined as *branleurs* (jerk-offs) who primarily do highly technical tricks to impress other magicians without much pretense of enchanting audiences. (Of course, this category probably does not refer to a specifically stigmatized group, but reflects general standards of negative assessment.)

Alternately, several of the professional and semi-professional magicians I grew closest to in Paris were seeking to transcend trickery altogether and dreamed, strangely enough, of progressively eliminating tricks from their magic shows. As they began to see tricks as a distraction from their ultimate goal of entertaining, one pair of magicians I met was developing a stand-up comedy routine with complex wordplay taking the place of illusionary feats.

But between the opposing poles of tricks-without-magic and magic-without-tricks lie infinite degrees of nuance. It is in this ambiguous middle ground where most magic is made, and aesthetic controversies played out.

One evening, I found myself in a café with two expert magicians locked in a heated aesthetic debate. Both were devotees of card tricks, or *cartomanes*, but they had vastly different approaches to making meaningful magic, one self-identifying as "figurative," the other as "abstract." Figurative cartomanes personify playing cards in order to tell a story, in which, for example, the Aces stand for gangsters, cannibals, or some other characters. Abstractionists do not present the cards as representations of some other reality. Instead they want the audience to focus on the cards themselves as a system of interrelated objects. For example, an abstractionist might have an Ace appear when the audience is expecting a King.

The author (right) and a magician friend discussing "cartomagie," or card tricks, at an all-night magic meeting, Paris 2004. (© Zakary Bellamy.)

As their discussion intensified, the two friends improvised mocking, but hilarious, caricatures of each other's on-stage patter. "These Jacks are two brothers from Marseilles," began the abstractionist, "and they are going to screw these four prostitutes, represented by the Queens of course, and then gorge themselves on this pile of frogs." This impersonation ingeniously uses trite stereotypes about French appetites for sex and food to imply that storytelling trivializes the intellectual interest of magic effects in and of themselves.

The figurative magician did an equally scathing imitation of his counterpart, one suggesting that without a narrative framework, magic tricks degenerate into vacuous athleticism: "If I take these four Kings, and make this magic gesture, and then this one, and finally this one, *automatically* they are transformed into Aces!" He seemed to be saying that such talk, at best, serves to underscore the incomprehensibility of the magician's technical prowess; at worst, it is an insult to the audience's intelligence.

Despite their mutual respect, these two opinionated conjurors could not agree on a common vision of the *really* magical. Meanwhile, some of their colleagues sidestep these essentializing debates altogether by characterizing the meaning of magic relationally, in terms of the social connections it establishes between audience and performer (and sometimes between audience members themselves).

Once again, cabaret magician Pierre Brahma's autobiography provides a paradigmatic example. After losing his hearing as an adolescent, Brahma's only way to break the barrier of silence was with magic. "In prestidigitation," he writes, "I discovered the pleasure of self-overcoming, and especially the joy that comes from delighting and entertaining my peers, when I had thought myself a diminished being" (Brahma 1998: 28). A friend planning to teach magic classes for at-risk youth at community a center in rough-and-tumble suburban Paris hoped his students would have similar experiences of self-validation.

Another striking illustration of magic's power to connect people emerged from my pre-field research. I was visiting a magician in a historical town to the south of Paris. Making our way home from a café in the wee hours of the morning, we came across a pack of scruffy teenagers lurking in the shadows of a celebrated gothic cathedral. "Let's go talk to them!" my companion said. Horrified, particularly at a time of strong anti-American sentiment in France, I trailed timidly behind as he charged into the breach. "Name an animal!" he cheerily began, digging into his backpack.

"A dog," one of the youths mumbled suspiciously between world-weary puffs on a cig-arette. Within minutes, my friend had made not only a dog (a poodle, to be exact), but a ver-itable Noah's Ark of multicolored balloon animals for the astonished teenagers, as well as a flower, a sword, and caps adorned with disconcertingly realistic phalluses for us all. We lin-gered on, talking amicably about their experiences growing up in the idyllic town they called "boring" and about my life in a New York I described as "hectic," seemingly worlds away.

Disappearing back into the night, we could hear their youthful laughter echoing along the ancient cobblestone streets. "That's what magic is all about: giving people a gift," my friend reflected. "They'll remember that forever."

"Me too," I whispered, my green boner helmet glistening in the moonlight.

Lightening Up

Several days before my return to the U.S. in June, the group of young magicians I spent most of my time with proposed to throw a going-away party on the banks of the Seine. I had been so preoccupied with the intellectual challenges of working out my research strate-gies that I was as surprised as I was touched by this unexpected affirmation of our emerg-ing friendships.

We planned to meet at six o'clock in front of the Arab Institute, but most everyone was late because of a transportation strike. I had been in the chic district of Saint Germain and arrived on foot with hummus and baba ganoush from a gourmet grocer; both proved win-ning novelties. Others straggled up with melon, chicken, cheese, bread, and sweets.

In my experience, magicians generally avoid alcohol and anything else that could detract from their mental or manual swiftness. Working with them, I found it doubly impor-tant to maintain a clear head. First, I needed to keep pace with nonstop verbal play and a constant barrage of magic tricks, while remaining ready to perform, however falteringly, in both genres. Second, I wanted to remember as much detail as possible to later include in my fieldnotes. For everyone involved, though for different reasons, late-night magic get-togethers in bars and cafés were trials of self-mastery. I often longed for a (tantalizingly close-at-hand) drink to quell the nervous strain that goes along with the *really-not-belonging* of participant observation, but I generally abstained.

On this particular evening, however, basking in the red glow of the setting sun as the fabled river flowed languidly past, I decided to partake in the wine, champagne, and pearly Pastis passing round. And as a further act of symbolic rebellion, I even vowed not to write anything down afterwards! My advisor had often told me not to worry because "it's all data." While I recited this phrase to myself mantra-like for reassurance that I was indeed gathering useful information whatever went wrong, I suddenly realized I had only half understood: everything you collect is data, but that doesn't mean you have to collect *everything*. Sometimes it isn't all data, sometimes it's just your life.

In the encroaching darkness, two elderly men unexpectedly set up a PA system on the quay before us and began playing loud Tango music.

> No despiertes si sueñas amores
> niña hermosa, que amar es soñar!
> despertar es quebrar ilusiones
> y hallar entre sombras la amarga verdad. . . .

Before long, colorful eddies of dancing couples encircled our picnic blanket. In a perfect waking dream, I relished my remaining hours with people who were teaching me so much, so generously, about appreciating the miraculous in and of everyday life—all the way down to the lowly rubber band.

The next morning, I broke my vow, typing up hung-over fieldnotes in the airport. "Au revoir, pays de merveilles," I wrote simply. So long, world of wonder.

—For H. B.

Note

[1] The ethnographic present of this essay is, roughly, summer 2003. As I revise it for press over two years later, having, in the meanwhile, gone on to complete an additional 12 months of participant observation in the same setting (with generous support from Fulbright and the Social Science Research Council), I am resisting the temptation to make anything more than minor changes for the sake of clarity.

References

Bamberg, David. 1991. *Illusion Show: A Life in Magic*. Glenwood, IL: Meyerbooks.
Brahma, Pierre. 1998. *La Malle des Indes: Les Nuits d'un magicien*. Paris: Editions de Fallois.
Nelms, Henning. 1969. *Magic and Showmanship: A Handbook for Magicians*. New York: Dover.

Bonding with the Field: On Researching Surrogate Motherhood Arrangements in Israel

Elly Teman
Hebrew University

This essay addresses my perspective during the course of fieldwork on the topic of surrogate motherhood in Israel. In a surrogacy arrangement, a woman is contracted to bear a child for a couple to whom she will relinquish the child, usually in exchange for monetary reimbursement. Gestational surrogacy—the variant that I studied—refers to a specific variation of the process in which a fertilized egg, created through in-vitro fertilization from the intended couple's gametes, is surgically implanted in the surrogate's womb.

Surrogacy is considered a highly controversial topic in most of the world on moral, ethical, legal, and religious grounds (Rae 1994; van Niekerk and van Zyl 1995). This has led many governments to enact regulations outlawing the practice entirely or carefully "ignore it" by maintaining that surrogacy contracts can be pursued in the free market economy but will not be enforced in a local court of law (Cook et al. 2003). The case of surrogacy in Israel interested me particularly because Israel is one of only a handful of countries that has legalized the practice, and because it is the first in the world to pass a specific state law that endows surrogacy contracts with full legal standing. Whereas surrogacy agreements are undertaken privately in the U.S.—where the majority of such agreements take place—in Israel the state is intimately involved in every contract. Specifically, a state approval committee awards couples and surrogates the right to enter such agreements only if they meet the strict criteria of

179

the surrogacy law: both parties must be Israeli citizens, share the same religion, and cannot be related to one another. Surrogates must be single and raising at least one child, while couples must be married and be childless or have only one genetic offspring.

The strict directives of the Israeli surrogacy law have resulted in my "field" being made up of a distinct population. All of the persons partaking in surrogacy contracts in Israel to date have been Jewish, permanent residents and citizens of Israel, between the ages of 22 and 52. Moreover, all of the surrogates have been single mothers raising between one and five children of their own, and all of the couples have been heterosexually paired, mostly married couples, with long histories of female infertility, or in which the female partner was either born without a womb or lost her womb to hysterectomy.

I have been researching surrogacy since 1996, shortly after the passing of the law. After completing my M.A. thesis on this subject, I continued to research it towards my PhD. What interests me most about surrogacy are the personal experiences of those involved in the process and how Jewish-Israeli culture shapes their experiences. This interest also frames my methodology, which has followed several complimentary methodological tracks. These include narrative interviewing, textual analysis of media and legal documents concerning surrogacy in Israel, and online participation in a Hebrew-language discussion forum in which Israeli surrogates and intended mothers share their surrogacy experiences.

Unlike an anthropologist who travels to a foreign country or conducts research for a limited period on a group to whom he or she is foreign, I am a Jewish-Israeli woman and live no more than six hours away from any of my informants. Therefore, my research has not been limited by time or place. As a result, I've been "in the field" for over seven years. During this time, I have kept in close contact with many of my informants, reinterviewing them repeatedly and taking part in their lives, to the point that many of my initial informants have turned into personal friends. It is the precarious anthropologist–informant relationship and the friendship that these relationships sometimes span that I address here.

Beginnings

A little background on the general framework of the surrogacy process in Israel will be helpful at this point. Couples and surrogates find one another through ads in the newspaper, private agencies, or online surrogacy discussion boards. Looking for the appropriate partner to proceed with takes time. Some couples I met interviewed over fifty women before finding their surrogate, while surrogates usually met several couples until they felt the right "chemistry" with a particular couple. Together, all three submit forms to a government-run approval committee that decides whether they can continue with the process. Merely obtaining the committee's approval is a very trying event in itself, sometimes lasting up to a year because of the bureaucracy.

After receiving permission to proceed, the trio begins upon the equally difficult task of achieving pregnancy. The law does not allow the surrogate to become pregnant with her own egg. Therefore, the technology of in-vitro fertilization (IVF) is used to implant an embryo created from the intended father's sperm and the intended mother's egg (or an anonymous donor egg) into the surrogate's uterus. The IVF technology, with a success rate of roughly 30 percent, does not always deliver quick results: some of the surrogates, although very fertile, conceived through IVF only on the fifth or sixth try. Sometimes, after finally achieving pregnancy, the surrogate would suddenly miscarry, and the whole cycle of IVF attempts would start over again. Other times, after six IVF attempts—the limit of standard contracts—did not result in pregnancy, the surrogate and couple would part ways, and each would have to decide whether or not to look for a new partner in the process and then approach the committee for approval yet again.

The fragility of attaining a surrogate pregnancy forged a "make or break" situation in the cases I studied. Participants either gave up somewhere along the way or became intensely involved with one another. In most cases, an intimacy formed between the surrogate and intended mother. The two women would "bond" with one another during the various stages of the process, forming a type of camaraderie similar to that of soldiers in battle—a comparison that they would sometimes make themselves.

In a parallel manner, my own relationship with informants has often mimicked the surrogate–intended mother relationship. The basic issue of both relationships was the same: establishing connections and maintaining distance. Surrogates and couples sign a contract according to which they will enter into a joint project where they will work together closely for a limited period of time. The same type of limited yet involved connection is part of the anthropologist–informant relationship. Moreover, surrogates attempt to maintain emotional distance from the pregnancy and fetus-cum-child even as they forge this close camaraderie with their intended mother. They feel that this distance is crucial in enabling them to eventually relinquish the child. Similarly, the anthropologist must achieve a careful balance between establishing trust with his or her informants so as to gain an insider (or emic) perspective, and maintaining an emotional, objective (or etic) distance so as to gain theoretical insight and create a realistic representation of their case study.

I have experienced challenges in maintaining the balance between involvement and distance during my fieldwork. I have found that my close involvement in my informants' lives and caring deeply for them has become a problem as I attempt to "exit" the field—mentally and emotionally, if not physically—in order to write about it. In this way, I relate to an issue raised by Fox and Swazey (1992: 199) when they wrote about ending their fieldwork on organ transplantation in the United States. As the result of their close relationships with their informants, they found that "the process of disengaging ourselves from the field has made

The author (top center) and one of the families she accompanied through their surrogacy process. Their daughter (bottom left) was born from surrogacy in October 2002. The photo was taken at a birth celebration for my son (who I am holding in the photo) in Israel, October 2005. The couple's surrogate (not pictured) also attended the event. (© Avi Solomon.)

us feel at times as though we were getting a divorce, departing from a religious order, or forsaking comrades in crisis."

This, in turn, has made it especially challenging for me to present an objective ethnography: even if the ideal of objectivity has been tempered in contemporary anthropology by the reflexive approach, I continue to believe that one must step away from the "field" in order to gain theoretical insight. This essay is written as I try fitfully to exit the field after seven years of fieldwork.

I will represent this conflict within the text by using two different voices—the distant, academic writing style that urges me to maintain objectivity and a theoretical, analytical perspective and the subjective, emotional voice of my very personal feelings during this research. I have found that writing a divided text is a good strategy for keeping this conflict integral to my representation of the data as well as for keeping my overinvolvement in the field from coloring my data. These subjective notations, which I have recorded throughout my fieldwork, are interspersed within the text as block quotations.

> I feel unable to break away from the women that I have met through this project, and
> see it my duty to remain an active part of their lives. I feel the need to prove to them that

I don't only think of them as research subjects and to show them that I care about them because of who they are. This is not the first time that I have conducted fieldwork, and yet it is the first time that I feel so personally involved in the lives of my informants. Here, I am constantly being pulled back toward the field—not wanting to let go, and not wanting to let the field let go of me.

In many ways, my life has come to simulate the field. The women tell me of how quickly they become involved in one another's lives, become partners in the surrogacy process, partners in the pregnancy. I too have experienced the feeling of entering into a reciprocal relationship where each person gives the "Other" a part of their Self. These women share their stories with me and I share with them my concern. They give me their stories, and I give them my caring. My partnership with these women accompanies my retelling of their partnership.

Yael

Although I became involved with the stories of surrogates and intended mothers alike, my understanding of the intricacies of these relationships first developed through my involvement with my first informant, Yael, an intended mother whose only son was born by a surrogate, Tali, in 1999. Yael's story, and my involvement in it, serves as a stage for discussing the issue of becoming emotionally involved in the "field," an issue that has continued to preoccupy me over the years of my research. In this case, I refer to the "field" not as a physical site but as an assortment of people, places, and sources that Marcus (1995) describes as "multi-sited ethnography." Thus, when I talk about the field, I am talking about an imaginary community that I, the anthropologist, have imagined (Kahn 2000).

February 1998

I think of my first informant, Yael. She has seeped into my conscience more than any of the other women. I have known Yael for a relatively short time. Still, I feel so intertwined with her fate. I do not meet her regularly, and yet I feel as though I have become part of her life, part of her experience, as though I too hold a personal stake in her happiness.

I met Yael for our first interview in a coffee shop on a Sunday afternoon. After telling me about the long process she had been through finding a surrogate, she told me about the pregnancy in a whisper. A whisper that said "if I say it out loud, it might disappear." Leaning forward, I immediately became a partner in her conspiracy. I too whispered each time that I mentioned the pregnancy.

That first interview began with one simple question. Tell me your story from wherever it begins. Instinctively, she began the day that the army doctor had told her that she had been born without a womb. Imagine, she said, finding out that you could never have children when you were only eighteen years old.

That had been the beginning, her most important day, the day that her story began. Each of her days since then became devoted to having a child. "I had planned on going to university," she told me, "but somehow my life became so wrapped up in having a child that the years just slipped by." And it wasn't easy, she repeated twice, even though she spoke with a smile. It wasn't easy at all.

Thinking about adoption, choosing surrogacy. The ups and downs of finding the "right" surrogate. One asking for too much money, one too young. The worry, the wait. The changes that she and her husband had to incorporate into their lives. "It was strange," she said, "giving up part of our personal life as a couple and letting a third person in." Learning to stop living as two, beginning to live life as three. "In some ways," I said, "it was preparation for parenthood." "But different," she replied.

Tali was the fourth surrogate with whom they had approached the committee. She recalls the day they met and the day that the answer to the pregnancy test returned positive. That was a joyful day. "We didn't know then what lay ahead," Yael said. "Now I know not to get excited at least until the first months have passed." Tali miscarried that first time five months into the pregnancy.

The emotional buildup of Yael's narrative curved my posture forward and twisted my emotions up and around and back again along with hers. We cried together at her memories of the most desperate moments and laughed at the little ironies of her life. Ten years older than me, and at a different point in life, I still left Yael that day feeling that I had made a friend. I too had a stake in her happiness. I understood how someone could say that she would do everything she could to give this woman a child.

Nobody tells you about this part when you go out into the field. You may find yourself immersed, embroiled, even drowning in the intricacies of other people's lives. That while surrogates are able to cut themselves off from their wombs so that they won't bond with the child that they carry inside, this anthropologist found herself bonding with the field, carrying it on my shoulders, dreaming about it at night. I am pregnant with the field and as it grows within my stomach I feel it weighing down my heart.

Fears

Having babies in Jewish-Israeli culture is a delicate matter. Most people don't announce their pregnancies until the second trimester and don't prepare the baby's room until after the birth, for fear of the "evil eye." The fear of a pregnancy not resulting in a live baby seems to pervade the women's stories that Tsipy Ivry (2004) has collected in her research on pregnancy in Israel. When it comes to assisted reproduction, where women experience repeated reproductive failures, these fears become even more acute. When I approach a woman to interview her about her surrogacy experience, I am often told that she would be happy to comply, but only after the birth, for fear that something may go wrong if she even speaks to the baby's existence before it is born. This fear dominates the field and has become a key for me in understanding its underpinnings. The field speaks loudly with its silences.

March 1998

A friend of mine stops me in the hall. We haven't seen each other in a long time. We begin to tell one another what we have been doing since we last met, and she asks me about my dissertation. Then we play out a scene that it seems I have been through a thousand times. "Surrogacy," I tell her. "I am writing my thesis on surrogate motherhood."

Immediately she reacts. "Who will talk to you about that? No one will let you inter-view them." Pausing a minute, she takes on a thoughtful look. "Actually," she tells me, "I know someone whose sister has hired a surrogate to carry her baby." My response to such remarks has become one of instinct: could she introduce us? "You must know how much easier it is to establish trust with an informant when you are introduced by a friend," I explain. Refusing, she relates, "Of course not, people say it is bad luck to talk about babies before they are born." Anyway, she adds, "I don't want to be responsible for stirring anything up in case something goes wrong."

Thinking about this, I wonder whether my talking to these women about such deli-cate matters as a surrogate pregnancy could bring bad luck. Once again I feel the responsibility for the outcome of these women's pregnancies lying on my shoulders. Because it is me who has asked them to say aloud what they otherwise only whisper or think to themselves. It is me who asks them to tell me their stories and thus make them concrete, objectified truths, instead of just quiet half-imagined notions that one can observe from a distance, only touch upon sparingly, and make every effort not to disturb.

Involvement

The problem of "bonding with the field" became a central issue during my fieldwork. Trying to understand why the "field" has had such an effect on me led me to ask: is this par-ticular to the issue of surrogacy? It is hard to say. In Helena Ragone's (1994) comprehensive ethnography of surrogacy in the United States, I found no clues that she experienced such confusion between herself and her informants. Could it have something to do with research-ing reproduction? Anne Oakley (1979: 4) writes that there were times during the course of her research into women's childbirth experiences in the United States that she began to con-fuse her roles as researcher, pregnant woman, mother, feminist, and participant observer. She claims that "academic research projects bear an intimate relationship to the researcher's life, however 'scientific' a sociologist tries to be" (ibid.).

Could such emotional involvement be the product of conducting research on sensitive topics related to life and death? At one point during my fieldwork, I met another student in my department who shared her difficulty conducting research on HIV-positive migrant workers in Tel Aviv. I asked her how she dealt with the deaths of her informants. She hoped that her research would end before she had to face the first death.

April 1998

After the last miscarriage, another IVF embryo transfer was attempted, and Yael's surrogate, Tali, became pregnant with twins. It is now three months into the pregnancy and the doctors are keeping a close watch to prevent another loss. I feel apprehensive calling Yael to find out how the pregnancy is progressing. On the one hand, her experience is data for my study. On the other hand, this is her life and I identify with her hopes that this time it will be okay. For days I put off calling her, but I think about her and her situation all the time. I think that she knows that I am thinking about her. I go to the phone and cannot call. I make myself feel better by telling myself she understands.

A few days later I decide to attempt phoning her again. I sit in front of the phone for a few hours. Should I or shouldn't I. What if. . . . What if? I call her. "What's new?" I ask tentatively. "Is there anything I should know?" "Elly," she responds, "what an opening line!" "Sorry," I tell her. "It's just that I worry." "We're taking it day by day," she replies and tries to make light of it. I knock on the table three times for good luck, my heart falling to the bottom of my stomach. I think how short a time I have known Yael and how involved I feel in her fate. Like I am part of her experience. How afraid I am that something might go wrong. My words become an echo of the rhetoric of the field. "I won't ask any more," I tell her. "It could arouse the evil eye." "You believe in the evil eye?" she asks, laughing. "You're Ashkenazi (of Eastern-European descent) with blonde hair!" "Of course," I respond, and anyway, the blonde hair isn't real.

August 1998

After I return from spending the summer abroad, I call Shoshana, a friend of Yael's. "Have you spoken to Yael lately?" I ask her, hoping silently that her answer will not bring bad news. "Not since she lost the twins," Shoshana answers. "I told her not to call me until she has a live baby in her hands. I can't take the bad news anymore."

My heart drops. She lost the twins. I remember the day that she showed me the ultrasound photos that documented their existence. She passed the small square ultrasound photos of white fuzz on black over to me across the table. I touched them. Three photos, none of them clear. "Do you see them?" she asked me. I didn't see a thing. "Wow," I answered, pretending I did. "I try not to look at them too much," she told me. "I don't want to believe it yet. Just in case."

I passed them back across the table to her and she retrieved them with a careful hand. "Are you going to frame those?" I ask her, "or put them in an album?" "No," she answers, "I keep them here," and puts them back into her bag, in an envelope. I watch the way she inserts the photos into their package. It is like she is putting them to sleep. She holds the envelope gently but firmly, securely tucking the photos into her bag. Her babies. They are with her all the time. In her bag. It occurs to me that she is almost really pregnant. Her babies, in a bag, that falls near her stomach. Those little bleeps on the ultrasound monitor. Now they are dead.

I think about what Shoshana said. I wonder how she can stand the tension, how she can wait and not know. She told Yael not to call her until there is a live baby. What if a live baby never comes? What if. . . . What if? I feel the fear and expectations of the wait. I am pregnant with Yael. Yael is pregnant with her surrogate. I wonder if all of Yael's friends are pregnant with her too. In spirit. In heart. In wait.

Connections

Still looking for answers as to what makes this field so potently involving, I ask: is this not the effect of doing research on difficult topics, but instead something that has to do with being a member of the same culture one studies? Is this an effect of doing ethnography at home, in general, or is it particular to doing ethnography in Israel—such a small country—where collectivism is still so strong? The research of both of my advisors, Meira Weiss and Eyal Ben-Ari, provide me with some answers. Writing about his fieldwork among the soldiers of the military reserve group he served with for many years, Ben-Ari (1998) notes that he had to go all the way to Singapore to detach enough from the field in order to write his ethnography.

Weiss' (1994; 2002) work also focuses on different sites of Israeli culture that are fraught with emotional repercussions, such as the grieving families of fallen soldiers, parents who abandon their appearance-impaired babies in the hospital, and the daily workings of the national forensic institute that identifies and pieces together the body parts of soldiers and citizens killed in terrorist attacks. In a reflexive article on her fieldwork experiences, she considers the country itself as her field and imagines the country entering her veins and watching her. She finds this field inescapable even when she travels to Berkeley, California, for a sabbatical.

September 1998

Meira writes that she cannot find a sealed room to cut her off from her country, her field. I too feel eaten up by the field. How can I feel so involved with the life of a woman I hardly know? I feel tension. Pressure. I begin to add a prayer for Yael into my nightly prayers. I wonder how it got this way that I too feel so part of a life not my own. And yes my own. Why I share Yael's fate. Why my hand shakes.

I call Yael on Rosh Hashanah, the Jewish New Year. I feel responsible. Maybe if she hadn't shown me the photos. Maybe if she hadn't told me about them. Interviewing her and recording her voice talking about them may have made them more real for her, may have given her false hopes, may have brought bad luck. Maybe I had something to do with her babies being dead.

"Hi Yael. Happy New Year." "Elly!" she recognizes my voice, "How are you?" "I heard from Shoshana," I tell her, "I was afraid to call, if you are wondering why you haven't heard from me." "Day by day," she repeats. "We take each day as it comes." "We won't talk about it," I say. "So how are you?" We exchange a few items of small talk, but the real conversation is exchanged underneath the surface of our words. It is the loud silence behind the empty words that I hear most clearly. She feels it as strongly as I do. I can tell because there is a tension on the line that is uncomfortable and painful. "My heart is with yours," I tell her, and I mean every word. She replies with a simple but fully aware, "I know." She does not tell me that Tali is already pregnant again. Two weeks later she calls me to tell me the news. They just had an ultrasound. It's a boy.

October 1998

I call Yael every week and a half. I have it down to a science. I call, ask how things are in general, and she signals back that things are going smoothly. But sometimes they aren't. Sometimes Tali is in the hospital and then the worries are even more real. There are complications in the fourth month and another pregnancy is almost lost.

"The baby wants to come out," Yael tells me. "Of course he does," I answer, "his parents have been waiting for him for over ten years. He wants to meet you already!" We exchange blessings and words that aren't meant for each other but for G-d. It doesn't seem strange to me until I hang up that we have just danced around each other with our words, never touching real ground, for fear of it ruining something. We speak in code.

Disconnections

One thing that I have found in my interviews with surrogates is their ability to disconnect emotionally from the baby growing inside of them. Part of my research focuses on ways in which surrogates manage to be pregnant while eluding the persuasive, hegemonic cultural script that dictates that a "good mother" will naturally "bond" with her baby while she is pregnant. In my analysis of the personal narratives of Israeli surrogates, I have explored the way that the women strategically maneuver around this cultural assumption that women necessarily *do* "bond." I focus on how they maintain a conforming identity as dutiful, normative mothers to their own children while erasing any maternal connotations from their relationship with the baby they birth for the couple (Teman 2001). At some point, I wonder whether my fascination with the surrogate's disconnection strategies is in response to my own inability to disconnect from the field. Other times, I see the surrogates' distancing practices as a tool that could help me achieve objective distance.

Early December 1998

I wonder how surrogates are able to disconnect emotionally from the baby growing inside them during the pregnancy. Connect, but disconnect. Bond, but unbond. Be in their bodies and out. I wonder if I can ever disconnect. I need to get out of the field already. I have been there long enough. Stop interviewing. Unbond. But I can't. I am like a surrogate, both in and out of the body/field, and surrounded by questions. In many ways, anthropology itself serves as a variation on surrogacy. Because you get into a relationship with the field for a specific purpose, and you know that it is temporary, that eventually it will end. You try not to get too attached. You try to prepare for your exit when your nine months are up.

December. I call Yael. She tells me that the pregnancy has become complicated. Tali has decided to stop working and stay home. They ran to the hospital the other night because Tali was bleeding heavily. "You cannot imagine what I saw that night," she tells me. "Pieces of congealed blood falling out of her onto the floor. We almost lost the baby. And of all nights, when Miki (her husband) was in reserve duty and had taken the car. We got to the hospital in a taxi. Just in time." She had taken out her book of Psalms and prayed and prayed, she said. This time it had to work. "And to think, just that night, Tali had called me with a craving for a certain type of soup that Moroccans make." "Is she Moroccan?" I asked. "No, I'm Moroccan," she answered. "She is Iraqi. And I didn't know how to make that kind of soup. So I called my mother, and she made her a pot. I said, 'Mom, don't you mind?' and she said, 'No, Yael, it is just like I am making it for you. I *am* making it for you. It is your son who is making her have the cravings.'"

A son who already has cravings for Moroccan soup, I think. A son like that is already real. A son like that knows who his parents are. He has a personality, an identity. All I can do is hope for them. I hang up with Yael and also say a prayer.

Merging

Surrogates' distancing techniques take place alongside and in conjunction with a type of "merging" that occurs between the two women. This merging is the result of identity constructing practices undertaken by the women that are aimed at designating the intended mother as the only mother of the child. Surrogates actively try to pave the intended mother's entrance into her new identity by encouraging her to take part in all of the medical checkups and by communicating any bodily symptoms of pregnancy to her throughout. As the pregnancy continues into its later months, many of the intended mothers begin to actually "feel pregnant," some of them even showing physical manifestations in and upon their own bodies of pseudo-pregnancy, such as gaining significant amounts of weight during the surrogate's pregnancy.

As the intended mother and surrogate begin to increasingly realize the interconnected purpose of their bodies in constructing the intended mother's maternal identity, they begin to describe themselves as "one body" that is "pregnant together." Their narratives of "two who are one" dominate the latter part of the pregnancy until after the birth, when they are once again constituted by one another as separate individuals. During my fieldwork, I have attempted to look into the way that the doctors and medical personnel who attend to the two women during the pregnancy and childbirth support the "shared body" construction by treating them as a combined patient up until the birth, and then begin to relate to them individually after the birth so that only one "real" mother emerges in the end. As I relay below, I too found myself supporting their performance of the shared body:

Late December 1998

I think of the women's rhetoric of "we." I too adopt the vocabulary of the field—this "field" that is their lives. I reread my fieldnotes, look back at revision upon revision of each written draft of this thesis and realize the meaning of my own choice of words and punctuation. "Yael's surrogate," I have written in one section, "is Tali, and their pregnancy is in the sixth month." Their pregnancy, her surrogate, and my desire for their partnership to succeed.

I reread my words that suddenly seem to have taken on a life of their own: my words have intention. How innocent these words that empathize so fully with the field, as I perceived it during their recording, not distinguishing between the different players involved and the interests at stake. My words that describe "surrogates" and intended "mothers." Only now do I realize the "mother" noun has been curiously removed from sentences where I write about the "surrogate" and attached to every reference that I make to the intended "mother." My words that empathize so fully with the reproductive cause and urge the two women to belong to one another. The characters that run across these sheets of paper want Tali's pregnancy to be Yael's and for everyone involved to be happy in the end.

I look at the papers strewn across my desk and circle all of the apostrophes that I have used with a red pen. The possessive pronouns that fill each page silently shift the responsibility for the surrogate pregnancy into the intended mother's hands and erase the surrogate's power over her own pregnant outcome. My language encourages this woman to take over another woman's body. And as I look at my words through the prism of time elapsed, I see myself, the anthropologist, blind to the dynamics of power involved and blind to the question of whose interests I silently promote. And I wonder whose voice has become my voice, and attempt to decipher for whom the red circles that decorate my pages are rooting for down the road, forgetting the element of competition involved.

Blindness

How does one manage to maintain the precarious balance between emotional involvement and analytical distance? Is acknowledging the issue enough? Is keeping textual divisions between the voice of the emotional participant and the objective observer sufficient? Or does overidentification with one's informants cause one to create a biased representation of the data? I have found that as I increasingly empathize with my informants, I simultaneously struggle to critique the practice of surrogacy and the way that the Israeli case serves as a prime example of the way that states control women's bodies. I have tried not to overlook the darker aspects of what surrogacy in Israel is: an unmarried woman signs a contract to be paid for leasing out her body to a married couple for nine months in exchange for money. There are power struggles involved, both muted and explicit, that my research reveals, such as a surrogate who was pressured by the couple's doctor into having a caesarian section for the good of the baby, even though she was against it. Most of the stories are good stories, but one surrogate I interviewed told me an absolute horror story about her experience. Her couple convinced her to move in with them during the pregnancy and monitored her every move. She told me how she felt like a prisoner in her own body. She finally threatened to harm herself if they refused to agree to an early caesarian section. It was the only way she saw to escape from her occupied body.

Early January 1999

I feel torn between representing all facets of each story and the picture that I want to paint. I don't want to write anything against surrogacy. For despite the critical nature of all of the articles that I have read on women's wombs in service of the nation-state, on motherhood as a culturally constructed practice, and on the controlled nature of repro-duction in Israel, I cannot release my own empathy with the intended mothers who have tried for so many years to have a child. I want each Yael in Israel to be able to have the baby they desire. I want anyone who wants a surrogate baby to be able to have one and for the process to become less complicated, not more. Surrogacy is a miracle. How can a miracle subordinate anyone? As the different shades of the picture become clearer, I try failingly to filter out only the bright rays of light. To be blind. But that is not good anthropology.

Afraid of what I might find, I spit out the taste of bitterness when it infiltrates my data. The stench of one woman sacrificing her body for another could ruin the miracle waiting for Yael. Could ruin the miracle I have been waiting for with her. For her.

Giving Birth

A final word is in order to conclude upon how I have tried to straddle the precarious balance of involvement versus distance in the anthropologist-informant relationship. First, I have acknowledged the challenge so as not to lose the analytical perspective that enables me to achieve the most accurate representation of my data. Then, I have chosen a writing style that allows me to represent the conflicting voices that inform my perspective and to keep them separate within the text. Next, I have tried to look beyond my identification with my informants so as not to overlook data that conflicts with the portrayal that I would ideally like to create. Finally, it is with these tools that I try to achieve the desired distance necessary to write, even as I struggle to exit the field completely.

Late January 1999

I come home at nine o'clock at night and listen to my messages on the answering machine. The third message takes a minute to register. I press the button and listen to it again. Yes, that is what she said. It is Yael. "Hi Elly. Our son was born an hour ago at eleven o'clock this morning. We are here at the hospital. Tali is feeling well. Bye." I look at my roommate. "One of my informants had a baby boy," I say in an excited voice and begin to jump up and down. I dance around the room. My roommate smiles and I sing a little tune. How can I be critical of a procedure that has just given life to a baby boy whose parents have wanted him so much for so many years?

I call Yael the next morning from my parents' home, where I am visiting. We scream together and laugh and talk in high-pitched tones. My mother walks by me while I'm on the phone and asks me what happened and why I am squeaking. "My friend gave birth," I tell her. "Your friend," she answers, "or one of your wombs-for-rent."

Both, I guess. Informant and friend. Me and you. Me as you. Me with you. The baby was born premature, two months early, and will be in the incubator for at least a month. He is having trouble breathing. I ask her if they have named him and she tells me his name. I think of a gift to give the baby at his circumcision ceremony. I want to give him a hand painted birth certificate by a friend of mine who is an artist. I order the certificate but ask him to hold on to it and not yet fill in the name. Wait. Wait until he gets out of the incubator.

I realize that I have become permeable with the field. I have let my informants seep into my life. And I have encouraged the blur. Lived it like them. Let the borders between us become unclear. Anthropologist. Friend. Me. You. I feel like I have bonded with the field. Let the "other's" experience enter into my own.

At first, I wanted to call my dissertation "Sharing Bodies, Sharing Lives" and talk about the disintegration of the whole, maternal body. But although these bodies are enacting a new type of embodiment, that doesn't mean they are disintegrating. Instead, I see it as two bodies collaborating, actually being strengthened. Puzzle pieces fitting together. Each body helping the other. Each life becoming part of the next. And my life too being . . . their life. Their life becoming part of my life. Because creating life is what surrogacy is all about.

A final word must be dedicated to what I have learned about doing fieldwork from studying surrogacy. I have learned as much about fieldwork as I have about surrogacy by examining the way that, as an anthropologist, my relationship to my informants has mirrored my informants' relationships with one another. From the surrogates' careful juggling of boundaries between attachment to the intended mother and detachment from the fetus, I learned how important it is to maintain a balance between identification and distance with the research population—a major challenge in being an anthropologist. From my immersion in the women's lives, I learned a lot about the development of relationships during the surrogacy process, and the fears, the waiting, the hopes and the disappointments. Most of all, sharing their stories with me made me realize my own responsibility as an anthropologist in retelling their stories, and to appreciate further the commitment that the anthropologist has in undertaking such a task.

References

Ben-Ari, Eyal. 1998. *Mastering Soldiers: Conflict, Emotions and the Enemy in an Israeli Military Unit.* Oxford: Berghahn Books.

Cook, Rachel, Shelley Day Day Sclater, and Felicity Kaganas. 2003. Introduction. In *Surrogate Motherhood: International Perspectives*, ed. R. Cook, S. D. Day Sclater, and F. Kaganas, 1–22. Oxford: Hart Publishing.

Fox, Renee C., and Judith P. Swazey. 1992. *Spare Parts: Organ Replacement in American Society.* Oxford and New York: Oxford University Press.

Ivry, Tsipy. 2004. *Pregnancy in Japan and in Israel: A Comparative Study,* PhD. diss., Hebrew University of Jerusalem.

Kahn, Susan Martha. 2000. *Reproducing Jews: A Cultural Account of Assisted Conception in Israel.* Durham: Duke University Press.

Marcus, George E. 1995. Ethnography in/of the world system: The emergence of multi-sited ethnography. *Annual Review of Anthropology* 24: 95–117.

Oakley, Ann. 1979. *Becoming a Mother.* Martin Robertson & Company Ltd.

Rae, Scott B. 1994. *The Ethics of Commercial Surrogate Motherhood: Brave New Families?* Westport: Praeger.

Ragone, Helena. 1994. *Surrogate Motherhood: Conception in the Heart.* Boulder: Westview Press.

Teman, Elly. 2001. Technological fragmentation and women's empowerment: Surrogate motherhood in Israel. *Women's Studies Quarterly* 24: 11–34.

van Niekerk, A., and L. van Zyl. 1995. The ethics of surrogacy: Women's reproductive labour. *Journal of Medical Ethics* 21: 345–49.

Weiss, Meira. 1994. *Conditional Love: Parents' Attitudes toward Handicapped Children.* Westport, CT: Bergin & Garvey.

———. 2002. *The Chosen Body: The Politics of the Body in Israeli Society.* Stanford, CA: Stanford University Press.

Acknowledgements

I would like to thank David Hoffman, Andrew Gardner, David B. Sherman, Eyal Ben-Ari, Meira Weiss, Tamar Elor, Adi Kuntzman, Lauren Erdreich, Danny Kaplan, Tsipy Ivry, and Juliana Ochs for their comments on earlier drafts of this paper.

Erasing SARS:
Outbreak Reflections on the Ethnographic Process

Megan Tracy
University of Pennsylvania

The essay that follows relies on excerpts from e-mails, letters, and a journal that I have kept alongside formal field notes taken during fieldwork in the People's Republic of China (PRC) during 2003. These sources, where I often spoke more candidly about the frustration of coping with the unforeseen appearance of the SARS (Severe Acute Respiratory Syndrome) epidemic, add richness to what I experienced during this period. I have added commentary written while in the field that seeks to capture this unpredictable field experience—how it changed my field research and continues six months later to have a significant impact. Now in the final stage, what seems peculiar to me is that my research project, like everyday life here, has largely returned to normal despite the widespread disruption brought about by SARS. Leaving aside for the moment its effects on Chinese society and focusing just on its impact on my own research, the virus prevented me from following my project as originally planned and has led to a constant reshifting and refocusing of my project. Coping with these changes and moving forward with a "new" project has become the central dilemma of my last few months in the PRC.

My first trip to the PRC occurred during another period of social upheaval in the spring of 1989—a few weeks before the Chinese government sent troops to dispel public protests, leaving a disputed number of people dead or injured. I would later return to China as a Peace Corps volunteer, a teacher, a student, and a researcher—all valuable experiences that supplied me with practical knowledge of China's recent rapid economic and social changes and their day-to-day effects on my friends and colleagues. The initial journey, however, provided a brief window into the rupturing of daily life in China's capital city, Beijing. While quite different in nature, the events of 1989 and 2003 possess some analogous aspects, though I was slow to consider what, if any, similarities there might be between them. Another anthropology graduate student who had also been in the PRC for both events made this connection in one of our numerous phone conversations in which we compared life and fieldwork concerns. The major interruptions to daily life in the city strike me as somewhat similar, as does the way which each event seized a complete and uncompromising hold on the public's attention and imagination. One key distinction, however, between SARS and the events of 1989 is that SARS (or, rather, concerns and anxiety about it) was publicly discussed and circulated through the efforts of the government, the media, *and* rumors and gossip. In contrast, the events of 1989, as I understand them, were available to the public mostly through personal networks. The "publicness" of SARS (once the government in Beijing acknowledged there was a problem) created a situation where it was impossible to ignore the very public responses of the government and its citizens. In advertisements, on billboards, on community notice boards, in restaurants, and in shops, all of us were reminded that the country was in a state of emergency.

A municipal-sponsored billboard posted in Haidian District, Beijing, May 2005. (© Megan Tracy.)

Uncertainty in the Early Days of the Epidemic

When I arrived in Beijing in January of 2003, there was little news of a strange pneumonia that had broken out in the southern part of the country. The greatest problem that I faced was how best to go about implementing a "studying up" project that was to take place partly in Beijing and partly in China's Inner Mongolian Autonomous Region (IMAR) to the north. My field research was to focus on a state-generated environmentalism in the PRC that sought to address concerns and anxieties over the environment and people's well-being through the promotion of environmentally oriented policies and programs and the classification of certain areas as being more appropriate for sustainable development. I based my research approach on Gusterson's (1997) idea of "polymorphous engagement," a term that refers to a focus on dispersed sites, both real and virtual, and the collection of disparate data. This strategy seemed appropriate for tracing the linkages between government institutions, corporations, the public, and the media that I was hoping to pursue. Tracking these connections is part of a broader call within anthropology to focus on the organizations, institutions, and processes that affect our lives in addition to small-scale, localized studies that were traditionally the discipline's domain (Nader 1972). In Nader's words, anthropologists need "to study up"—that is "to study the colonizers rather than the colonized, the culture of power rather than the culture of the powerless, the culture of affluence rather than poverty" (289). This is not to say that we should only study the powerful, but that anthropologists should think of the entire social field and study the powerful as well as the powerless.

In his follow-up piece two decades later, Gusterson observed that the continued rarity of such studies was due to the inappropriateness of anthropology's classic methodology of participant observation in situations where, for example, access to a site (or even the lack of a tangible site) could be an issue (1997). What I did not know when formulating my research was that when SARS hit Beijing the traditional anthropological methods we are taught to rely on became not only inappropriate but also impossible to use; we (my husband and I) would come to rely on other sources of information during that period. On the one hand, we had the quintessential "front seat" participation experience during SARS in the sense that there was no palpable difference between our experiences and those of my colleagues, friends, and informants. On the other hand, with normal life and routines stopping and with people shuttering themselves behind gates and doors, the pieces of everyday life that we had been focusing on were no longer there to observe. The restrictions and virtual shutdown of the city affected us as much as it did others. The premium placed on seclusion during the SARS epidemic (see below), however, still rendered it impossible to participate in or observe day-to-day life with others.

April 5, 2003 (e-mail)

Try not to worry too much about SARS. Guess you guys saw that they finally gave a news conference here. :) [My husband] heard a rumor that one of the students on our campus has it—exactly what the government here was trying to prevent. The recovery rate is decent so we're not modifying our lives that much. No public buses . . . and the avoidance of really crowded spaces. We check in at WHO's [World Health Organization's] website every so often. If we get sick, it's off to the clinic right away. I guess that's the key element in recovering. Most of the cases either didn't report to the hospital (or were sent home) or had complicating factors (other diseases). I wouldn't avoid coming here [because] of it unless the numbers get really high (and how would we know that anyway).

April 7, 2003 (e-mail)

We are okay. Really! Since the government acknowledged "feidianxing feiyan" [SARS], at least the people at large seem more aware of it. . . . [A friend] warned me to be careful last night. Twenty or so reported cases in Beijing. Probably in the 100s. Only 5% of the people die from it and they usually have some other disease. We're really not that concerned. Honestly. We check WHO's website every day for updates. Who trusts what the government here says???? We aren't taking buses or the subway or eating in small, closed restaurants.

At the beginning of the first week in April in a government guesthouse in rural Inner Mongolia, the news on the TV looked much less serious. Neither I nor the people (Chinese scientists and environmentalists) I was traveling with were concerned, and instead, they seemed confident that the virus would remain in southern China. When I returned to Beijing at the end of the week, as the e-mails I sent around that time indicate, that feeling was already beginning to change. Just four days later, we had begun to question the reliability of our information and assess the reactions of the people around us. In retrospect, it seems impossible that we didn't realize that something "bigger" was going on. A distinct lack of information and distrust of what information was available made it difficult for us to see. International news sources, especially in the early weeks of the outbreak, provided little additional help as WHO, the CDC (Centers for Disease Control) and other health agencies struggled to contend with what would be the emergence of a new virus. The idea that SARS might have a greater impact on our lives and on my research was only beginning to become apparent.

April 9, 2003 (e-mail)

We are watching the SARS news pretty carefully. They say that there are only 19 cases in our city of 13 million. Doesn't seem quite possible, does it? But what can we really do? Getting on a plane out of China seems a more likely way of contracting the disease. We are taking some but not excessive precautions. It's finally on the front pages here. I see some people wearing masks but not many. People seem to be going about their normal lives, which is what we are doing. It hasn't curtailed our lives that much yet. If it continues, I guess we'll really stop going out except to work and such.

April 12, 2003 (e-mail)

I think this week will probably be the worst week in terms of the SARS issue. People here are nervous but it is more because they suspect the government is holding back information about the situation in the north. They've been surprisingly upfront about the south but that has only caused more concern about the lack of transparency in the north. Of course, until this week, the vast majority of the population had little information about SARS. They've been broadcasting information all week—even airing the question/answer sessions with the media in their entirety. . . . So I think the agitation felt elsewhere is really only beginning here. Lots of rumors about people having it and how to prevent it . . . we don't really see any need to leave and are taking the precautions suggested by the WHO. . . . I might delay a research trip, partially because of SARS and partially because of the difficulties traveling due to the upcoming holiday.

Rumors were flying both in day-to-day conversations in the early days of the epidemic and in what would become the preferred method of sending information—text messaging on mobile phones. I began receiving text messages from friends about what hospitals to avoid (those already perceived as epicenters of disease transmission), what face masks were the best to purchase and where they could be found, when to stay indoors to avoid "dangerous" air quality from the supposed transfer of SARS patients from one hospital to another, and so on. Faculty at my host university encouraged me to turn to Internet chat rooms as another site where information about SARS was being disseminated, discussed, and critiqued. The Internet itself had become a vital resource and connection to the "outside world" so that we could feel we had a handle on information about SARS. Sources, usually evaluated somewhere in the chain of communication as being "better," were passed along among the remaining foreign community in Beijing. Often, I was asked to "report back" to Chinese friends and colleagues what we were reading in international news sources and hearing from this expatriate community. In what were generally phone conversations, my friends and colleagues would then compare differences in what the local news was reporting as opposed to the international news. They also took an interest in what was being said internationally about China's responsibility for the control and dissemination of the virus.

As far as our own personal health was concerned, we attempted to evaluate what was true, what wasn't, and where grains of truth might lie in the entire set of rumors. Were they really spraying chemicals from airplanes over the city at night as one text message (received from several sources) described? As a researcher, I had to reconcile the facelessness of many of these sources with anthropology's penchant for richer data based upon the nuances of intimate and personal interactions. I quickly came to recognize that evaluations of the reliability of information were made in the transmission of information from person to person. This recognition highlighted for me the manner in which we anthropologists always evaluate our data in some respect: who is the source, how reliable are they, is one source a "better" source than another, who is telling the truth, is it is so simple to divide things into true and not, does it matter in the end or is it the act of telling more important than its veracity, and so forth.

Rethinking Methods during SARS

The ratcheting up of the public's unease crept into my e-mails as well as a growing realization that there would be an repercussions for my own research.

April 20, 2003 (journal)

SARS panic is growing here. They shut our university down yesterday (or so I've heard unofficially). We're not concerned but the residents of Beijing are quite nervous. It's sort of "wait and see" to see how much of this will impact my core fieldwork.

Same day (e-mail)

My guess is that the news out of Beijing is going to get worse for the next few days. There seems to be a bit of mass panic going on in the city. We still feel as safe as ever. Just in case you read the story in the *Washington Post*, yes, there is a confirmed case of SARS in our university with another case likely to turn out to be SARS. [I] have talked to my good friend that works in the clinic here just to make sure. She seems to feel much the same way that we do—take precautions, stay out of crowded areas and relax. :) On the plus side, I've never ever seen Beijing this clean. They are distributing disinfectant all over the campus and university . . . on the downside, lots of widespread rumors and misinformation. [People in general] don't seem to have much basic health knowledge (about how viruses work and such).

April 22, 2003 (journal)

SARS is in FULL swing here. It seems as if the entire population of Beijing (no small number) is panicked. The rumors are flying and people are leaving the city, despite warnings against traveling. [I] came very close to yelling at friends of mine who went back to a relatively remote area. . . . [I received] a text message yesterday reassuring me that they tried very hard not to take the virus back with them. . . . People seem to think of SARS as an entity here—something that you can see and touch. We get warnings about not going to this and that place because SARS is there and [we] joke about "SARS" hanging out in the local department store, chatting with people. Most of the population lacks a real understanding of basic health/disease issues. If only I was a medical anthropologist! Home remedies and other cures abound. I get lectured at least once a day for not taking Chinese medicine. . . . The government has started broadcasting very detailed instructions with regards to prevention and such. I can only imagine what it is like in the rural areas. I have indefinitely postponed my next trip to Inner Mongolia. The Swedish embassy sent out a message that the situation in Inner Mongolia and another province is quite serious. Beyond my trip, however, I didn't think that it would really impact my research that much until the last few days. . . . I hadn't had that experience [of postponing meetings] until yesterday when I went to get some materials from an extension of UNESCO and the guy lectured me about coming to get them instead of having them send them. And then when I asked about getting together to talk about their project, he said, "just call." . . . I think SARS will factor into my project in more ways than I had anticipated. It's tempting to shift gears (and I may have no choice in the end) and study SARS but to be honest, I'm already sick of hearing and talking about it. . . . The university that I am at has had 2 confirmed cases (1 teacher and 1 grad student) but for the moment, they are still holding classes. I've been told . . . that this is just the official position. . . .

By mid- to late April, it became evident that SARS would indeed have a significant impact on the city and, by extension, my research. As the journal entry above indicates, access to buildings *and* people became increasingly difficult. The meaning behind the "just call" comment of the person above was that it would be better to call rather than meet face to face. After asking about the situation at the university with which I am associated and receiving a reply that it had several suspected cases, the man referred to in the e-mail above practically ran back inside the building. Although by this time the university's campus was closed, our own movements on and off the teachers' compound where we lived were not restricted, though I was now required to produce a university ID upon entry to the main campus. Several days later, the situation would become more intense and we would have to secure IDs that would allow us to enter and *leave* the campus as well as to enter our own compound. We were now forced to seriously contemplate our fears of being completely restricted to the compound. Though I am not sure how likely closure of the compound really was, I was nonetheless forced to consider what kinds of data I could collect under these kinds of constraints. Would the data be worth the restrictions and my husband's peace of mind, and should I leave and return at a more opportune time? Moreover, I was struggling with my own reluctance to shelve my original project, even for the time being, for at the time I felt I had to make a choice between one project and a "new" project based on the current situation. After several discussions, my husband and I made the decision to stick it out. Helpful, practical replies from department faculty back in the U.S. to a troubled e-mail or two suggested several strategies for continued research.

April 23, 2003 (e-mail)

Everyone is gearing up for the "explosion period" that is supposed to take place in the next few days. People are running scared. We're up to about 75% of people wearing masks and people look at us like we are crazy not to. . . . People are now saying that things will return to mostly normal by the beginning of next month, but there is no real commitment behind those statements. My research is at a virtual standstill in regards to meeting anyone new.

April 27, 2003 (e-mail to faculty members)

I was somewhat optimistic at the beginning of last week, but over the weekend, the situation here has gotten more difficult. While I (we) have no plans to leave Beijing (SARS is just not that serious a threat), the city and my research have come to a halt. And when things will pick up again and start to get back to normal is also unclear. All offices, agencies, companies, etc. are closed or have restricted access to their buildings. As a result, no one is willing or able to schedule meetings. Because the situation remains unclear, I can't even get commitments for several weeks from now. The other major impediment is that individuals don't want to meet either, preferring to remain at home with family members . . . travel to Inner Mongolia is unadvised for some time to come. The health care system in provincial areas is just not up to dealing with the issue. The outbreak in the countryside will get worse over time rather than better.

SARS differed from other types of disasters, such as earthquakes and floods, because what people feared was face-to-face, especially unprotected, contact with anyone they knew. Fear was blind in a sense because one's ethnicity, social status, and education level were not determining factors in how one reacted to others or how one assessed the likelihood of someone else having the virus. Instead, the majority of people sorted the world by family and nonfamily—the front door became one's boundary. Being invited into someone's home was a rare event. Unfortunately, access to people's homes was necessary to gather data from households as outlined in my original project. (I would later conduct some of these interviews once SARS subsided.) The advent of SARS required a reevaluation not only of fieldwork strategies but also a reassessment of the "field" in which I could do research. A multisited "studying up" approach was difficult to pursue when confronted with various new restrictions on movement, decreased access to buildings and communities, and the reluctance of people to meet, along with the likelihood that many people would not be in their office, choosing instead to work from home.

The prospect of reassessing my methodology was less difficult to accept than the growing certainty that I was circumscribing my study for the indefinite future. Where originally I had planned to conduct research across Beijing and in Inner Mongolia, I now felt unable to travel because of stories of enforced quarantining of traveling Beijing residents

Shopping district in central Beijing in early May 2003. A paint company is distributing masks free of charge to the few shoppers on the street. (© Megan Tracy.)

and because of concerns about access to health care. My research area became limited to my compound and neighborhood with occasional trips to other parts of the city. Most public spaces such as restaurants and stores had shut down, partially out of people's general fear of the epidemic and partially due to the lack of patrons at the height of the SARS outbreak.

This time period, however, was also oddly liberating. Traveling within the city became much simpler as people stayed home and traffic lightened correspondingly. I find myself longing for SARS these days as it takes one hour to travel the same distance that during SARS took fifteen minutes. Reactions to SARS differed significantly depending on where one was in the city and to what kind of place one wanted to go. Instead of approaching the city as a unified whole, SARS highlighted how various districts reacted to the virus in different ways. For example, there were severe restrictions in the district where I live, while at the same time in another area of the city, outdoor restaurant seating provided a venue that people considered to be relatively safe to continue their normal life. The epidemic also changed my own perceptions of the compound where I live, causing me to consider it in ways that I had not quite frankly been interested in before—as its own miniature community.

The epidemic challenged me to find other methods to gather the kinds of data that would capture the immediacy of what was happening. It led somewhat counterintuitively to the most intensive data gathering period I have experienced in the field. The period required not just a dependence on alternative media but also a greater dependence on phone interviews. This change in mode of communication meant the loss of some of the "extras"

present in face-to-face interviews—body movements and gestures, cues that are an important source of confirmation for the researcher, especially when interviews are conducted in a
second language. Recognizing that people's homes, offices, and even some businesses
were "off limits," I had to evaluate what public spaces would be fruitful to observe changes
in people's behavior and patterns and where I might still be able to have face-to-face interaction with people. I charted flows of people both at the gate of our compound and at one
of the large retail department stores in the area for several months, attempting to gauge the
impact of SARS over time. The former activity not only gave me an opportunity to have casual
exchanges with friends and colleagues but also to mark on how these restrictions eventually
took their toll on people's patience and tolerance of the changes to their lives. As we moved
further away from the height of panic, restrictions at the gate chafed against residents'
nerves. In May and June, I observed behavior in a campus restaurant at set times twice a
week to examine if the changes people were claiming to make in their hygiene habits coincided with their actual behaviors. I conducted interviews with the tenacious restaurants that
remained open throughout the SARS period when 32 out of 40 of the restaurants in a three
block-radius closed for some period of time. With the help of the now liberated graduate
students of my host university, I later conducted a survey of all these restaurants after most
had reopened in July. I became obsessed with photographing each installment of notices
placed on the compound boards, which served to inform us about the measures that the
university community and the municipality were taking. I also sought out SARS public service
announcements and advertisements throughout the city.

June 23, 2003 (journal)

Like most other people I know here in Beijing, SARS just kind of crept up on us. And as it
was slow to come to Beijing, it has been slow in leaving.

Moving On After SARS

Once SARS left, it was like it never happened. As the fear of SARS faded, so did people's
interest in discussing the impact of this event on their lives. In the random comment now
and again, six months later, SARS will come up but its absence in general conversations
causes me to perk up just at the mere mention of its name. I literally may sit up and take
notice now if someone mentions "feidian." As anthropologists, it is our inclination to want to
revisit the ruptures of social life. Unfortunately, our informants, friends, colleagues, and
neighbors may not share our desire.

June 29, 2003 (e-mail)

Everyone is SARS-weary here making eliciting responses about [the impact of SARS]
more and more difficult.

July 11, 2003 (journal)

Tackling SARS is getting more difficult as people continue to move further away from it. I thought, mistakenly, that businesses hit most by SARS might have more of a continued interest but that doesn't seem to be being borne out in the restaurant survey. Taxi drivers haven't moved beyond it, though, and still seem quite open to answering questions with regard to SARS.

Anthropologists have remarked on communities' capacity to forget (or leave unmentioned) violent events in order to repair breaches in the social fabric and overcome trauma (Last 2000). While SARS was not a violent event as such (despite the large amount of martial expressions used in government posters to promote SARS prevention), there appears to be something similar going on here. The methodological impact is significant. Having your informants perform the equivalent of rolling their eyes at you when you bring up a topic does not encourage the researcher to pursue that path of inquiry. Likewise, I felt uncomfortable pushing people to recollect and reengage with a topic they seemed unwilling to discuss. This situation heightened my awareness of anthropology's own sticky problems with the tenuousness of the data-collecting process—that is, concerns about the data we cannot collect for whatever reasons and the reservations each of us has about what we might be missing.

I, too, was SARS-weary, especially in the months following the core epidemic period, largely due to media saturation and the continued inconvenience of things like the restricted access to our compound. Doggedly, through the largely post-SARS months of July and August, I continued to pursue different research strategies (like the restaurant survey mentioned above) and continued to add SARS-related questions in interviews. Even now in late November, I engage taxi drivers in conversations about what, if any, continued impact they experience. Despite the government's continued low-level campaign to improve people's knowledge about health, disease transmission, and sanitation, as well as the recent news about new outbreaks in labs in Asia, it seems that Beijing's population has moved on. My gut instinct provides me with two plausible explanations. First, sustaining that level of anxiety was just too much for individuals and the population at large. Secondly, over time, people realized, largely through the government's triumphant "conquering" of SARS and the government-sponsored media blitz about the control and prevention of disease transmission, that the risk to themselves and their families was minimal. Recognizing the time-sensitive nature of the topic, my research has also had to move on. Poised to leave the field, I face a future problem of integrating—or not integrating—my SARS data within the larger body of my dissertation research.

Finally, SARS underscored the increasingly common difficulties with anthropological fieldwork in complex societies in general, and "studying up" projects in particular. Just as one may not be able to "hang out" at an office or a laboratory (although there are successful examples of this) and will have to do fieldwork surrounded by doors that open only for brief formal interviews, during SARS—and I suspect other epidemics—"hanging out" with other people became much more difficult. In this context, hanging out became mostly fruitless, possibly dangerous, and at times socially unaccepted. There are, of course as Markowitz points out, advantages to "not asking to hang out" (2001: 43). For my research in particular, these advantages included a need to consider the larger network within which the participants lived. Equally important was the necessity of adopting flexible research tactics and theoretical perspectives. This is sometimes difficult to achieve when the researcher is loathe to put aside strategies planned and plotted out months or even years in advance. Finally, the contingencies of SARS prepared me for my return to the original "studying up" research project and drove home the necessity of knowing when to get in, when to get out, when I had overstayed my welcome, and when I had pursued a line of questioning as far as it could go.

References

Gusterson, H. 1997. Studying up revisited. *PoLAR* 20: 114–19.

Last, M. 2000. Reconciliation and Memory in Postwar Nigeria. In *Violence and Subjectivity,* ed. V. Das, A. Klienman, M. Rampheley, and P. Reynolds, pp. 315–32. Berkeley: University of California Press.

Markowitz, L. 2001. Finding the field: Notes on the ethnography of NGOs. *Human Organization* 60: 40–46.

Nader, L. 1972. Up the Anthropologist—Perspectives Gained from Studying Up. In *Reinventing Anthropology,* ed. D. Hymes, pp. 284–311. New York: Pantheon Books.

Initiating Change:
Doing Action Research in Japan

Akihiro Ogawa
Cornell University

A gardener said one day, "We are going to plant a flower garden."

However, the flowers of the garden never fully bloomed.

The trimming is only an appearance.
The arrogant gardener prunes according to his taste.
He never considers each individual flower.
The gardener gives water and fertilizer haphazardly.
The flowers can't get their necessary nutrition.
The roots have begun to rot.

The garden has beautiful stone walls.
However, the stone walls hurt the flowers' roots.

To make matters worse, the walls disturb the draining.

The gardener wondered why the flowers were withering.
Without serious consideration, he pulled out the flowers,
although some of the flowers had buds.
He bought new flowers and planted them.
But the newly planted flowers again started withering.

The day after a heavy rain fell, the garden lost all of the flowers,
leaving only the beautiful, but cold, empty stone walls.

—Ms. Andō, SLG Volunteer

I received this poem from a female volunteer during the initial stage of my fieldwork at SLG (pseudonym), a Japanese third-sector, nonprofit organization. This poem confirmed to me what I needed to do as an action-minded anthropologist: to become deeply involved in helping SLG get out of a deadlocked situation and to facilitate change so the organization could operate more effectively for its members. Suspending my objectivity as a researcher, I set off on a mission of action.

Research for Social Change

The research strategy I chose is called Action Research (AR)—a social research strategy that combines collaborative research and an impulse toward social change with a strong democratic emphasis. I am not a silent, passive observer, a note taker, or even just a participant. I am actively involved with my research subjects. I do socially relevant research, that is, research for social change.

I came to know AR when I was extremely frustrated with positivistic social science research—the positivistic, number-oriented, rational-choice based knowledge production, a dominant trend in social science in the U.S. academia. When I did assigned readings, I felt like they were something far from the real world. I even felt like it was knowledge for the sake of knowledge, just looking for a linear causal relationship as a form of theory. While thinking about my real-world experience as a journalist before going back to graduate school, it seemed to me that positivistic research would never be directly related and relevant to daily lives at the grassroots level. Further, I believe that everyday life is a dynamic texture of social meaning. Where is the meaning as human beings in such positivistic theory making? I definitely needed another research paradigm.

On snowy winter days one December, I spent a lot of time at the methodology section of the Olin Library at Cornell. At that time, I happened to encounter a book titled *Introduction to Action Research: Social Research for Social Change* (Greenwood and Levin 1998). I had never heard the term—"Action Research"—but the word "action" definitely sounded attractive to me. While reading chapter by chapter, I felt very comfortable with the content, thinking this might be what I've been looking for. I was even surprised that this kind of research would be accepted and published by an academic press. The book was on a style of cogenerative knowledge production whereby researchers and members of a community jointly identify a problem, gather information, analyze the collected data, plan for transformation, take action, interpret the results, and have reflection. The research aims at achieving positive results through broad participation of the stakeholders in the research process.

One of the authors of the book was a Cornell professor of anthropology, and luckily enough, he offered a course on AR in the upcoming spring semester. Without hesitation, I attended his course. The course was fascinating, and something I had never previously experienced. The course had no preset syllabus. Instead, the students wrote a syllabus based on what they wanted and what they could offer. We formed several groups based on our interests. Each group chose readings, presented materials to the class, facilitated the discussion, and led the reflection. The professor also joined the group based on his interest. I felt that AR democratized, even destabilized, the conventional classroom learning. This AR strategy came naturally to me: it reflected my dual role as involved participant and friendly outsider; it was well suited to my being a native anthropologist interested in democratizing my own society through social reform; and it defined my research style as a scholar from that point. My encounter with this research strategy motivated me to transfer to the anthropology program.

I decided to do research on Japanese civil society, or the voluntary third sector, which is associated with neither government nor businesses and is called NPO. The NPO was formally institutionalized in the Japanese civil society following the surge of disaster volunteerism in the post–Great Hanshin-Awaji Earthquake in 1995 and was incorporated under the Law to Promote Specified Nonprofit Activities (the NPO Law) in 1998. I have been researching the transition that Japanese society has undergone at a grassroots level since this groundbreaking law began allowing thousands of civic groups to be acknowledged as proactive participants in Japanese social and political life.

Civil society has been a popular topic among postwar Japanese political scientists. But, I, as an anthropologist, argue that most of the work in the field contains normative theoretical formulations or analyses of high-level political institutions and a small number of political elites. The predominant conceptions of Japanese civil society are very monolithic; it is seen as having weak political advocacy, little international linkage, and close symbiotic relations with the state. One of the conventional arguments is that postwar Japan has been an "activist state," institutionalizing only specific kinds of civic groups, which significantly supports a state ideology—developmentalism.

The research agenda that runs through my project is that the civil society argument needs a grounded analysis or "studying up" of grassroots values and practices expressed by local actors struggling to frame common definitions of what Japanese "civil society" is. We need to analyze the dynamic micro-politics of everyday interactions between the state and ordinary people. In order to explore the meaning of "civil society" in contemporary Japan, I thus chose the NPO as a dissertation topic. What do Japanese grassroots people experience under the new civil-society making? This was my immediate research question.

In this essay I offer a reflexive account about my struggle with a research strategy framed by the interconnection of my three identities as: a Western-trained or American university graduate student, an action-minded researcher, and a native (Japanese) anthropologist. One of the products I sought from my research effort was an ethnography of the new

Japanese NPO movement. I hoped that my ethnography might transcend being merely descriptive and serve the larger agenda of generating movement toward the democratization of the institutional environment of civil society in Japan.

Establishing the Field Site

In the summer after finishing my coursework, I returned to my native country, Japan, to conduct my fieldwork on the Japanese NPO movement. At that point, I had targeted no specific organization as a pertinent example of the emergent third sector. I wanted to set my field site in Tokyo, or the greater Tokyo metropolitan area, where my wife had begun her job. Initially, I attended gatherings for people who were interested in the NPO movement. The 1998 NPO Law had encouraged a number of salon-style gatherings across the country for people who wanted to know more about NPOs. The gatherings were advertised on the Internet and in newspapers and were open to the public. At the initial stage of my fieldwork, I attended many of these events, exchanging my business cards with as many NPO practitioners as I could. I asked them about what they were doing at the grassroots level so that I could get a real sense of these types of activities. If a particular NPO sounded interesting to me, I visited its offices.

At the first salon-style gathering I attended I happened to sit next to Mr. Hasegawa, general secretary of SLG. We exchanged business cards, along with a brief self-introduction. In early August, I e-mailed him, requesting a meeting, since I was still in the process of data collection on several types of the NPOs. In his response, he asked for information on my research. I simply told him that I wanted to conduct research on the voluntary citizens-based NPO (I did not use the term "ethnography." I did not think that Mr. Hasegawa, as a member of the general public, would be familiar with this research method.) I told him I was looking for an NPO to use as a basis of my research, which was to analyze the dynamic development of third-sector organizations. I wanted to be involved in the NPO as much as possible, if possible, as an unpaid staff member. Further, I wanted to establish some collaborative relationship with NPO participants. I did not want to be treated like a visitor or an outsider. In his response, however, Mr. Hasegawa rejected my request on the grounds that his NPO was not in line with my research purpose. According to him, SLG was a "quasi-governmental organization" and was not part of the dynamic movement of the third sector in Japanese society. Although I did not exactly understand his use of the term "quasi-governmental" at that time, the term itself intrigued me. I sent him an e-mail, saying, "I want to see various kinds of NPOs in the initial stage of my research. Even quasi-governmental organizations, as you said, are a reality of the Japanese NPO sector. If they are less dynamic, I would like to think about why these types of NPOs are less dynamic. Anyway, I would like to see you and know your NPO."

In mid-August, I took a train to a tiny station on a minor metro line, two stops from Asakusa, a downtown area on the northeast side of Tokyo. One-story Japanese houses and various kinds of mom-and-pop shops dot the landscape, spreading out in clusters around the metro station. It is a busy, crowded area with narrow streets and not much space between homes and buildings. The district is a major industrial area in Tokyo, for medium- and small-sized manufacturers of products such as toys, soap, and shoes. As I was approaching the neighborhood, I suddenly saw a modern building rising above the landscape. As I got closer, I could see that all of its walls were made of glass and every door was automatic. At the entrance, there was an artificial river. The contrast of this contemporary compound against the traditional flavor of the neighborhood was striking. The building was SLG. Mr. Hasegawa's office was on the second floor.

Mr. Hasegawa soon appeared, and we spoke briefly about the typhoon that had hit the Tokyo metropolitan area the previous day. He then gave me some information about SLG. According to him, this organization provides lifelong learning courses in the local community. More specifically, local residents are organized as volunteers under the NPO, and the volunteers plan such courses as foreign language, literature, haiku (Japanese-style poetry), sculpture, pottery, social dance, and so on, for all the residents. The volunteers are expected to decide the content of the courses, look for instructors through their networks, organize the courses with the instructors, and help in the routine course-related activities, including taking attendance. This sounded to me like an independent, community-oriented, lifelong learning project. "But," Mr. Hasegawa told me, "the municipal government fully funds all of the business operations of SLG. What we are doing in the name of the NPO are social services formerly provided by the municipal government."

I was aware that the Japanese Law for the Promotion of Lifelong Learning enacted in 1990 articulates that both national and municipal governments must support the promotion of lifelong learning. In 1994, the municipal government in downtown Tokyo opened a public facility for promoting lifelong learning in the ward where SLG is currently located. In order to operate the center, the fiscally ailing government, which did not want to spend more money for the social services, decided to ask that course-content creation be done by local residents as volunteers. The government initially organized the local volunteers as a citizens' group, and it functioned as a part of the government. Following the enactment of the 1998 NPO Law, the government decided that this citizens' group should apply for NPO status. Lastly, Mr. Hasegawa honestly told me that he was frustrated with the way the government implemented cost-cutting measures in public administration by employing voluntary NPO activities. He wondered if the government had made any serious efforts in reducing the administrative costs, before transferring the business operations to this third-sector organization.

One of the most important revelations in my conversation with Mr. Hasegawa was that SLG had been established by the municipal government, not by a voluntary third sector of the community. "What was the government doing creating a third-sector organization?" I thought to myself when I went back home by train. In my graduate coursework, I read a lot of literature on Japanese civil society. Much of the reading focused on the rosy discourse of the emerging Japanese NPO movement. The literature often argued that Japanese society had finally matured through the institutionalization of the NPO since 1998. It stated that Japan has formal, functionally differentiated, and professional nonprofit or third-sector organizations that actively interact with the state and private businesses. (While reading, I was wondering if Japanese society, usually known as having a strong state, could easily have experienced such changes in such a short time.) On the other hand, what I heard today sounded very different from the rosy discourse described in the formal writings. While thinking about my conversation with Mr. Hasegawa, I thought that SLG was indeed a case of the state-led institutionalization of civil society, which was primarily argued in the Japanese civil society literature. The phenomenon itself might be nothing new. But I wanted to know what opinions the grassroots people had to offer about the operation of the SLG. I confirmed that my key interest was to go beyond the formal discourse and to study up values and practices expressed and conducted by grassroots people. I thought that SLG would be a great case study for my research.

Later in the day, I sent an e-mail to Mr. Hasegawa saying that I was strongly interested in his organization. I would like to study his organization, since I could share in his frustration, in particular. I wrote to him that I wanted to be involved with his NPO and help initiate some change, if at all possible, through my research involvement. Further, I asked him to accept me as a staff-researcher. Of course, I would not expect to be paid.

One week later, I received an offer to act as an unpaid staff-researcher at the SLG secretariat. Mr. Hasegawa had negotiated with several directors at SLG and created the position especially for me; I accepted it. I was told that I would be in charge of course planning at SLG and had to be at the office from 9 AM to 5:45 PM from Monday through Friday and every other Saturday, like other regular staff. I was told that, in exchange, I would be free to conduct research there. The next day, I visited SLG to submit my curriculum vitae and proof of enrollment at Cornell, upon his request. Thus, SLG became the focus of my research.

Knowing My Field Site

I joined SLG in early autumn, one year after its official incorporation as an NPO, and continued my fieldwork for 20 months. I started my research by attending every meeting held at SLG and arranged as many interviews as possible. The following spring, I also planned lifelong learning with the SLG volunteers.

At my field site, I expected that the meetings I observed and the stories I heard in the organization would yield significant information about the organizational culture. I regularly attended weekly staff meetings, course-planning meetings, and monthly directors' meetings. At these meetings, I observed and collected evidence of basic organizational values, such as dominant rationality and power relations. Further, I collected stories through open-ended interviews. I usually spoke with people at SLG in informal settings over coffee. The interviews might be better called informal chats, as we relaxed and enjoyed conversations. My primary interest at this stage was: Why did these people participate in SLG? How did they feel about their activities? Did they see any difference between the previous citizens' group affiliated with the government and the current NPO style?

While continuing to make observations and collecting stories, I realized that the volunteers were very frustrated, or even extremely weary, with their environment. Ms. Imai, one of the oldest volunteers in the organization, voiced her concern.

> This organization has become more bureaucratic ever since it got the NPO status. I imagined we would act more actively and freely. However, we cannot. In particular, I even feel that the relationship between volunteers and the secretariat has become rigid. We were more flexible before.

When I spoke to Ms. Tajima, a housewife volunteer, about the difference between the former entity and the current NPO style, she told me,

> After becoming an NPO . . . everything is driven by a theory of organization. SLG as an organization is the top priority. Many people say, "We have to do this since we are now an NPO." Instead of what we are doing, the organizational form—NPO—seems important. Before becoming an NPO, we really enjoyed discussions. All kinds of decisions were made in free, open forums. Anybody could join the discussions. Now we volunteers are divided, based on our interests, into four divisions, like the course planning division. I am sure it is an easier way to control us in the name of organization. All we often hear now are orders from the SLG president. He said you should do this, and you should do that . . . We are not his subordinates.

What SLG volunteers complained about most was the inflexible, bureaucratic decision-making style inside the organization, led by the government-appointed president, all of which materialized after SLG changed its organizational style to NPO. The poem, which I introduced in the beginning of this essay, was part of this story collection. In particular, the volunteers faced certain difficulties due to their confusion under the president, described in the poem as a gardener whose methods lead to the garden's ruin.

Even though the SLG volunteers were organized under the NPO rubric, I realized that they did not understand why they were organized this way. Some volunteers even thought that the arrangement of SLG was improper for a third-sector organization. SLG was an atypical NPO because it was organized by the government, not by the spontaneous will of citizens. Further, many volunteers had strongly expected that the transition to the NPO would bring about an organizational structure different from the exiting government and businesses; they felt that the operations of the NPO should be in their hands. Instead, it seemed the organization was becoming increasingly inflexible, isolating its members. In fact, the NPO was ironically run in a more bureaucratic way. They even were annoyed with the term NPO and the concept behind it. Many people asked me, "What is an NPO?" Since I was introduced to SLG's volunteers as a researcher in the area of the NPO, I was supposed to know a great deal about NPOs and how they work. Furthermore, there was one point that the volunteers never said but I realized: SLG was even losing sight of *manabi*, or learning—SLG's primary agenda as a provider of lifelong learning opportunities in the local community. I did not hear any active discussions on their philosophy of learning from the members. Under such circumstances, several volunteers left SLG due to disillusionment. The remaining volunteers struggled to understand their position in the hasty NPO-ization of Japanese society, led by the government.

Initiating Collaborative Inquiry

Confronted with this context, I decided to actively employ an AR strategy to address this issue. AR was already embedded as my meta strategy. But, from this stage, I believe I implemented the strategy in a more direct and specific way. It seemed to me that the current organizational deadlock at SLG stemmed from a lack of self-reflexive evaluation of the organization's activities. I hoped that the AR approach could be useful in resolving this central issue; hopefully a self-evaluation system would be a good starting point for initiating changes. I thought that creating such a system would require generating a reflexive space for the organization to think about itself and its activities. I was wondering if I could start the evaluation process in the area of course planning, instead of in the whole organization. SLG volunteers and I would collaboratively begin to accumulate concrete knowledge and explore solutions on our own. As a researcher, I could provide feedback from the ethnographic data I collected on the organization to help them understand the reality they faced. Although most of the people at SLG had never encountered an anthropologist, I believe they found the evidence I collected on the organization and its needs to be extremely helpful.

An immediate goal was to establish a collaborative inquiry group made up of SLG members who shared a desire to change this situation while pursuing new possibilities for the organization. For the past three months, I had been establishing solid networks among the volunteers through my involvement. The first person I had in my mind was Mr. Harada, one of the directors in charge of course planning. Mr. Harada, in his 50s, was a professional architect. He was one of the most influential directors at SLG and had a rich background in community development. He also seemed to have a strong sense of SLG's purpose. He had said many times that SLG should offer high-quality, interesting courses to its "customers"— that is, local residents—and monitor their satisfaction through course evaluations. Otherwise, SLG as a business would not meet the need for which it was established.

At the end of November, I went to Mr. Harada's office and honestly and directly told him about my concerns. I told him, "I have observed that many people are frustrated. I was wondering if we could make a more open, diversified discussion space in the organization through the evaluation process. I remember that you mentioned several times the necessity of creating an evaluation system within SLG. I think that would be the first step. That is why I came here today. I would like to participate in evaluation activities as a part of my research activities here at SLG. How about if we create a path to make a breakthrough?" I explained this, drawing a flow of actions of the linear relationship—clarification of problems, problem-solving process, and then reflective evaluation. While listening to my proposal, Mr. Harada agreed that a bottom-up style of discussion would be interesting. Further, he drew up a more developed cyclic and dynamic diagram to represent his way of thinking. I thought that his diagram was more evolved than mine. It showed a dynamic learning process that was circular, moving through recursive processes of planning, action, and reflection. While drawing the diagram, Mr. Harada said to me, "What we need is more active and positive interactions and reflections among us—volunteers. I want to generate such flows within the organization, too."

Mr. Harada and I then started to recruit group members for this evaluation project. We thought that the most crucial point was to diversify the group. Up to this point, I had had many chances to talk to the SLG volunteers about our shared concerns. Among the SLG volunteers, in particular, I wanted to invite Mr. Iwata into the group. Over the past months, I had built a strong relationship with him. He was an engineer from Okayama in western Japan and was around my age. Mr. Iwata joined SLG primarily because he wanted to meet people in the community where he now lived. He positively participated in SLG activities; he attended the meetings, planned a couple of courses, and organized an event for children. Through the SLG activities, he got to know local people; he became a member in the local community.

It looked like Mr. Iwata enjoyed the activities, but, on the other hand, I knew he was frustrated with SLG because of its organizational culture—its top-down decision-making style and government-dependent stance. He and I spent a good deal of time exchanging ideas about what we could do to make changes at SLG. In late November, I asked him to come to the secretariat office after he finished his work, and explained to him what I wanted to do. I mentioned that he often said, "We, as an NPO, could do things in a different way." That night, I said to him, "If you feel frustrated, why don't you initiate change? Let's start something together, instead of just being frustrated." I was sure he could be a key person in the evaluation group, but I observed that he hesitated.

Mr. Iwata said to me, "I am not sure this project will go well; recently, we volunteers have become very tired and have lost motivation and autonomous attitudes, as you know." But, I pushed him to make a positive decision asking, "Why don't you work with me? I want to offer everything I can. Otherwise, nothing will be changed." He finally said, "Okay, I can work with you. Nothing will be changed without action."

Mr. Harada and I then invited five other volunteers to be the core members of the evaluation group, taking into consideration the balance of gender and age. At the December directors' meeting, Mr. Harada asked the board for approval to set up an evaluation group under his direct supervision. He obtained the board's consent.

Taking Action

Shortly after the evaluation group received the directors' approval, as a facilitator of the group, I started building relationships with its core members through e-mail discussions. I realized it was extremely difficult to get all of the members together in one place at one time, since they were volunteers who were participating in SLG activities during their free time. Thus, e-mail was a convenient device to enhance our discussions, and through e-mail discussions, we gradually reconfigured the purpose of the group. We formulated the premise that self-evaluation would improve the planning and offering of the continuing education courses, the main business of SLG. By strengthening the foundation, the organization would improve. Thus, we started the evaluation process by focusing on the course planning with other volunteers from the course planning division. We also agreed on our strategy: first, we would know our current situation—identify problems; second, we would prioritize objectives—which problem should be solved first. We emphasized that we would solve the problems by ourselves, which we believed would lead to empowering ourselves to function better in the current oppressive atmosphere.

It was time to move ahead. A regular meeting of the course-planning division in February was scheduled for that night. As I distributed notepaper and colored markers to the 12 people who were present, including the core members of the evaluation group and some other volunteers, I said to them, "Write down anything you want to change. Bring to the table the causes of your frustrations. Otherwise, we can't solve anything." At the beginning, it seemed that the volunteers hesitated a little bit. However, after Ms. Kunimatsu, one of the core members of the evaluation group, said, "This is interesting. Hmmm, I can write whatever I want to change," other volunteers gradually participated in this process. The participants appeared to enjoy the process, changing the color of the markers they used every so often. Surprisingly, in 15 minutes, we had collected more than 50 pieces of notepaper from the attendants. We divided them into various topics, such as items related to course planning, volunteers themselves, directors, the secretariat, and so on.

A discussion scene in the collaborative inquiry. (© Sumida Gakashu Garden.)

In the next meeting, 10 days later, we classified all of the problems that the volunteers wanted to solve. Based on their interests and their areas of expertise, they formed small groups. For example, volunteers interested in setting a mission for course planning next year comprised one group; those who had accounting backgrounds formed a group to work on the budget for the next year. We agreed that each group was expected to analyze the problem, identify the cause, and write a proposal on how to improve the situation.

From March through July, I facilitated monthly meetings to address the problem-solving process. I also attended the subgroup meetings as much as possible and helped them write a proposal and present the material. This collaboration was a highlight of my fieldwork experience. I felt that it was a joint learning exercise among us. It was not just a problem-solving process. It was a process in which we discovered ourselves, I helped write and rewrite proposals and led discussions in the series of monthly meetings. I felt the grassroots participation was meaningful for the organization. These activities reflected our sincere wishes for SLG; they were not just a process to resolve frustration. We confirmed to each other why we were here and why we participated in SLG, although our reasons varied. Mr. Iwata was looking for friends in the local community; Ms. Tajima wanted to use her free time for the good of the community; Ms. Andō wanted to learn about her own community through planning literature and history courses related to the community; and I was doing research on the Japanese NPO but wanted to improve the organizational situation by my research involvement. Despite the different motivations, everybody shared a common interest in doing something positive for the local community. The SLG activities were not only for the local residents, but the activities themselves were actually for us. The activities would enhance our own quality of life, and we wanted to enjoy the activities.

After five months, we had a reflection session. We confirmed what we tried and achieved. I asked the participants of the evaluation process whether they wanted to continue this problem-solving process. Ms. Andō said, "I want to repeat this process. If we stop at this level, we will have frustration again. I am sure that we are moving ahead through this process." "I don't want to postpone dealing with problems, either. We need to do it again," Ms. Murase added. We thus started another cycle of the problem-solving process. Meanwhile, the government-appointed president of SLG was aware of this activity. Although he did not express any interest in participating in this process, he watched from a distance and he seemed bothered by it. As the process went on, he would not even make eye contact with Mr. Iwata or me. He finally directly intervened in my research.

My Positionality

Being an action-oriented researcher is overtly political, and surviving organizational politics is a key issue in this approach. Apparently, some people had difficulty understanding my active stance as a researcher. They expected me to be a conventional researcher who collected data but did not participate in the activities of the subject being researched. I was just expected to be a silent observer. One experience I had in my field site drove this point home. That was a conflict with Mr. Nakamoto, president of SLG. Here is an excerpt from my field notes.

> Field notes 90
> Name: Am I being blackballed?
> *File Number: 060302*
>
> This afternoon I was told by Mr. Kuroda, general secretary of SLG, that Mr. Nakamoto said that I am no longer allowed to attend a monthly strategic meeting, which I had been attending from last October to June. Some board members, including the president, vice presidents, the director in charge of course planning, and the director of recruiting and training, had been attending the meetings. I had been allowed to attend as a staff-researcher of the secretariat. I deemed the meetings to be a crucial part of my fieldwork because I could observe active interaction among the members who take initiatives in SLG management. As the board of directors was not functioning well at SLG due partly to its big size, the strategic meetings had become a significant place for making decisions.
>
> As a reason for my "exclusion" (I was surprised that some people used this term to describe my situation) from the meetings, Mr. Kuroda said that the next meeting was going to deal with an entrustment contract with the municipal government. Mr. Kuroda

said, according to Mr. Nakamoto, "It should be a secret meeting because it deals with how SLG talks to the government. The content of the meeting must not be leaked. Thus, Mr. Tanase from the government would not be allowed to attend the meeting either."

I was very upset by this decision. I had never disrupted the meetings. I was only an active listener. Sometimes, some members asked me to make comments. Only in those cases did I say something. I have no idea what I should do as a researcher. Later that afternoon, I had a chance to talk to Mr. Aota, vice president of SLG. He already knew that I would be "excluded" from the meeting. He was also upset. I asked him, "Was there any discussion about my position in the meeting among the meeting members?" He said, "No. We didn't have any discussion about this decision. Mr. Nakamoto made the decision by himself. I don't understand why you are not allowed to attend the meeting. A possible reason I can guess is that you presented some questions at the annual shareholders' meeting in mid-May. The question was exactly a point that Mr. Nakamoto did not want to touch upon. He is scared of you." Showing me the agenda for the next strategic meeting, which Mr. Nakamoto had faxed to him, Mr. Aota continued, "Now nobody controls him, even the municipal government that assigned him as president of SLG. See this agenda. It portrays a one-man style of management just as medium/small-sized companies have. All decision making is concentrated around Mr. Nakamoto. The agenda even mentions expanding the SLG president's term of office. He seems to have misunderstood his position. He is parading around like the emperor with his new clothes."

I was thinking that this kind of situation might happen some day. However, I never expected somebody to be offended by my research activities in such an unconcealed way. Facing this situation, I was mainly concerned about keeping my position at SLG, primarily because of my commitment to the volunteers' cause, and also because of continuing my dissertation fieldwork. My collaborative involvement in the evaluation group had just begun. My mission of action was not completed yet. Also, I could not leave SLG at this stage, since I wanted to know more about this NPO as a research subject.

I asked the general secretary if I could attend the meeting, while reiterating my research purpose. He gave me permission to attend and said that I was under his direct control as a secretariat staff member. On the next Monday night, the strategic meeting was held. Mr. Tanase, an official from the municipal government, did not appear at the meeting. The discussion was primarily about how to deal with negotiation of an entrustment contract between the municipal government and SLG. During the meeting, Mr. Nakamoto proposed creating another committee to prepare the negotiations. The committee was to be organized by the SLG president, three vice presidents, the general secretary, the vice general secretary, and two more directors; He excluded me from this group. At that time, I asked Mr. Nakamoto, "I would like to attend the meetings as an observer. May I?" He promptly said, "Of course not." There was no explanation.

I was doubly shocked. First, I was surprised at the fact that I had just been excluded from the list of attendees of future sessions of the newly organized strategic meetings. Second, I was dumbfounded by the fact that my request was turned down so quickly, with a sharp "No" in a public discussion. I had never experienced this kind of reproach. Furthermore, I was not given a chance to reply to him. Others in attendance also said nothing. The way I had understood it was that all meetings at SLG should be open, as it was an organization operated by volunteers and most of its funding came from taxpayers via the municipal government.

The next morning I faxed Mr. Nakamoto in order to clarify my purpose of research at SLG. I wrote to him, "I am doing research on the Japanese NPO. SLG is a case. But, I do not intend to just observe as a researcher. Since I am here, I want to be involved with activities as much as possible. You might not accept a researcher like me. No, I am not a conventional researcher. In a sense, I test a research style. Through my research involvement, I want to improve the situation I observe and experience. I test my own possibilities about whether I can do something to improve the situation for the people with whom I work. This is an action I am taking not only as a scholar but also as a citizen. I am testing what it means to be here." Due to some help from the general secretary in negotiating with Mr. Nakamoto about my further involvement, I was then allowed to attend the meetings again. After this experience, I tried to speak up clearly about my research stance whenever I had the chance. In so doing, SLG volunteers, and I also confirmed the meaning of my involvement with SLG activities. Meanwhile, Mr. Nakamoto never spoke to me again.

During my fieldwork I was always thinking about my positionality in this field site. "Who am I in this organization? What kind of role am I expected to play? How do I define myself? I am a doctoral researcher from an American university," I told myself; "but I am also a secretariat staff member at my field site." Even though I was from an American university, I was not just a "visiting" researcher. I was a Japanese anthropologist doing research on his own society. I always confirmed myself like this: "Thanks to this action-oriented approach, I believe I can be involved with making positive changes happen at my field site instead of just formulating arguments from afar (like an armchair theorist). By actively participating, I can generate small but solid moves with people at the grassroots level to effect positive outcomes with regard to the state's deliberative effort to institutionalize civil society." There was a crucial responsibility I had to take in doing this type of research as a native anthropologist.

Now, as I finish my fieldwork, I believe that my research results will, more or less, meet my expectations. It became possible to build collaborative research relationships with people at the grassroots. In fact, what I actually did in this research was to help empower ordinary people and to forward the democratization of my field site NPO by practicing action-oriented social research. In one sense, achieving these results, or at least discovering whether I could, was my research. I tried to facilitate moves that the grassroots volunteers in my field site could use by themselves and for their activities, as a gardener waters flowers for them to freely grow. I wanted people in my field site to have a chance to speak up and empower themselves. Further, I believe that the knowledge I generated on the Japanese NPO under the AR strategy will definitely contribute to the overall academic scholarship on Japanese civil society.

My hope is that when I am able to return in the near future, the evaluation process we started collaboratively will have taken root, giving the people at SLG more colorful flowers within their beautiful stone walls. I was there to act with them. We initiated a spark of change.

Reference

Greenwood, Davydd J. and Morten Levin. 1998. *Introduction to Action Research: Social Research for Social Change.* Thousand Oaks, CA: Sage.

The *Other* City of Angels:
Ethnography with the Bangkok Police

Eric J. Haanstad
University of Wisconsin–Madison

กรุงเทพมหานคร อมรรัตนโกสินทร์ มหินทรายุธยามหาดิลก
ภพนพรัตน์ ราชธานีบุรีรมย์ อุดมราชนิเวศน์ มหาสถาน
อมรพิมาน อวตารสถิต สักกะทัตติยะ วิษณุกรรมประสิทธิ

The city of angels, the great city, the residence of the Emerald Buddha, the impregnable city (of Ayutthaya) of God Indra, the grand capital of the world endowed with nine precious gems, the happy city, abounding in an enormous Royal Palace that resembles the heavenly abode where reigns the reincarnated god, a city given by Indra and built by Vishnukarn.

The full name of *Krung Thep Mahanakhon* (Bangkok)

Abort, Retry, Fail

I am a bad anthropologist. That was the fear, anyway. What was first-time fieldwork like for a person like me, a bad anthropologist? The auguries were not good. I thought about the project ahead of me as I flew 20,000 feet over the Pacific Ocean. I was flying to Thailand to study a group of armed agents of the state whom most people treat with a mixture of distrust and hostility. Once there, I was to observe, interview, and conduct "participant observa-

223

Metropolitan Special Patrol Police, Bangkok 2001. (© Eric Haanstad.)

tion" with the Thai police. My research proposal read: "The project will show how the lived realities of national policing intersect and collide with the growing networks of international law enforcement relations." Funding agencies seemed to like the idea.

I spent eight months in Thailand a few years ago doing predissertation research, building language skills, securing permission and site access. That experience was different, however. Those eight months were my first time abroad. Like many Americans, my international experience was limited to some trips to Canada and the occasional Native American reservation ("Welcome to the Menominee Nation," the sign read, as I watched cars with tribal license plates pass our station wagon on a family camping trip to northern Wisconsin). Thus, with access to another continent, predissertation research was an adventure filled with excitement and possibility.

By contrast, this trip to Thailand was the culmination of an unexpected half-year in my parent's basement. Twenty-eight years old with a master's degree, funding from two major sources for conducting dissertation research, and I was living with my ever-supportive parents, waiting. Why? Because I didn't have the tactical mind it takes to be a good anthropologist, I suppose. I didn't plan on the seven months it would take for human subjects' approval. Didn't think through the time it would take to get a preliminary committee to meet (the council of supportive elders). Didn't count on the proposal rewrite that resulted from this meeting. Didn't know that all these things would need to be completed before funding could be released for a plane ticket, and by that time it was Christmas. In the first few days of January, as I pressed my forehead against the pressurized window and watched the plane chase the sunset for hours, I nailed down an unfamiliar feeling: I was completely and utterly terrified.

That first night, landing at midnight, I didn't have a room reservation in Bangkok. I don't know if that conveys confidence in my knowledge of the city or sheer stupidity. Regardless, I found my way to my old apartment building that, thankfully, had a vacancy. I was happy that I had an old but functioning Thai Internet card. I still had no response to my heartfelt and desperate follow-up letter to a four-day holiday romance. This situation served as a harbinger of the assured initial loneliness to come, despite one of my friend's assurance that, "you are never alone." As I tried to sleep that night, exhausted, I wondered over and over again, "How am I going to *do* this?" The next morning I woke up to a crashed hard drive. I've heard other tales of electronic ruin from friends, but the shock and dislocation of this event seemed much more devastating in person. Sometime during that first morning as I tallied the lost files, electronic memories and events in progress, my brain's internal fuse box suffered an overload of incoming stress and flipped a switch.

Captain Willard in *Apocalypse Now* describes one of his companions, Chef, as "wrapped too tight for Vietnam," and that analysis applied equally well to me. It's not just Chef and I; many self-described expats in Southeast Asia seem to be experiencing, often by choice, their own personal Vietnam. I thought that predissertation research abroad and reading numerous accounts of culture shock in the field would make me immune to its effects. Despite this preparation, physically encountering "the field" with its infinite possibilities and probable terrors led me to quite literally question my sanity—not in the trite way that this phrase is usually intended, but in wondering if all the symptoms of manic depression, obsessive compulsive disorder, Tourette's, and paranoia add up in small quantities to form a new diagnosable syndrome.

Bangkok is a "global city" and has some of the best medical facilities in Asia. However, the day after my arrival and my hard drive crash, I found, not to my surprise, that the channels of Western psychological counseling were completely unavailable, often in darkly comic ways. In my detachment, a living movie screened to my mind's empty theater:

1   **INT. MODERN HOSPITAL, PSYCHIATRIC OFFICE, BANGKOK (SUBTITLED)**   1

YOUNG ANTHROPOLOGIST. I need to make . . . see a doctor; I am feeling very . . . sad.

HOSPITAL SECRETARY, *stares at him with a look of utter confusion.*

YOUNG ANTHROPOLOGIST, *switches to English.* Can I make an appointment?

The secretary looks through a large schedule book.

HOSPITAL SECRETARY. We have appointment on 29th.

YOUNG ANTHROPOLOGIST. Of January?

HOSPITAL SECRETARY. February.

YOUNG ANTHROPOLOGIST. Two months from now?

HOSPITAL SECRETARY. Yes.

YOUNG ANTHROPOLOGIST. Is there someone I can see now? It's a bit of an emergency.

HOSPITAL SECRETARY. I'm sorry, sir. Doctor is finished.

YOUNG ANTHROPOLOGIST. What, ma'am?

HOSPITAL SECRETARY. Doctor is finished. You have an appointment?

YOUNG ANTHROPOLOGIST. No, ma'am.

HOSPITAL SECRETARY. How long you been in Thailand?

YOUNG ANTHROPOLOGIST. One day.

I watched my "self" disintegrate in that conversation at the hospital and in the hours that surrounded it. It was as if I knew the receptionist's responses before she said them and could see the futility and tragic-comedy of my own responses. I watched this happening as if "I" were sitting slightly outside of my own body. Buddhists might call this the "appearance of the witness" and physicists might call it awareness of holographic reality (Talbot 1991). In Vedic philosophy all experiences are *maya* (illusion), simultaneously "real" and unreal. These are the spiritual underpinnings of the Thai national religious system, an amalgam of Theravada Buddhism, Hinduism, and animism. I was conducting participant observation, after all. My conscious identification of these revelations of perception would come much later, unfortunately. In Western psychoreligious systems (the categories available to me at the time), at worst this was the onset of schizophrenia, at best this was simply losing my mind.

It took a few weeks after that initial crash to reintegrate into a form of mundane normalcy, and every day that passed I felt more guilty, lazy, and unprepared. Those feelings are not new among anthropologists. In the late sixties, Wintrob (1969) coined the term "disadaptation syndrome," a combination of stress, fear, and feelings of incompetence that often accompany fieldwork. My situation is not unique, but because of the way our myths are transferred professionally, we are often left to blindly inhabit secret personal worlds of discomfort and alienation. As students, we routinely slog through the overgrown paths of our mentors and anthropological heroes. On the way, the most rudimentary tools (support networks, research methods, and means of expression) must be reinvented, crafted from sheer willpower and basic necessity.

Riot Therapy

> When we are absolutely certain, whether of our worth or our worthlessness, we are almost impervious to fear. Thus, a feeling of utter unworthiness can be a source of courage. Everything seems possible when we are absolutely helpless or absolutely powerful.
>
> —Bruce Lee, *Tao of Jeet Kune Do*

It was none other than Bruce Lee who helped me get into graduate school. I included the "absorb what is useful" quotation attributed to Mr. Lee in most of my entrance statements, and for a time its inclusion embarrassed me. Graduate students are supposed to perform the role of serious academics. In Bangkok, however, after experiencing what St. John of the Cross famously called "the dark night of the soul," I began shedding the pretensions of what I *should* be doing as a fieldworker in favor of actually working in the field. Flexibility—absorbing what was useful—would be key.

At the end of my first month, a Thai soap opera actress was quoted in Cambodian newspapers as claiming the ancient Khmer site of Angkor Wat rightfully belonged to Thailand. The remarks later proved to be misquotes, but the damage to Cambodian national pride was done. I heard the news the following morning that the Thai embassy and a number of Thai businesses in Phnom Penh, Cambodia, were burned in riots the night before. Despite the "Land of Smiles" moniker in Thailand, there is a Thai expression, "*naahm ning lai leuk*" (still waters run deep), that describes the often volatile feelings beneath the calm and silent cultural veneer. A half-century campaign of Thai nationalism, a long history of military politics, combined with a number of other factors (including the U.S.-led anticommunist programs between the 1950s and 1970s) created widespread xenophobia, mistrust, and in certain situations, outright hatred of foreigners. This animosity is especially expressed towards Thailand's closest cultural and geographical neighbors. With this in mind, knowing my goal to study the state construction of order and chaos, I rode the elevated train to the Cambodian embassy in Bangkok to witness the backlash to the riots in Phnom Penh. I arrived too late for the immediate and more violent protests in the morning, but by noon there was a massive buildup of police vehicles, media vans, and protesters in the wide street near the embassy.

Leaving the train platform, I talked to someone who had a large camera and asked him if he was going to the embassy. He said he was, and in the same breath invited me to model for his agency as he showed me his prints of Thai models. What? With this surreal exchange behind us, later he showed me a grainy photocopy that was widely circulated at the protest. It depicted a scene supposedly taken from the Cambodian riots: a smiling man driving a stake into a large picture of His Majesty, the Thai king. This act of symbolic violence and lèse-majesté is a capital offense in Thailand, and this image alone provoked intense rage for many Thais.

As the afternoon wore on, a number of Cambodian flags were burned along with countless effigies of Cambodian Prime Minister Hun Sen. Later, a police general gave a ten-minute speech from a police fire truck, which vocally competed with a few chants from the crowd of *"Aawk bpai!"* (Get out!) addressed, presumably, to Cambodians still living in Thailand. This chant was used as a kind of default rallying cry throughout the course of the day by the most visibly angry and/or intoxicated sections of the crowd. Riders on passing buses, clearly sympathetic Thais, were handed pictures and literature from the smiling and cheering crowd who waved Thai flags (some of which were distributed by uniformed police officers). The police general finished his speech and the crowd cheered enthusiastically. He said that the king of Thailand himself sent a message asking the crowd to disperse. By the end of that day, I had two hours of video, many pages of notes, and a renewed confidence that I was in the right place at the right time. The embassy demonstration underlined the necessity of keeping the settings and subjects of my research flexible. From then on, even when the police weren't cooperating with me, there was always a dispute or protest involving the police to provide equally rich data. Like Bruce Lee said all along, "It is like a finger pointing towards the moon. Don't concentrate on the finger or you'll miss all that heavenly glory."

"Give Up and Get Out; Get Caught or Get Killed": Life During (Drug) Wartime

In my research proposals, I consciously avoided two social phenomena because they were so massive, so complex, and so "obvious" in a study of the Thai police: drugs and corruption. I thought that any examination of either one of these topics would be too broad and all-consuming. Predictably perhaps, I immediately discovered these initial plans of avoidance were naïve and impossible. Suddenly, many police officers were unavailable for interviews because of "drug planning" meetings. I began to see antidrug ads on billboards, television, and in movie theaters. These included the constant image repetition of skulls, dead drug dealers, and dramatizations of a "crazed" methamphetamine addict holding a knife to a child's throat. Clearly, the public was being conditioned for something beyond the routine constructions of fear expected from the modern state. Newspaper accounts confirmed this by announcing a government antidrug campaign. I wanted to study state "displays of order," and it appeared that this campaign would be a spectacular fulfillment of that desire.

Thus, in the tradition of many anthropologists before me, I began to abandon many of the topics I originally planned to study for topics of greater immediacy and relevance. This process was both frightening and liberating; a dormant seed opening in alien soil. In February 2003, the first day in the Year of the Goat, the Thai prime minister unveiled a three-month operation to "rid drugs from every square inch of Thailand." As one of the world's major transit points for heroin and opium and with a domestic methamphetamine production problem reaching epidemic proportions, this quixotic campaign seemed immediately destined for failure or tragedy. The Thai interior minister, Wan Nor, declared, "In our war on drugs, the district chiefs are the knights and provincial governors the commanders. If the knights see the enemies but do not shoot them, they can be beheaded by their commanders." Within days, bodies began piling up throughout the country as the police acted on blacklists of drug dealers, users, and addicts. The government and police claimed that rival drug dealers were killing each other to avoid the risk of betrayal by their accomplices. These were lies: power tends to occult itself.

At the end of the three-month campaign, close to 2,500 people were dead, with no investigations into the murders. For me, the grisly paradox of the drug war is that this national tragedy couldn't have been timed better for my research. Prior to its launch, I was not planning to make drug suppression a major focus of my research. Now it became impossible not to study this massive spectacle of chaos and order. I was a witness to a series of political operations designed to fulfill a similar function: creating the necessary enemies of the state, whether they are drug dealers, criminals, terrorists, or rival states. In Thailand, as in many nation-states, a constant demonstration of coercive force is integral to state legitimacy. The state demands sacrifices.

What was amazing to me is how willing certain police seemed to be to openly talk about a drug war that has brought international criticism from governments and human rights groups. One officer, at a small metropolitan station where I did initial survey interviews, unexpectedly launched into a discussion of extrajudicial killings during my questions about his role in the drug campaign: "It is called an *wisaamaan* (irregular or extraordinary) killing when police accidentally kill a suspect. . . . This kind of thing only attacks one police officer—lower ranking ones—not the commander, not the policy makers, even if there is more than one cop there."

"Did this happen in this station?" I asked. Without pause, he said, "Yes it just happened recently." When I asked follow-up questions about the drug campaign, again he reiterated his statement above, providing a chilling non sequitur. In his mind, the drug campaign and extrajudicial killings were intimately linked. "I know my duty, I know I have to be polite with everyone. If I have to deal with thieves, killers, and criminals, how can I act polite all the time? Sometimes the commander orders an arrest for actions that aren't illegal—we have to follow even when we know it's wrong—it's a tradition (*praphenii*) to do this."

Interesting. This was a moment of pure human honesty in the middle of all of the government and media deception. This man was not an automaton of the state, despite his occupational position as a state agent. We were talking at a picnic table outside the police station, watching a hand-to-hand combat training seminar. Twenty or thirty officers were paired off, smiling and laughing as they applied choke holds to each other. Later, I would reflect on the surreality of this scene (seriously, was this a dream?), but at the time I was overwhelmed with the value of the pure human interaction the officer was presenting to me. "How deep do you want to go, college boy?" his responses seemed to be asking. He wouldn't tell me any more, perhaps realizing the trouble the human proclivity for honesty might cause him. It didn't matter. In that moment, a strange empathy connected us. Through the liberation of information, the differences between us faded.

On the taxi ride home from that interview, I thought back to my first meeting with the police when I felt the magic of that shared understanding. Sympathy and empathy got me further than thought and judgment ever could. During the predissertation stage, when I was trying to obtain permission from various police departments, I went to the Metropolitan Special Patrol Police headquarters. I wore a freshly tailored suit that I hoped would provide me with instant cultural capital. Plus, I could invisibly sweat into it without attracting attention to my Nordic incompatibility with the Bangkok heat. When I went to the office of the then-commander of the Metropolitan Police, I was surprised that he also invited the Special Patrol division commander and the Bangkok SWAT team commander.

In this moment of intense stress, I had the sensation of moving slightly above myself observing this odd scene (I would encounter the same sensation several years later in the Bangkok hospital). Why were these people willing to meet with me? At the time, I barely spoke Thai. Eventually, one of the commanders realized we would need a translator and called his son by cell phone who tried to explain my research to his amused father. I realized I was also the receptive son, a role that would serve me better than the one of social scientist trying not to be intimidated by all that brass. It was immediately apparent that my "status" as an American academic was simply not compatible with their power. These men were police commanders; they could have easily refused this meeting or sent me to an undersecretary. Yet they met with me that day as uncles and opened their bureaucracy to me. They did this knowing that I might uncover embarrassing (or dangerous) information. It was an early testament to the tendency towards honesty and the value of pure emotional connection I would rediscover while talking to the officer at the picnic table. The drug warrior, his victims, the commanders who gave him his orders, and me: we are the same. We are divided only by an illusion of separateness. Like children, we subvert this illusion constantly and often unconsciously.

Dark Influence, Snooker Bars, and the Value of Lunacy

At the conclusion of the drug campaign, on the neopagan holiday of Beltane, the Prime Minister immediately launched another three-month campaign to eliminate "dark influence" from Thailand. This sinister-sounding phrase (in Thai, literally, "persons with influence") contained a convenient flexibility, allowing government officials to target mafia-like figures, certain sectors of the illegal economy and, more disturbingly, "opinion leaders"—anyone from *chao pho* (godfathers) to NGO workers and academics.

During this time, I solved a problem I wasn't able to solve previously: finding a research assistant. The fact of the matter remains, despite years of studying Thai, my language abilities remained below what I thought I needed to do the job. This fact alone caused much of my initial anxiety about the project. There is nothing more frustrating than having access to a meeting, event, or interview and not having complete verbal comprehension of what is said. At first, I thought I would seek out a graduate student or senior undergraduate student from the criminal justice program of the local university I was affiliated with.

My initial searches proved fruitless as I couldn't find anyone with the time, talent, and tolerance necessary to work on a relatively unconventional topic with a rather unconventional foreigner. Also, without really examining why, I assumed that the research assistant should be male, to ensure access to the predominantly male occupational world of the Thai police. I was talking to one of my friends about the lack of viable candidates when she suggested, "Why not Pitcha?"[1] the wife of one of my close friends and neighbor. Why not, indeed? I only had to think about it for a few moments: her English skills are incredibly advanced, she's interested in my project, looking for work, and practically lives next door.

Pitcha was able to bridge a major gap of fear in my research: the seemingly simple act of calling offices within the police force and making appointments. These phone calls for me were always a confusing and frustrating experience. I would try to communicate bizarre demands in a language that was not my own, to people I could not see who would usually do anything to ensure that I simply left them alone. Inevitably, they would want a formal letter in Thai directed to the commander of the division, explaining what I was trying to say. Sometimes, despite my best intentions, weeks would go by as my will to get interviews dwindled. My research assistant, with her command of bureaucratic Thai and polite tenacity, thankfully eliminated this fundamental problem.

Nevertheless, the occupational world of the police still had many taboos. I wanted the personal intimacy that I imagined would be critical to finding the "lived experience" I often described in my research proposals. A professor once told me, "You want to find the fat cop with three wives. That's the guy to talk to." So I went looking for him. I knew that each police station usually had a restaurant and snooker bar that would open each evening. Yes, the cop bar, certainly this is where I could find informal friendships and easy camaraderie I needed for a full cultural portrait. The first time I walked into the florescent lights and smoke of a local police station's attendant snooker bar was an exercise in dumb courage. By then, I was used to the weight of the collective gaze at the out-of-place *farang* (white guy), but this felt suicidal. I quickly identified the brand of rum that most of the off-duty officers clad in t-shirts and black jackets were drinking as they stared at the walking freak show that was me.

With nowhere to run, I ordered a bottle and a bucket of ice, feeling momentarily confident. Eventually, I convinced some young cops to drink with me. They immediately wanted to put some money on a game of snooker. I had no clue what snooker was. I knew it was like pool, but I'm terrible at pool. They taught me how to play—I was in no position to bet. We talked a bit about the Dark Influence campaign, but I didn't learn anything beyond what I read in the papers. I returned many nights, trying to develop my meager snooker abilities, but despite my best efforts I never got much more from the experiences than some rambling stories and quite a few hangovers from the cheap rum that Thais like to call whiskey. It was the dark side of research flexibility. In other words, to absorb what is useful, serious time is spent experiencing what is not. I devoted long hours performing the role that I imagined would eventually lead to great revelations that never materialized, and I'm still terrible at snooker.

Undaunted, I sought other ways to gain this imagined research intimacy. Through a friend, I was invited to visit a provincial police station in Northeast Thailand and stay in the police barracks for a weekend. Serendipitously, this visit coincided with a village festival during a full moon. Taking the train up, I was just getting over a rare bout with food poisoning resulting from my penchant for cheap sushi. By that night, watching the full moon rise over a hilltop temple, I felt fairly well after taking the obligatory short course of antibiotics offered for nearly any stomach ailment in Southeast Asia. I went to the village festival where, unbeknownst to me, I was to be a guest of honor seated next to some sort of provincial administrator. Any foreign visitor to the village was not only a strange kind of celebrity (all day people were smiling while gawking at me unabashedly), but also a genuine honored guest. I did my best to answer the administrator's amiable but relentless questions on public health in the United States, straining my Thai ability beyond its outer limits. As we watched a beauty contest (an inevitable accompaniment to any festival), I realized I was relapsing and would need to locate a bathroom immediately. The administrator sent someone to accompany me, and we went looking for appropriate facilities.

After 10 minutes of fruitless searching, we finally came to a hut with a porch where a group of men were drinking (and apparently had been doing so for the better part of the day). "Could I use your water room?" I asked. "Only, if you drink with us," they said and smiled. In no position to bargain, I accepted a short glass of *lao khao* (white liquor—essentially moonshine made with fermented sticky rice). I dutifully drank the greenish liquid hoping to impress them by not grimacing. I asked them again to use their bathroom. They laughed uproariously, "This is just a hut—we use the field!"

I shambled off quickly and did the best I could in the circumstances. I returned to the festival, feeling embarrassed and sick. Then I remembered it was generally not advisable to mix antibiotics with alcohol, much less sticky rice moonshine. As I realized this, a camera crew appeared at our table. A local news team with blinding lights and multiple microphones were there to interview us. The provincial administrator and a random old man were happily presiding over this spectacle. I did my best to answer their questions and smile for the camera while quietly losing my mind.

Eventually they left, and I excused myself to find a few moments of privacy. After minutes of searching, I eventually squatted near a rice paddy. The alcohol and antibiotics continued dancing in my seizing guts and I began uncontrollably sobbing. Some kids discovered me and summoned, of course, the village police whom I was staying with! About five officers descended on me with flashlights asking concerned questions. I tried to explain my situation as tears rolled down my cheeks. A crying and agitated man is incompatible with the Thai version of masculinity. Thankfully, they assumed I was simply drunk. I was escorted back to the police barracks in a pickup truck filled with drunks and people arrested for fighting. Embarrassed and defeated, I fully submitted to the overdetermined circumstances that led to this particular public breakdown. I stayed that night in the apartment of the young lieutenant who was hosting me. In the same room where I slept, I saw an assault rifle leaning in a corner. Although I didn't realize it at the time, this was an obvious indication that I was among friends.

I woke up the next morning planning to quietly slink away on the next bus out of town. Unfortunately, there was a group of young officers nearby and I couldn't avoid them. "Hey, Eric!" one officer called. Walking over to the smiling group I tried to summon the best wording for an apology. "Did you have fun last night?" they asked. I realized then that maybe my situation wasn't as dire as I supposed. In fact, we spent the next hour recounting the night before. They shared stories of fights and debauchery and then reveled in reenacting my bizarre display. It became immediately apparent that this was the intimacy I was looking for all along: in my temporary "drunken" madness, I demonstrated my humanity. Everyone wants to hang out with the farang—he knows how to party! The new amicability they showed me went beyond my status as a freak outsider—I felt a genuine friendship with them. Beyond that I sensed something absent from my relationship with any police prior to this: they absolutely loved me, and it was mutual. Howl at the moon, brothers. Good times.

Perseverance Furthers ("Be like water, my friend. Be like water.")

Ethnographic research in the field, any field, can be depersonalizing, but that depersonalization can be useful. I am convinced that most first-time researchers, who are left to float on a sea of isolation, are in the same boat—we just can't see each other. I shared this part of the story because I don't think it's unique. I'm hoping stories like this will help us understand our common experience, the common patterns of fieldwork. Despite the widespread fears about graduate school and research projects ("I don't belong here, I'll be found out, and I'll fail"), in this experience there are countless daily occurrences that add up to an

The author, after a police ride-along, Bangkok 2003.
(© Brian Gylling.)

easy flow of discovery sitting just below the surface of worry, guilt, and anxiety. This discovery is the light illuminating the labyrinth of fieldwork, a sometimes exhausting, paranoid, and utterly exhilarating place; it's what Robert Anton Wilson (1977) and others call "Chapel Perilous." The passing months and years of field experience offer levels of deeper understanding as old paths of understanding are abandoned and new paths are revealed. Some of the many paths of "The Field" offer nothing less than personal disintegration, transformation, and rebirth.

Fieldwork for me, in the context of an ethnographic examination of the police, is piecing together a slightly shocking lived reality from a pulp narrative. This "reality," however, can always be interrogated. The cops I was involved with are real people who carry guns and arrest other real people. An internationally notorious pedophile captured in Bangkok based on a tip from *America's Most Wanted* was the ex-husband of someone I talked to at a party. The Police Major who committed suicide under mysterious circumstances was the same grouchy person I interviewed a few years ago. An 11-year-old boy who was killed in a shoot-out during a police sting died near the same spot where I stood with a video camera, trying to find street vendors who saw the incident. Many developments shaped my first half-year with the Thai police: the drug campaign, the dark influence allegations, and the growing Thai response to terrorism. As I think back to my first morning in the field, the overwhelming sense of submission seems liberating now, necessary to the progression of my research. This liminality should come as no surprise; modern man-children still need rites of passage. The core of what it takes to do this kind of work is discovered through practice and failure as each day brings with it a new confidence.

I learned the truly roundabout way that progress in the field can become apparent. Familiarity develops: in the simple act of watching Thai news on television and realizing that a police station looks like police stations I've seen before; recognizing a group of high-ranking police officers in plain clothes at a coffee shop based on pictures in the police directory; understanding the policy shifts that cause the day-to-day police responses. Furthermore, almost daily, my research assistant and I are learning what works and what doesn't. We've compiled piles of documents, police histories, rumors, anecdotes, and field recordings. I've fallen into the habit of obsessively writing down or recording notes about "the project" during any given moment. I guess that's one of the strangest personal transformations taking place: I no longer fear the vastness of this topic. Wintrob's disadaptation syndrome has given way to another more adaptive mental peculiarity as I scrawl notes on odd pieces of paper:

> THAI JUSTICE SYSTEM LACK "OF MIRANDA RIGHTS" TYPE OF CULTURAL PHENOM is indi-cation of commitment to types of justice—example Police below Lt. cannot search. . . .
> I'M AN ACADEMIC—A REASON FOR CRAZINESS BECAUSE YOU HAVE A PLAN. HIDING from the definition of insanity. I have a crazy project.

I am now beginning to enjoy that craziness. After all, the cops don't know where I live. Looking out my balcony, the August monsoons are bringing sheets of rain. My field record-ings of the rain hitting the roof are some of my best. The countless travelers who despise this city don't understand that Bangkok's world-record-length name that is perfectly apt. "The city of angels . . . the happy city . . . the heavenly abode"—it's all here. When I wake up in the morning, I'm eager to see what I'll learn, who I'll talk to. This is a mystery school. As the Delphic oracle commanded, "know thyself." Perhaps that's all we ever find: ourselves watch-ing ourselves knowing ourselves. This is good. This is enough.

Note

[1] Pitcha is a pseudonym my research assistant chose for herself, and I used it in all my field notes and interactions with the police. While I was convinced that my status as a foreign researcher "protected" somewhat by sympa-thetic contacts within the police and my official research permission, I remained healthily cautious.

References

Lee, Bruce. 1975. *Tao of Jeet Kune Do.* Santa Clarita, CA: Ohara Publications.

Talbot, M. 1991. *The Holographic Universe.* New York: HarperCollins.

Wilson, R. A. 1977. *Cosmic Trigger I: Final Secret of the Illuminati.* Tempe, AZ: New Falcon Publications.

Wintrob, R. M. 1969. An Inward Focus: A Consideration of Psychological Stress in Fieldwork. In *Stress and Response in Fieldwork*, ed. F. Henry and S. Saberwal. New York: Holt, Rinehart & Winston.

Contributor Affiliation Changes since Publication

Although only a few years have passed since the first printing of this volume, many of the authors' affiliations have changed. **David M. Hoffman** was, at the time his chapter was penned, a graduate student at the University of Colorado–Boulder. He is now an Assistant Professor of Anthropology at Mississippi State University. **Kate Goldade** has finished her PhD and is now a Visiting Assistant Professor of Anthropology at Carleton College. Like Kate, **Andrew Gardner** was a graduate student at the University of Arizona at the time this volume was prepared. He is now an Assistant Professor of Anthropology at the University of Puget Sound and at Qatar University. **Nathalie Peutz** wrote her chapter while a graduate student at Princeton University. She is currently a Visiting Instructor in International Studies at Middlebury College. Both **Greg Simon** and **Caroline Conzelman** have completed their PhDs. Greg currently teaches in Southern California, while Caroline is now a visiting lecturer in the Department of Anthropology at the University of Denver. After completing her dissertation at the University of California–Berkeley, **Gwen Ottinger** was the John C. Haas Fellow at the Chemical Heritage Foundation and a Lecturer in the Department of Science, Technology, and Society at the University of Virginia. In 2008, she returned to the Chemical Heritage Foundation as a Research Fellow in the Environmental History and Policy Program in the Center for Contemporary History and Policy. **Graham Jones** completed his PhD at New York University. He is now a postdoctoral member of the Society of Fellows at Princeton University, where he is also Lecturer in Humanistic Studies. At the time her chapter was written, **Elly Teman** was a graduate student at the Hebrew University of Jerusalem. She is now a postdoctoral researcher at the Penn Center for the Integration of Healthcare Technologies at the University of Pennsylvania. **Megan Tracy**, at the time a graduate student at the University of Pennsylvania, is now an Assistant Professor in the Department of Sociology and Anthropology at James Madison University. Her current research interests build on the work from this volume, examining another moment of crisis in China's dairy industry. **Akihiro Ogawa** was a graduate student at Cornell University when he wrote his chapter. After doing postdoctoral work at Harvard University, he moved to Sweden to take an Assistant Professor position in Japanese Studies at Stockholm University. The research based on this chapter was culminated as a book entitled *The Failure of Civil Society?: The Third Sector and the State in Contemporary Japan,* forthcoming from SUNY Press. Finally, **Eric Haanstad** completed his dissertation in 2008 and is now an honorary fellow with the University of Wisconsin–Madison's Center for Southeast Asian Studies.